Transgender Realities.

An Introduction to Gender Variant People
and the Judgments About Them

G. G. Bolich, Ph.D.

Press

Psyche's Press

Raleigh, North Carolina

©2008 G. G. Bolich

ISBN 978-0-6152-0055-2

Table of Contents

Preface

Greetings. I'm glad you are interested in meeting a special group of people. They go by various names—and not all of them are complimentary. For one reason or another, these people not only excite curiosity, but they sometimes also arouse strongly negative feelings. Because such emotions are often expressed in hostile behavior, this group of people is especially at risk for rejection, discrimination, verbal abuse, and physical violence. The hope behind this volume is that better information about these persons will not only satisfy the curious, but also reduce the kinds of misunderstanding that may generate harmful behaviors.

In this slender volume you will find a brief introduction to a subject area that has exploded in scope and size in recent years. If you are interested in learning more there are many fine materials available through books, journals, and the internet. Here you will find in very abbreviated fashion some of the ideas and research presented in much greater depth in my own five volume series on this subject. Unlike that work, which introduces a large amount of material and uses extensive notation, this little book is a simple overview of some select areas of particular interest and importance.

One word we use much is 'crossdressing.' While this volume gives center place to the word 'transgender,' the two words share a complex relationship. Many of the people called transgender are so labeled because others perceive them as crossdressing. In fact, a strong argument can be made that crossdressing is the hallmark behavior of transgender people. But transgender realities cannot be reduced to any one behavior. In this book we will explore many aspects of transgender, including crossdressing.

As we seek to understand transgender people our emphasis will be on *people*. In other words, the tone used throughout will be encompassing as 'we' and 'us' includes both gender variant and gender conforming individuals. A constant aim is to help those of us who are not transgender connect with those of us who are. Toward that end, there is a fair amount of talking about gender in general, as well as specifically talking about transgender.

Actually, I prefer to use the idea of 'transgender realities' rather than the simple word 'transgender.' For one thing, 'transgender' is a word used in many different ways and can be very confusing. If and when I use it, I want to be very clear about what I mean. For another matter, referring to 'transgender *realities*' reminds us that we are dealing with very real people and their actual experiences, feelings, and behaviors. It also demands we recognize that what we call 'transgender' is not all of one kind. There are significant differences among people who are called by this label, and 'transgender realities' embraces diverse identities, roles, and behaviors. This leads to a final point about the value of the word 'realities.' There are different kinds of realities—physical ones such as we find in biology, and social ones that construe physical realities in many ways. Transgender realities are both physical realities anyone can observe and social realities variously interpreted, explained, shaped and responded to by different folk in different places. Because of the social dimension, transgender realities are also about *judgments*. We shall look long and often at these judgments, especially with respect to morality.

The notion of different kinds of realities interacting with each other is the crucial center of this book. Life as lived is not simply linear or narrow. All of us know firsthand that life is round, goes in many directions simultaneously, and involves realities of many different kinds. We may find ourselves focusing on one or another reality, whether it be Nature or society, but we ignore any at our peril. Our goal must be to glimpse how these interact and perhaps find some way to balance these realities in our calculation of gender variant people.

Whatever else we might say about these people, we must start with the fact that they are recognized by their societies as at variance from the gender experience and expression most of their fellow citizens demonstrate. They are 'gender variant.' But all this means is that they are males who do not identify and act like what their society expects and approves of masculine men, or that they are females who do not identify and act like what their society expects and approves of feminine women, or they do not have bodies easily distinguished as either male or female and this reality is accompanied by problems they or others have as to what gender they belong to. If this *sounds* confusing, imagine *living* it!

We shall do our best to clear away as much confusion as we can. The material covered sacrifices some depth to gain breadth. The coverage is intended to spark interest that will motivate discussion and further research. Discussion, in particular, is needed from the very start. This book tries to be conversational, but it depends on its readers to talk to anyone who will listen and respond. These are matters affecting us all and we all need to be conversing on them.

My hope is that by speaking clearly, appealing to reason and evidence, and trusting in your sense of fairness we will together reach a better understanding of transgender realities and the people who live them. I believe that in so doing we can enrich our experience and appreciation of the human condition. We can challenge our own limitations and biases, thus growing as persons. We may even learn that acceptance of differences is just the first step to celebrating them. A world characterized by such celebration has to be better than the one we presently live in, doesn't it?

So let's get started.

1.

Gender Logic . . . or Illogic as the Case May Be

We must begin with the gender in trans*gender*. These realties cannot be comprehended unless we have a solid grasp on what gender is all about. Unfortunately, most of us assume we have such a grasp. Our confidence that we understand gender comes from the central place it occupies in our lives. From the moment we are born we are put in a gender box ('boy' or 'girl'), and over the course of a lifetime this box provides guidance at the heart of our sense of personal identity and social relating. With so much at stake we cannot afford to feel shaky on this matter.

And yet some of us do.

Despite what we think we know, and how we conclude we are supposed to be, a fair number of us experience feelings of doubt about our gendered self. What a remarkable thing! When we consider all the messages we receive—from parents, siblings, friends, peers, teachers, the media, and so on—how could any of us fail to know what is expected of us with respect to being either a girl who becomes a woman, or a boy who becomes a man? Yet all the teaching in the world, all the knowledge of how we *ought* to be, may not suffice. Try as we might, our own sense of our gender might not conform to what we have been told it must be.

Realizing that truth of our experience can shake us to the core of our self.

We most likely first conclude, 'There is something wrong with *me*.' Certainly, that is the message sent whenever gender nonconformity pops up. Enormous pressure exists to fit within the gender box we have been put in. Most of us spend a lot of time trying to fit. Most of us succeed well enough that we feel a sense of mastery. We not only gain gender confidence, but because gender is so central to identity and relating, we gain a confidence in who we are and how we are meant to be with others.

Some of us, though, despite all our efforts, never feel comfortable in the box we were put in. Because gender is so crucial to who we are, we can hardly just live with the discomfort. So we come to a second conclusion: 'I have to change this situation.' We feel internal pressure to *do* something to try to relieve the pressure from outside us. None of us prospers when we are caught between pressure inside and out, so it makes sense to try something different when what we have been doing isn't working. For some of us, that means moving to a different gender box. That act provides the *trans* in *trans*gender. We *trans*form ourselves as we *trans*it from one gender box to another. Or, perhaps we feel we *trans*cend the boxes all together. However we may interpret it, we have done something creative to end the chaos from being in the box that is wrong for us.

Many of us also notice what a surprising number of folk there are who seem discontent with where they were put. Gender nonconformity, in fact, appears among even those who accept the box they were placed in. Such observations may prompt a worrying suspicion that our culture's gender boxes have problems. The size, shape, and perhaps even number of gender boxes found in our world do not seem to match up all that well with the experience and practice of gender we see in the lives of people all around us. So somewhere down the line we may come to a third, rather startling conclusion: 'Maybe it wasn't *me* that got this gender business wrong, but my *society*.' This conclusion is usually a very tentative one. After all, virtually every message from birth on has been consistent, and what it consistently proclaims is a certain notion of what gender is.

But is that idea necessarily correct?

To answer that question we must be willing to do some things we may find hard. First, we have to open ourselves to the possibility that everything we think we know about gender may not be the truth, the whole truth, and nothing but the truth. Good science starts with what we actually observe—and that may force us to a reappraisal of ideas we grew up with. Second, we have to accept that opening ourselves up to rethinking gender may stir up some strong feelings. We must recognize that our feelings alone cannot tell us all we need to know. In fact, new learning may even change our feelings. Finally, we must be willing to entertain new ideas, to try them on and patiently consider whether we—and our society—might be better by adopting them, or at least granting them a measure of legitimacy. After all, the greatest truth is one that sets people free.

Why Gender Matters

The effort suggested by these three acts may seem to exceed the value that might be gained from doing so. Because most of us take gender so much for granted, rethinking gender may seem unimportant. This is especially the case for those of us most comfortable with our assigned gender because it would seem we have the most to lose by looking too closely at the subject. Our task, then, is to see why gender matters. Let's ask ourselves, 'What does gender actually do that makes it something anyone cares about?'

1. Gender Divides People

At it's most basic level, *gender divides people*. We'll learn more about that in a moment. But we already know that it is true. We all have had it drilled into us that 'men and women are different.' We hear about a 'war between the sexes,' and best-selling books tell us that 'men are from Mars, women are from Venus.' However we appraise the value of being divided, we can hardly protest it hasn't happened. We all live with the consequences every day of our lives.

2. Gender Arranges People

Why divide people? An answer comes from the effect of division: people are arranged into smaller groups. *Gender arranges people.* Why? One possibility comes from the logic of conquest: 'divide and conquer'; 'a house divided against itself cannot stand.' Divisions promote a stratification that makes it easier to control some groups of people if the stratification is vertical in nature. Although it isn't inevitable that the arrangement be hierarchical, it mostly tends to be that way. This is why gender scholars refer to a 'gender hierarchy,' an order in which one kind of person gets higher status than another kind of person.

3. Gender Facilitates Social Role Differentiation

Another possibility for dividing people is to promote social functioning. *Gender facilitates social role differentiation.* In conjunction with the first possibility— social stratification—one basic social role differentiation is between leaders and followers. As the old saying goes, 'We can't all be chiefs.' One gender group can lead, while any other follows. Yet the idea of social role differentiation can be (and is) much more complicated than just that. If we divide social tasks and kinds of jobs by gender, then perhaps we cut down on the confusion of who can do what, thereby greasing the wheels of society. To the degree that a culture can persuade its gender groups that certain social roles fit them better than do other ones, to that same degree there will be relative harmony as each gender plays its assigned part.

4. Gender Predisposes Personality Development

The way these possibilities interact produces certain outcomes, one of which is the development of predictable traits within gender groups. *Gender predisposes us to develop personalities consistent with our social place and role.* Right from birth a host of cues inform us what we can realistically expect from life. We are cued as to our status, the kinds of possibilities open to us for work and play, and the sort of behavior expected of us—all because we belong to a certain gender and not another. These cues work with other forces to shape our personality in directions generally consistent with what society desires.

5. Gender Crafts a Sense of Personal Identity

Finally, all of the above culminate in crafting within us a sense of personal identity based on our gender membership. *Gender tells us who we are.* This is more fundamental than social role or personality. Society intends a basic sense of self that has at its core a realization that we are forever a member of one gender— only one—and always constrained by what belongs to it, while forbidden from

5

what belongs to other genders. For most of us this social goal is met. We resonate with our gender and embrace the sense of self it brings.

Conclusion: Gender Serves Society

In sum, *gender serves society*. There would be no pragmatic purpose served by gender if it did not do so. We must fully realize that gender is not a trivial or purposeless concept. It is a utilitarian one. Gender debates are social debates precisely because gender is enlisted to serve society.

We shall see when we look at gender logic that the very notion of gender presumes *groups*. Being able to group individuals is what makes society possible, but by itself doesn't quite do the trick. We must be able to coordinate the group, and that is easiest when we can divide them logically and accomplish the other tasks we have just named. Gender is a central way our society divides us, arranges us, organizes us, and tells us who we are and ought to be.

Does all that seem important enough?

Gender Logic 101: The Importance of Being Different

So, how did our society decide what gender is?

The question itself may seem odd. *Decide?* Is there really any decision involved in gender? Actually, there are a number of decisions involved with gender, including one we already have considered—being put at birth into one gender box ('girl') or another ('boy'). That choice, made by others, is called *gender assignment* and comes complete with color-coding and a set of instructions to be learned and followed over a lifetime.

Lesson 1: Decisions Constitute the Heart of Gender

However, we want to get back to an even more basic choice: the decision among possible alternatives of what gender *is*. The notion that there might be alternative ways to define gender may be startling, even unsettling. That is because we hardly ever think about our society's choice; it seems so obvious. Most of us are so sure about the choice our society made we don't even think of it as a choice. It seems like an inevitable acknowledgement of truth.

However, in light of what we have talked about thus far we should now know better. *Gender represents a set of decisions flowing out of a fundamental one about what is the most useful way to separate people into groups.* Logically, we need not assume every society would make the same choice. To the extent that societies are a reflection of their cultures, any given society's decision as to how to gender its people will be mostly consonant with its culture's perspective.

Western culture's choice, of course, has been to regard gender as how we ought to respond to the fact of being born male or female. In short, our society agreed to a choice made by other societies that belong to Western culture to base gender on sex. To understand this choice we must step back from it and consider the logic involved. One way to do that is to spend a minute contemplating how the ancients in Western civilization approached this matter. We can do that by reviewing the history of our word 'gender.'

Lesson 2: The Definition of Gender—Deciding Groups Based on 'Kinds'

As we think about our word 'gender' remember that what society wants is the most fundamentally useful way to put individuals into groups. This desire forms the root sense of the word. Our term 'gender' traces its lineage back a long way through a Latin word (*genus*) to a Greek noun (γένος) and its corresponding verb having to do with 'kinds' and 'sorting into kinds.' A gender is a kind of something and gendering is the sorting of things into the kind they belong to.

We do this with all sorts of things, though our interest here is how we do it with people. In a very broad definition of the word with respect to people we can say that 'gender is specifying the kinds of persons there are.' Put more personally, 'gender labels the kind of person *I* am.' We all have been sorted into a box designed to identify us in a particular and important way. With this in mind, our formal definition will be, *gender is the decision that the most fundamentally useful way to group people is to place individuals in groups according to the kind of person each individual is.*

Lesson 3: Deciding 'Kinds' Depends on Differences

But back up. Let's not go too fast when the logic here needs more exploring. The idea that there are *kinds* of persons requires us to recognize that there are *differences* among people. That isn't much of a stretch. Obviously there are many, many differences among people. Theoretically, we could use any of them as a basis for choosing how to separate people into 'kinds.' Let's look at how we might proceed if it was up to us how to sort people.

Choosing a Difference that Matters

First, we might decide we want to sort folk according to some *important* difference. At the same time we decide this difference needs to be fairly obvious, one we can spot right away. We might think of height in that regard. Clearly this is a difference that makes a very real difference in how life is lived. It is a difference that matters. So we can 'gender' everyone by height, sorting short people from tall people. But we encounter some realities that force further decisions from us. For one thing, the gradient in height is so steady that we might have trouble deciding where to draw the line between 'short' and 'tall.' Another problem is that all people start out short. Some become tall, meaning they leave the 'short' box and join the 'tall' box. So height is a dimension of difference that can potentially yield many boxes with people moving from one to another to another. Even though our difference matters, sorting people in this way is hardly simple.

Choosing a Difference that is Discrete

Based on our first experience we may decide that we want a difference that is not so relative. We now see the desirability of finding a difference that creates boxes that are clearly different and that people will stay in. We ponder once more what we see when we look at people, something obvious like height, but not so changeable. Aha! Eye color springs to mind. We tend to notice people's eyes and though there is some variation in eye color, we mostly think in terms of eyes being 'blue' or 'brown.' Now we have a way of deciding what kind of person one is by sorting according to eye color. Brown-eyed people go into the box on the left, blue-eyed people into the box on the right. Yet we are left with a serious problem: how important is eye color? It doesn't seem to matter in any practical way.

Choosing a Difference that Both Matters and is Discrete

Scratching our heads, we return to the differences among people, searching for one that like height matters, but like eye color offers a clear and stable difference. As we muse on the matter, we pass a room full of students taking a test. Excitedly we realize that some are writing with their left hand, while others are using their right. In fact, when we think about it, handedness seems both to matter and to be stable. In practical terms, many things are made for either a right-handed or left-handed person. In sports, being one or the other way can provide a distinct competitive advantage. Moreover, right-handed people are that way consistently in things that require a hand choice, and so are left-handed people. So we can sort people—gender them—by handedness.

Unfortunately, we haven't escaped our problems. First, handedness is not readily apparent. A room full of people watching television probably won't let us see who belongs to what kind. Second, although generally stable, handedness is not absolutely fixed. Because there are so many more right-handed people the world seems built to help them more, thus providing incentive to left-handed people to become right-handed. Finally, there are some people who don't seem to stay in one box. These ambidextrous people use one hand sometimes and sometimes the other.

Clearly gendering people in a way that yields boxes (or, 'categories') that provide all we want is hard. Our experiments reveal that we want 'kinds' that meet several criteria: first, we want them to matter in the real world; second, we want them to be pretty apparent; third, we want them to be relatively stable. In short, we want our boxes to mean something, be clearly different from each other, and to keep folks once they are put in one. Each of those criteria carries a value. We think meaningfulness important because otherwise we would be wasting our time sorting people. We think the difference should be apparent or we might make lots of mistakes. We think folks should stay put both because the difference matters and because moving from one box to another will confuse everyone and thus create chaos. If we have chaos, our system falls apart.

Gender Logic 102: The Western Solution

Civilization depends on order; order depends on coordinating people in ways they won't object to, or at least won't object to effectively. Societies either have to coerce or persuade their people to go along with the coordinating plan. An obvious solution is to institute a way of sorting people into kinds (gendering them) that seems to most people highly sensible. Once that occurs, the ways that we discussed earlier that gender matters can come into play.

The Ancient Western Solution

How did our forebears solve such problems? What difference did they decide serves best for gender? The ancient Greeks' choice how to gender people involves determining kinds and creating categories based on *origin*. They didn't have to make this choice, but it isn't a bad one. They wanted to get to the root of things in order to derive the most basic difference they could find. Reasonably, a truly fundamental difference must also be one that really matters.

Where do the differences we see among people come from? What is their origin? Western societies have been profoundly influenced by this ancient Greek culture's conviction that it is not enough just to sort things; inquiring minds want to have an implicit reason for doing so. If people differ from the very start, at their point of origin, then perhaps we have a difference that matters, is clear and stable, and is so fundamental that we can even call it 'natural.'

The Greek solution seems brilliant in its elegant simplicity. Any clear, obvious difference among people that we can detect at birth would suggest it is an *original* difference—a primary and basic one that matters and will likely persist. In looking at newborns one immediately obvious difference suggests itself: what they look like between the legs.

Sex names this difference.

Deciding that Sex Determines the Kind of Person (Gender) We Are

Our word 'sex' is a label that we qualify by other terms. So we say, for example, 'male' sex or 'female' sex. A male is one who has something different between the legs than what a female has. The ancient Greeks did not speak about genetics like we do, but they reasoned similarly that the difference between male and female exists right from the start. They further observed that this original difference persists. It thereby seemed a basic and reliable way to gender people.

If this sounds like 'sex' and 'gender' mean pretty much the same thing, that impression certainly will be bolstered by how interchangeably most people use the words. Even government forms seem arbitrary in which word they use, and whichever is employed the same two choices are always 'male' or 'female.' In fact, using certain words to refer to either sex or gender makes it very difficult to entertain the idea there is much separation between them.

No wonder that most of us find gender easy to grasp—it's all about sex! Determine the sex, color code with clothing to make it apparent, and move on. What could be more obvious, or natural? So accustomed are we to seeing things in only this way that it is very difficult for us to accept either that gender is a *choice* about how to separate people into kinds, or that *other* choices are possible.

Perhaps the role that decisions play can be made more apparent if we recall that this sorting we call gender is a reason. We don't divide people into kinds simply because some Greek was bored on a Sunday afternoon and arbitrarily devised a way to sort folk. Culture embraced gender as a socially useful way to coordinate human affairs. If people accept they are different by Nature from the very start, and that this difference matters, then the way it matters can be used to guide them into their 'proper' identities and roles.

Gender sorts us in a meaningful way, offering a preset notion of identity and setting out a preordained role for us to play on the stage of social relations. To the degree individuals buy into the system, order is maintained and things move relatively smoothly. Clearly there are advantages to sorting people if the way they live together is thereby smoothed.

Western Culture's Definition of Gender

In Western culture, which predominates in societies like our own, sex determines gender. In fact, *gender is very generally defined as 'the social and psychological ways we respond to the reality of our being one sex and not another.'* Following the ancient Greeks, our society views gender as a sorting of people into kinds based on their origin as members of one of two sexes—male or female. This basic decision leads to others.

Gender is Based on Sex, which is Based on Reproductive Roles

The subsequent decisions are largely judgments based on how we choose to regard what sex difference *means*. For the most part, especially over the last couple of centuries, this has meant understanding this difference in terms of *reproductive roles*. Since males and females have different reproductive roles, this difference can easily be attached to the basic difference based on sex anatomy. So a logic develops that says, more or less, 'Sex anatomy signifies different roles in reproduction, which in turn signify different social roles, which suggests varying social tasks, jobs and relations best suited to each gender, which is reflected in different gender temperaments and identities.' From a single difference in bodies, observed at birth, comes gender—with all that means for how we come to see ourselves and live our lives.

One Decision, Two Appraisals

The Western decision to base gender on sex and then largely articulate that difference with ideas about reproductive roles is neither inevitable nor necessary. It is simply a choice—one made by many societies and endorsed by many people, albeit usually without examination. But since our task is to examine that choice we can do so by starting with a simple observation: this decision can be appraised as either the best one available, or as one questionable in light of its effects and other possibilities.

Essentialists: The Western View of Gender is the Best Choice

Proponents of the view that our Western choice about gender is the best decision are typically identified as *Essentialists*. They earn this name for their argument that gender, as understood in their fashion, is something natural—even God-given—that merely names an internal, fixed and universal essence in human beings. Essentialists purport that a natural difference between the sexes accounts for differences in personality characteristics and proper social roles. Thus, because of her essence, a female's reproductive capacity means she should become a 'woman'—literally, 'a man's wife.' Her role is to be subject to his sexuality, bearing and rearing his children. In addition to her reproductive role, her menstrual cycle limits her ability to do many kinds of work, and makes her emotionally unstable. This latter quality constrains her ability to make moral judgments. All told, then, her essence dictates that her proper role is in the home, subordinate to her husband, whose natural domain is activity and leadership in the wider social world.

Many today would prefer not to put matters quite so starkly, but that basic sentiment prevails, whether in the stark form found in some other countries or the subtler biases of our own. Women remain in a subordinate position in a gender hierarchy justified on the grounds that such an order is 'natural' or 'God-given.' Contemporary sentiment in the United States tends to shy away from the crassness of the above depiction, but the internal logic and its attendant pressure to conform to certain ideas about how men and women should be persist. In fact, many of those who object to the idea that a woman's reproductive capacity should limit her place in the world still agree to the proposition that perceived differences between men and women in matters such as personality traits and personal preferences are essential, meaning they are both natural and fixed.

We continue to use a difference in body sex as an explanation for other perceived differences, whether they are real or not, and whether they actually have anything at all to do with having bodies with differing sexual anatomy. We may no longer be quite so comfortable with a formula that says Nature, perhaps divinely established, determines our destiny—but it hasn't stopped us from thinking along many lines that presume that very logic. What we have learned growing up in our culture is very resistant to change.

Social Constructionists: The Western Decision is *Not* the Best Choice

In fact, we may well wonder how anyone in our society could ever manage to question what is so entrenched that it permeates the cultural air we breathe.

To see how this is possible all we need do is return to where we started—our own lived reality may mean an uncomfortable, even impossible fit with the gender box we were put in. In fact, after the Second World War (1939-1945), an increasing number of people in the gender box reserved for women felt the box ill-conceived, poorly designed, and unfairly stacked under the one for men. The rise in discontent became a swelling tide today known as the 'second wave' of Feminism.

In the 1970s-1980s, these women challenged the basic logic of the Western view of gender as set out earlier. Their challenge was based on work they were doing in a number of disciplines, including psychology, sociology, archaeology, anthropology, politics, economics, and philosophy. The main thrust of their critique of Essentialism was that it misrepresented the facts and in so doing hid a value agenda whose main purpose was retaining a gender status quo with masculine men at the top. Many men concurred with this critique. In time those who found Essentialism fundamentally flawed developed their own perspective.

The alternative view put forth by the dissenters of Essentialism has come to be called *Social Constructionism*. As the name suggests, this perspective says that a better way to look at gender is to see it as socially constructed—made by and for a particular society. Proponents of this view believe our society has suffered under Essentialism. In fact, many societies influenced by the idea that sex determines gender through reproductive roles have developed *patriarchy*, a system that entrenches men in their roles as fathers and husbands in charge of all others both within the family and in the wider society. Social Constructionists do not agree that such developments are natural and inevitable, that gender is a fixed essence determined by biology, or that there is only one way gender can be and is decided.

Social Constructionists vs. Essentialists

To bolster their case, Social Constructionists have dismantled the logic of Essentialism piece by piece in order to make transparent the nature of choices made in building one particular sense of gender. By now it should be obvious that the discussion we have been having is one articulation of a Social Constructionist perspective. Let's continue it by proposing that the Essentialist position depends on three pillars: Essentialists regard gender as determined by biology ('natural'), invariant in goal ('fixed'), and found everywhere ('universal'). If any one of these pillars falls, the entire edifice crumbles.

Pillar 1: Gender is Natural (Gender is Determined by Sexual Biology).

The first pillar is that *gender is determined by biology, specifically sexual difference*. To get at this we must be a bit technical. Males derive from a 46,XY genetic karyotype and females from a 46,XX genetic karyotype. *If* only two types of genetic sex exist, and *if* they predictably produce male or female bodies, and *if* such bodies unfailingly deliver masculine or feminine gender in accord with body sex, *then* Essentialists are in an unassailable position on this pillar. Of course, Essentialists themselves admit this is not the case. There are other genetic karyotypes, such as those with extra X chromosomes associated with maleness (e.g. XXY, XXXY, or XXXXY), or those X chromosome differences associated with femaleness (e.g. X, XXX, XXXX, or XXXXX). So there are more than two types of genetic sex. Still, most of us are 46,XY or 46,XX.

A Social Constructionist Critique

Do such karyotypes always deliver only male or female bodies? The answer to that is a bit complicated. Genetics guides the unfolding of the body plan during development, but not just the sex chromosomes are involved. All kinds of things can occur prenatally that can influence how supposed 'maleness' or 'femaleness' ends up looking bodily or behaviorally. A person can be genetically 46,XX or 46,XY and still not appear 'typically' male or female. For example, in *androgen insensitivity syndrome* (AIS, also sometimes called 'testicular feminization syndrome'), a chromosomally normal male is insensitive to male hormones (androgens). As a result, the body develops with what looks like normal female genitalia. Here is a genetic male who appears female—and on the basis of that appearance is typically assigned to femininity and raised as a girl. Likewise, genetic males with *5-alpha reductase syndrome* are born with genitalia that look like a clitoris and labia. This typically leads to gender assignment as girls. But at puberty hormonal changes produce more male-like bodies. Many then move from a gender identity and role as young women to become young men.

It is not only genetic males who experience such things. A genetic female with *adrenogenital syndrome* (formally known as 'congenital adrenal hyperplasia') can be born with what appear to be male genitalia. In this situation, the fetus has been exposed to a bath of androgens that results in fused labia that look like a scrotum and an enlarged clitoris easily seen as a penis. Even when identified after testing as female, many of these children develop a masculinity not expected for their gender assignment. These kinds of outcomes suggest genetic sex is not as important as Essentialists maintain; what really matters is external appearance.

We could multiply examples, but it is clear that even if a person does look like an ordinary female or male in superficial ways, the brain may be configured such that the individual's behavior does not look like what is socially expected. That leads to the third link in our formula, namely that male and female bodies will unfailingly deliver a corresponding masculinity or femininity. Yet it takes little investigation to see this isn't the case. There are many individuals whose sexual bodies are at odds with their gendered minds. Most notable among such people are those commonly labeled as transsexuals—a population we shall turn to a little later.

An Essentialist Rebuttal

Of course, Essentialists have answers for these discrepancies. They point out that Nature can go wrong. They regard extra X chromosome types as 'unnatural' and genetic 'defects.' Similarly, any event that produces a body that appears different from the male or female genetically expected, such as babies born with AIS or adrenogenital syndrome, is judged 'abnormal' and 'deficient.' Finally, they see any male with a feminine gender, or female with a masculine gender, as having 'failed' to achieve Nature's (or God's) goal. They blame such failures on environmental forces that bend and distort the Natural plan. Thus, anything not falling into what they expect as a masculine male or feminine female is a product of unnatural influences, which ought to be corrected if possible to restore what Nature (or God) intends.

Essentialists are likely to maintain that their conclusions are driven by scientific facts, even if they use value-laden words (e.g., 'unnatural,' 'defective,' 'deficient'). For instance, they typically deny that their determination of abnormality is based on rarity of occurrence. Rather, they appeal to the idea that things like extra X chromosomes serve no useful purpose and, in fact, typically render the person infertile and thus cannot be what Nature intends.

Pillar 2: Gender is Fixed in its Goal.

This Essentialist answer leads to the next pillar, and is dependent upon it: gender based on sex is invariably fixed in its goal. The idea of a human essence is sculpted teleologically: our humanity not only has a design, but that design has a purpose. A purpose means one or more goals can be discerned. What is that goal, or at least the primary one, that Essentialists envision?

Essentialists: The Primary Goal is Reproduction.

At base it seems to be that *Nature intends reproduction, so gender becomes the psychological and social correlates that see to it Nature's goal is accomplished.* There is a linear relation between sex and gender. Sex comes first and determines gender not merely by body difference (the first pillar), but also by a fixed purpose inherent in that body difference (the second pillar). Put bluntly, sexual difference exists for reproduction and gender makes sure this intention is fulfilled.

This way of looking at things is commonplace in our society. When people are asked why sex exists, they don't generally answer that it exists to distinguish genders or to create them. Instead, they typically respond that it exists for reproduction. Once more, the answer seems like common sense. There would be no next generation if male parts did not get together with female parts.

Yet, again, such an answer has problems.

Social Constructionists: Prizing Reproduction Most is Just One Option

First, most of us forget something we probably learned in an early biology class: most of the reproduction we human beings engage in has nothing to do with sperm and egg joining together. Cellular reproduction occurs in our body throughout life and can happen by recombination of DNA strands, merging, meiosis, or mitosis. Reproduction is much more than merely producing a baby. Seen in this manner, we can truthfully say that most reproduction is not sexual in the way that we think of it as the procreation of a new human being.

Of course, that is likely to seem like mere quibbling. Let's turn the matter around and ask about the role of procreative reproduction in human sexuality. If procreation is the purpose of sexuality, then we might expect both that we would engage in sexual behavior for that reason and in doing so be pretty successful. Neither turns out to be the case. When it comes to reproducing ourselves, we humans are incredibly inefficient. On average, it takes about 100 acts of intercourse to produce a live birth. And that's assuming we are actually trying for one! In actuality, the vast majority of human sexual activity is nonreproductive not only in effect, but also in intent. From a scientific standpoint—based on actual behavior and what people report—a better argument can be made that the purpose of sexual behavior is pleasure than that it exists for procreation. So the proposed goal of sex differentiation is suspect at best.

Given the facts, maybe we would be more accurate if we admit that *putting reproduction at the heart of sex is simply a choice*. Other possibilities exist. The fact this choice seems obvious doesn't make it best. Perhaps it seems obvious only because we have heard it so often and haven't bothered to question it.

Essentialists: Sex Relates to Gender this Way—Sex Determines Gender

But let's suspend a final judgment and look at this second pillar more closely. Where the first pillar focuses on the body, this one focuses on mind and relationships. The relationship between the first and second pillar invites us to consider the relationship between sex and gender. We already know the Essentialist view: boys become men to suit their destiny, while girls become women to meet theirs. Since women's reproductive role is to carry and bear children, then nurse them and care for them, their sphere is the home and accordingly feminine gender means personality characteristics suited to such a role, which they naturally desire. Men, unconstrained by their reproductive role, venture into the world where they procure goods to benefit their family: in essence, they bring home the bacon their wives then cook.

Social Constructionists: Sex Relates to Gender this Way—Gender Determines Sex

We might think the Essentialist view so consistent with the obvious and with common sense that it brooks no dissent. But let's ask why one particular body difference (the genitals) *must* determine gender. In fact, let's ask if Essentialists haven't actually put the cart (sex) before the horse (gender). Maybe it is gender that drives sex, and not the other way around. On the face of it, that may seem an absurd notion. After all, we have said that 'sex' is simply the distinguishing of different body parts belonging to male and female. But is that all there is to the story?

What if gender socially constructs our idea of sex? There are a number of things that suggest that is exactly what goes on. A Social Constructionist case can appeal to a number of exhibits demonstrating aspects of this subjective process. Let us begin at the level of the origin of our word 'sex.'

Exhibit A: Tracing the History of the Idea of 'Sex'

How do we fit the Essentialist logic with the fact that our word 'sex' is much more recent than our word 'gender'? 'Sex' derives through late Middle English (14th century) from the Latin *sexus*, a grammatical term based on a verb (*secare*) referring to the 'cutting' (i.e., dividing) of human beings into two groups. In other words, quite literally, 'sex' is a word later than 'gender' yet serves the earlier word's purpose. Moreover, the use of the word 'sex' as a verb, as in 'to sex a baby,' is very late, first being used only in the late 19th century—barely more than a century ago. The use of the word 'sex' specifies gendering as the dividing of people based on apparent body difference, particularly the presence or absence of a penis. We might argue that the term came into the language as a reflection of the Western decision to make gender about a particular body difference. If so, it ratifies the earlier decision after the fact rather than justifying it beforehand as a logically inevitable basis. Put most bluntly, our word sex came about as a consequence of a particular way of gendering people.

Not merely the word but the idea of sex in actual practice is socially constructed. To see that clearly all we need do is look at our next exhibit.

Exhibit B: The Subjective Nature of Sex Determination

When we examine how sexing a baby is done it quickly becomes obvious that 'sex' is not as purely objective as we usually imagine. First, sexing a baby does not typically involve genetic testing. Instead, visual inspection looks for the presence of a penis or clitoris—a process we call *phallocentric*. Someone who appears to have a penis and testes is presumed not to have ovaries; someone with a clitoris and labia is presumed not to possess testes. Of course, the process all too often proves not as straightforward as one might like. Nearly 1-in-20 males at birth have undescended testes, leaving sex determination to a visual estimation of whether the phallus is long enough to be called a penis. At least 1-in-2,000 births are marked by ambiguous or mixed characteristics such that the infant can be termed 'intersexed' (formerly called 'hermaphroditic'). Despite the fact that sexing the baby usually goes on without incident, it does not always do so.

The important idea here is that *appearance*, not actual genetic sex, is what matters most in sexing babies. In fact, modern medicine traditionally has regarded a mixed or ambiguous appearance of body sex as a 'medical emergency.' What is really important is that a baby must look like either a girl or a boy. Once a judgment in that regard is made, then the child can be put in a gender box. Calling the need to do this a medical emergency highlights how weighty gender assignment is. But such assignment is a subjective decision based on appearance, and the nature of an acceptable appearance is determined by culture, not by biology.

Exhibit C: Choosing One Sex Organ Over Another

The social construction of sex also emerges in the choice of which body organ to prize most. This has two dimensions: first, in accordance with the gender hierarchy, a penis is valued more than a clitoris. Second, what sits between the legs matters more than what rests between the ears. Let's consider each choice.

First, *our society chooses the penis as more valued than the clitoris.* It is clear that our society, like many others, prizes boys over girls, men over women. Remember, according to Essentialists our place in a gender box is determined by Nature, and signified by having either a penis or clitoris. Throughout life bodies with penises enjoy more status, wider opportunities, greater power, and richer rewards than bodies without penises. In the early 20th century, Sigmund Freud observed in girls and women what he called 'penis envy,' and speculated that such envy drove members of the feminine gender to seek marriage so they could obtain a penis-by-proxy. Later theorists, like Karen Horney, agreed that penis envy might exist, but argued that if so it was driven by an implicit recognition of all the social benefits having one conferred. It seems clear that such valuation is social, not biological.

Second, *our society chooses the genitals as more important than the brain.* Essentialists expect the gonads to dictate how the brain thinks. However, the matter in reality is not as simple and linear as they might wish. The child developing within the womb experiences changes keyed by the sex chromosomes that initiate changes between the ears as well as between the legs. Earlier we talked about genetic females and males where hormones produced bodies—and sometimes minds—at variance with their genetic sex. But we need not focus on such rarities. The interplay of genetics with processes like hormone release is complex and variable, subject to critical periods during prenatal development, and susceptible to environmental influences such as the mother's stress level, drug use, and health. In short, there is no end to the diversity possible in forming a human being—and that diversity shows itself in matters of sexual development as it does in other things. A male brain, for example, can develop functioning more like what we would expect with feminine gender, regardless of what the external genitalia look like. The decision to fix gender by apparent genitalia is a social choice that ignores the reality that the brain exerts more power over how we develop both sexually and in respect to personal gender identity. Social Constructionists remind us this choice is not required by Nature; it exists because it benefits a particular social group.

Exhibit D: Stereotypes

Human psychology is guided by more than just biology. We are not a closed system; the social environment also shapes us. For example, all sorts of stereotypes creep into our understanding of sexual differences. These stereotypes may be argued to have roots in objectively real phenomena, but by the time they show up as a stereotype the subjective values imposed in interpreting and applying whatever really exists has taken control. Large books have been written on how stereotypes work, but we need only offer one example to demonstrate how they exert power over our perception of sex.

Essentialists argue that differences between boys and girls, men and women, stem from sex. One such difference is body size; as a group men are larger than women. This observable average is easily exaggerated by a social desire to apply large body size to our conception of masculinity. Real men are big men. Short men are often prejudged as more effeminate, a danger that motivates many to exaggerate their behaviors to increase the perception of their size. (Think Napoleon Bonaparte.) In fact, in our society we have it so fixed in mind that body size is a dependable sexual difference that we see male infants as larger than female infants even when they are not! This is just one example of how we fill a word like 'sex' with values and expectations that far exceed genetic sex difference. Those values and expectations are socially constructed, not inherent.

Summing the Exhibits: the Essentialist Decision Leads to Flawed Categories

Add all of these considerations together. The decision to gender people based on an apparent—and sometimes not permanent—display of genital difference does not yield dependable categories. Perhaps ratifying sex as the basis for gender was a poor decision. If so, we must return to the idea of difference and consider whether any other observed difference among people will yield a better way of gendering.

Pillar 3: Gender is universally the same.

These ideas bring us to the third pillar of Essentialism: that *gender is the same everywhere*. Essentialists maintain that two sexes (male and female) produce two genders (boy/man and girl/woman) in every society, and that everywhere these genders are predictably determined by the dictates of reproductive biology. A Social Constructionist need find only a single instance where this is not the case to refute the assumption that gender is a universal essence.

Let's consider each of two possibilities: first, that a society might construct gender in a way different from our own, and second, that a society might experience changes in the construction of gender over time. These possibilities yield a number of alternatives for how the choice to gender people can be made.

If even one of these is actually embraced by a society, then the Essentialist's third pillar comes crashing down. In fact, *all* of these alternatives have been embraced in one or another time and place. Our few alternatives here hardly exhaust the list, but they should assist us in our effort to see gender differently.

Alternate Choice 1: Gender Based on Some Other Body Difference.

Let's reexamine the broader notion of 'body difference,' but still keep the Essentialist idea that sex ('male' and 'female') plays a key role. What if other body differences besides genitalia matter more? After all, on average male bodies are larger and possess greater upper body strength making them well-suited to certain kinds of physical labor females generally find more difficult. Since our survival and well-being requires a wide range of tasks to be done (e.g., hunting, gathering, building), *perhaps gender is built to facilitate a division of labor to maximize social efficiency.* Thus, reproductive capacity and roles may be secondary to wider, more general survival and social needs. In this view, gender facilitates the construction of personality characteristics, personal identities, and social roles that help women and men best fit in to a complex society, thus advantaging all. Some Essentialists prefer this way of looking at things because its broader conception better fits what we see in the world. Sex difference remains the underlying determination of gender. Some Social Constructionists can live with this view because it at least potentially can weaken dependence on sexual anatomy and reproductive roles. A number of societies have been argued to embrace this idea of gender.

Alternate Choice 2: Gender Based on More Than Two Sexes

We already saw that even with two sexes, three or four genders might be constructed. Imagine the possibilities if we see there being more than two sexes. In some cultures, intersex people—often still called 'hermaphrodites'—are seen as a different sex from either male or female. One notable example of this are the *kwolu-aatmwol* of the Sambia in the eastern highlands of Papua New Guinea. Some are raised as boys, some as girls. In this case, these intersexed individuals have been variously construed as either occupying a third sex fitting into a two gender system, or a third sex in a three gender system.

Alternate Choice 3: Gender Based on More Than Two Reproductive Roles

Under the influence of Essentialism, we tend to think that gender is fixed not merely by differently sexed bodies, but specifically by the role such bodies have in reproduction. But as we have seen with other Essentialist ideas, this one is amenable to adjustment. Social Constructionists do not have to deny that reproductive roles can be instrumental in determining gender. All they have to do is demonstrate that our Western decision as to how this works is not the only possible choice a society can make.

What if there are societies where gender is determined in relation to reproduction, but the results are three or four genders rather than two? Thus, children are nonreproductive (one gender), most adults are reproductive in two different ways (men and women), but some adults are also nonreproductive (a fourth gender). In this respect archaeologist Rosemary Joyce points us to Mesoamerican societies like the Aztecs, who recognized reproductive men and women (two genders), and nonreproductive males and females (a third gender).

Alternate Choice 4: Gender Based on Energy Rather than Matter

Perhaps the most basic difference that sorts people is one of energy rather than body. In Africa, the Dagara people have decided the best way to gender people is by the energy they exhibit. Dagara shaman and scholar Malidoma Somé, who tries to explain this to Europeans and Americans, says that gender energy is independent of body sex. A male body can vibrate feminine energy; a female body can generate masculine energy. Somé maintains that gender marks a person's individuality without defining the person's social opportunities. However, the nature of the energy vibrated does motivate a person to seek out social roles and tasks that fit that energy. Masculine energy, says Somé, vibrates outward, a centrifugal force that needs expression in physically demanding work. In complementary fashion, feminine energy is centripetal, needing expression in relational roles that help hold home and community together. The Dagara conception of gender—their different choice—also gives an honored place to people who in our society are labeled homosexual or transgender, seeing in them the ability to serve as gatekeepers to realities beyond our ordinary mundane ones, realities essential to the well-being of all people. This gender choice demonstrates that people may be sorted into kinds without relying on some body feature.

Alternate Choice 5: Gender Based on Developmental Change

Though our Western minds love nicely drawn and stable boxes into which to put things, it is not absolutely necessary to sort people into kinds that are once and forever fixed. Some societies think a more realistic approach is to recognize how development over the course of life fundamentally changes the kind of person one is. Thus gender should sort us into kinds that recognize such change. This creates gender boxes that are stable with respect to themselves, but fluid with respect to individuals. In other words, the boxes don't change, but as people change they move from one box to another.

There are a number of ways this can be viewed. Some societies seem not to have our urgency in assigning gender; they may see infants and small children as undifferentiated, not yet exhibiting significant enough differences to be placed in any box. A child is perhaps 5 years old before the Igbo people of Nigeria assign gender, and the Mbuti pygmies of Congo—a remarkably egalitarian society—appear to find no need to do so before puberty. Or, consider the Dogon of Mali, in West Africa. They conceptualize the perfect human as androgynous. That creates an ideal gender box that depends not at all on sex difference for placement within it. Though they also link sex and gender, they do so in a way quite different from our own. An uncircumcised male child retains femininity as long as the foreskin remains; remove it and femininity flees, liberating a masculine drive to seek out a mate. In other words, a change during development (circumcision) creates a change critical to gender.

Gender fluidity may be a trait in adulthood, too. For example, among the Gabra people of Kenya older males may undergo a gender change accompanying reaching the exalted status as *D'abella* (ritual experts). They move from masculinity to femininity. What makes this transformation particularly remarkable to Westerners is not only that these males' gender identity changes, but that they are then revered in a society that denigrates females and femininity. In this society, in Western terms, the apex of a male's life happens when he becomes like a woman! Similarly, spiritual matters may be involved in other societies where gender change occurs. In each instance, gender fluidity allows a society to recognize that important changes experienced in life can be fundamental to identity and role, moving them from one group ('kind') to another.

Why So Many Possible Choices?

The few alternatives we have considered raise an important question: why are there so many possible choices? Essentialists cannot even comprehend the query, let alone answer it. Social Constructionists respond that every society decides gender based on its particular social environment and needs. The logic of gender—sorting people into kinds—may indeed be universal, but not along the specific lines developed in our society.

Conclusion

Social constructionists suggest we think of gender as *a sorting of people according to variable and changing social values, needs, and decisions.* This is a far messier idea than the notion of two apparent sexes. But it possesses the advantage of better accounting for the facts we observe in the world. The concept of gender isn't changed by this different basis. It remains true that all human beings are sorted by virtue of observed differences into different categories called 'genders.' However, now we have a flexibility that recognizes how in different times and places various societies have made distinctive choices about how to sort their people. Many societies have only two genders; some have more.

We aren't logically forced to regard sex as the key element. The key point in deciding gender may not be that differences in body generate differences in gender. The crucial point may be that *social needs construct gender*—on whatever basis—to best fit people together. If this actually proves to be the case, then gender does not have to be seen as invariant in goal. Instead of being fixed by

Nature, gender is socially constructed, meaning it has some flexibility to change as society changes. Exactly that appears to be occurring in our own society, though the process of that change is eliciting a stormy resistance by defenders of the gender status quo buttressed by Essentialism.

The present battles over gender in our society constitute an important reality for those of us who are transgender. We have a direct and critical stake in whether our society reaffirms a narrow Essentialism or a more pragmatic Social Constructionism. But we who are gender conforming also have high stakes. Our present allegiance to Essentialism has come at a steep cost. Any of us who are not masculine males are relegated to a subordinate status. Yet not even we who are masculine males are spared. Research suggests we experience inordinate gender pressure to be different in ways that justify our place at the top of the gender heirarchy. In fact, this tremendous pressure may be a contributing factor to what some see as a rise of gender variance among males in our society. In short, we all have much to gain through a reappraisal of gender. We have in our power the construction of better social realities for us all.

As we now turn our attention especially to transgender realities, we should keep in mind how the culture war over gender that our society is now in has important consequences for all of us, and most especially for those among us who are gender nonconformists. Part of that war has to do with the names we call ourselves—and others.

2.

By Any Other Name . . .

The contest over gender is much more than verbal jousting, but the importance of words cannot be underestimated. In this respect, Essentialists enjoy a substantial advantage. Our Western commitment to a certain set of decisions about gender has resulted in a very particular—and limited—way of talking. For example, deciding that gender is based on sex, deciding that there are only two sexes, and deciding that there can only be one gender per sex has resulted in a gender system that is *dualistic*. On one side we have masculine males and on the other we have feminine females.

Now few are crude enough to suggest that these gender poles are so fixed and far apart that there are no degrees of difference. Pretty much everyone agrees that males can be more or less masculine and females more or less feminine. But our society relies on a culture that limits the degree to which one can be different without paying a price through correction, censure, or worse. In our gender system there are only two recognized genders.

Sex and Gender Speech

Only *recognizing* two genders is not the same as only *having* two genders. The decision to only recognize two genders, though, means constructing gender language in such a way that talking about any other gender becomes very difficult. In fact, an important consequence of this decision is that our limitations in how we can talk about gender make it hard to mentally conceptualize more than two. To grasp this, try to imagine a fifth dimension, one beyond space (height, width, depth), and time. Without words for the possibility, thought is hindered.

Sex Words

In English we have two basic words for sex: 'male' and 'female.' We have no pronouns specifically for sex, so we borrow from the gender vocabulary to call males 'he' and 'him,' and females 'she' and 'her.' We aren't troubled by this because we have been conditioned to accept that sex and gender are pretty interchangeable. Our speech reinforces our culture's close ties between sex and gender. Our sex vocabulary begins at birth when we sex type a newborn.

Words for Speaking About Ambiguous Sex

When we occasionally encounter an infant who is not unambiguously male or female, we respond to the challenge within the confines of our decision about what is possible. We judge mixed or ambiguous sex presentations as errors of Nature, since we have decided only two sexes are what Nature intends. Leaving aside the dubious notion that we know enough to accurately discern what is 'natural' and 'unnatural,' we are regularly confronted by newborns whose genital presentation challenges the ease of identifying their sex. Unable to immediately type the child as male or female, some other label must be used.

In former times, the word *hermaphrodite* was popular. Derived from the name of an offspring of two Greek deities—the male Hermes and the female Aphrodite—the hermaphrodite appears somewhat like both sexes. A *pseudo-hermaphrodite* is more like one than the other, and so may be called a 'male pseudo-hermaphrodite' or a 'female pseudo-hermaphrodite.' A *true hermaphrodite* presents a picture of mixed sex such that an observer is baffled as to which sex the person should best be placed as.

The word hermaphrodite has had a checkered history and no longer enjoys favor. Today the term *intersex* is preferred. This word clearly shows the effect of our two sexes system. Anyone not clearly male or female is caught between the two sexes. This is *not* the same thing as being a *different* sex—a 'third sex.' The very term intersex depends on a dualistic sex system, two poles one can be between ('inter').

Expanding Our Sex Vocabulary

The choice to talk about things this way can be challenged. In 1993, biologist Anne Fausto-Sterling wrote an article for *The Sciences* provocatively entitled, "The Five Sexes." Although Fausto-Sterling was writing tongue-in-cheek when she suggested naming these sexes 'male,' 'female,' 'herms' (true hermaphrodites), 'ferms' (female pseudo-hermaphrodites), and 'merms' (male pseudo-hermaphrodites), her essay excited comment and controversy. Why *not* think of sex realities beyond 'male' and 'female'? The biological facts don't change, but using different labels helped Fausto-Sterling's readers imagine reality in a new way. Many believe this different perspective is better because it does not devalue those who are not unambiguously male or female.

What we need to see is that the words we use reflect and shape the way we think. The *physical* reality of a child's genitalia does not change by our using different ways of talking about it, but the *social* reality does change. Since, as we have discussed, we socially construct sex, and what we make we can change, then we should be motivated to change our construction of sex to create a better social reality. If we value diversity, champion equality, and believe in fairness toward all, then recognizing more than two sexes has genuine human value—and does not compromise scientific observation or explanation.

People labeled in our society as intersexual are sometimes numbered among the transgender population. Partly this is an artifact of linking sex and gender as we do; an ambiguity in sex is presumed to produce trouble in gender. Consistent with viewing intersex presentation as a medical emergency, a decision is typically made very quickly as to which gender the child will be assigned so that the medical team and the parents can get on with their respective tasks. The medical team works at making the sex appearance conform to what they think belongs properly to the assigned gender. The parents work at socializing the child to adopt the identity and act the role of the gender to which they have been assigned. Some children adjust well to the box they are put in; some do not.

Gender Words

Gender vocabulary presents us with a similar situation. Gender words are limited by their strong ties to the presumed two sexes. Our basic stock of nouns includes two general terms—'masculinity' and 'femininity'—with matching adjectives: 'masculine' and 'feminine.' These words are typically associated with stereotypes that embrace a number of personal characteristics. These various characteristics are in turn associated with members of the two genders, each gender being paired in a fixed manner with a particular sex: masculinity with being male; femininity with being female. Members of the two genders are further differentiated by their development into 'boys' (immature) and 'men' (mature), 'girls' (immature) and 'women' (mature). Pronouns match these nouns: 'he,' 'him,' and 'his' for boys and men; 'she,' 'her,' and 'hers' for girls and women. All of this is very familiar to us.

An Attempt to Broaden the Gender System: Androgyny

As we have discussed before, the limitations of our gender system and vocabulary have bothered people for some time. In an attempt to stretch the system and facilitate broader thinking by developing a more robust vocabulary, psychologist Sandra Bem, in the 1970s, proposed filling an old word with modern meaning to ease the system's rigidity. The word she chose is *androgyny* ('androgynous' is the adjectival form).

Androgyny is a calculated label derived from Greek words blending masculinity (*andro-*) and femininity (*gyny*). Bem's idea was that this word nicely points out a readily observable fact: many people blend characteristics associated with both genders. She designed a research instrument—the Bem Sex Role Inventory (BSRI)—to test whether people could be sorted according to their relative identification with positive stereotype traits strongly associated with masculinity and femininity. People who strongly endorse only masculine characteristics are grouped as 'masculine.' Those who strongly endorse only feminine characteristics are grouped as 'feminine.' Those groups represent folk at the gender poles.

The third and fourth groups were different. Some did not strongly endorse either masculine or feminine stereotyped traits and were labeled 'undifferentiated.' That simply means they couldn't be placed in one of the other groups based on their BSRI score. Whether it might mean anything more than that is an interesting idea, but not one that seems to have generated much attention.

The final group is the one Bem was most interested in. These individuals strongly endorse both masculinity and femininity. They are 'androgynous.' What makes them notable is not merely the label, but the finding that the people in this group differed from the other groups in generally enjoying better mental health, relationships, and success in life. In short, androgyny is a good thing.

Even though Bem's work was well-accepted and the concept of androgyny enjoyed respected use in the social sciences, some unforeseen consequences emerged. First, as Bem herself came to realize, androgyny in the way she discussed it did not really change the existing gender system since its very definition depended on there being only two genders. Second, androgynous people were not seen, even by themselves, as standing between or apart from the two genders. Androgynous males did not start calling themselves androgynes nor did androgynous females. They continued to see themselves as either men or women. A third consequence was that outside of its academic use, the word 'androgynous' proved to be used in popular culture to label milder expressions of gender nonconformity. The word 'androgynous' in our culture typically functions in social estimations as a modest counterpoint to being *too* masculine or feminine. In effect, it is often functionally used as a way to redefine what is normative masculinity or femininity so as to ease the obvious stress created by trying to adhere too closely to stereotype.

In societies with a rigid gender hierarchy, despite all we have just said, androgyny is likely to be judged as closer to femininity. This is why in societies like our own androgynous dress is much more acceptable for girls and women. Ironically, today many of the young people who are choosing to blend genders through androgynous dress (and use of makeup) are males. This probably reflects both protest against masculine stereotypes and the lessened distance between the genders—the very things desired under the promotion of an androgynous psychological profile. Nevertheless, particularly among other males, androgynous dress by men or boys commonly fetches disparaging comments.

Androgynes

Much less often, androgyny is seen as a 'third gender' and the person is labeled an *androgyne*. Just like the other genders, androgynes rely on dress to present themselves. In this case, the body is garbed to mask the sex and thus sever it from the social practice of pairing the perceived gender with an assumed sex. Androgynous dress either selects items that are socially considered gender neutral (or that are very weakly gendered), or consciously mixes gender differentiated clothing so that both masculine and feminine dress elements are very obvious. In either case, androgynous dress can be used to mark out a proclaimed 'third gender' appearance.

This strategy is not a new one or unique to our society. It is a strategy sometimes employed in societies where a particular group is separated from the dominant genders. For example, the *Xanith* of Oman in the Middle East present in distinctive dress that lies intermediate to the appearance of men and women. Thus, while men and *Xanith* both wear ankle-length tunics, those of the *Xanith* are cinched at the waist like a woman's dress. Where a man wears white and a woman wears bright colors in patterned cloth, the *Xanith* wear unpatterned colors. Even within our own culture this strategy has been used in another connection. Historically, when children were viewed as asexual beings, their dress often was androgynous. As well, at times other socially inferior people, regardless of their sex, were made to publicly appear in androgynous garb.

Gender Words and Social Roles

Gender vocabulary also embraces particular social roles our society has decided belong exclusively to one gender group. Thus, only girls and women can be wives, mothers, sisters, daughters, aunts and nieces. Only boys and men can be husbands, fathers, brothers, sons, uncles and nephews. As these terms suggest, gender is especially salient for family relationships. In Euro-American culture, the family is structured along gender lines with reliable pairings of sex (male, female) to gender (masculine, feminine) to family role (husband/father, wife/mother). But none of these words are determined by Nature; they are social choices. Other societies mix sex types and our Western gender relations in such ways that in our language result in, for example, the 'boy wives' (*ndonga-techi-la*) of the Azande people of the Central African Republic and Sudan, or the 'female husbands' (*nwanyi kwu ami*) and the 'male daughters' (*nhayikwa*) found among the Ibo people of Nigeria.

Our culture's choices limit our social perceptions and thereby constrain the possibilities for our relationships. Although in fact we may have within our society individuals who are 'male daughters' or 'female husbands' we do not use such pairings in our discourse. Our gender thinking precludes such choices, so we must struggle with other ways of speaking of such things. What another society might accept as a legitimate social role ('male daughter') our society denigrates as an 'effeminate boy.' This is but one example of the value consequences flowing from our culture's choices embodied in our own social construction of gender. Our words judge and they wound.

Transgender Words

Our society has made choices; we all reap the consequences.

For some of us, our society's choices about gender prove rewarding; for others they are tolerable; for some of us they bring pain. Despite the enormous pressure to conform ourselves to the gender box we are told from birth will forever be our home, some of us just never find ourselves able to fit. What shall we call such people given the rigid expectations of our gender system? One choice—which we can at least begin with—is to style them as *gender variant*. This does not mean *deviant*, though some provide that connotation. Its denotation is simply *different*—and some people like to say they are 'gendered differently.' Unfortunately, in our society being different with respect to gender tends to receive a negative evaluation.

From the standpoint of our society, gender variant people are *gender nonconformists*. That designation also carries with it different value weight depending on who uses it, but most who use it regard nonconformity in gender as a bad thing, so they aren't being complimentary when using it. Still, in popular usage neither 'gender variant' nor 'gender nonconformist' are employed. Instead, a number of slang taunts are used.

The Problem: An Abundance of Negative Words, a Lack of Positive Ones

Words can uplift or press down; taunting is meant to express disapproval and encourage reform. Early failures in gender conformity are met with censure and correction, though generally mild in nature since we are more forgiving toward the very young. Persistence in gender nonconformity meets with increasingly stiff resistance and mounting social pressure. This drives many gender variant individuals into a dual existence—apparently gender conforming in public, while nonconforming in private. This provides some measure of relief from what others say. Some gender variant persons cannot or will not accept such duality and pay the price for consistently not conforming to their assigned gender. They, in particular, are bludgeoned by a social vocabulary meant to sting them into submission. Such words include, for example, 'queer,' 'femme,' 'tranny,' 'homo,' 'dyke,' and 'faggot.' If words don't work, then often sticks and stones are employed.

Obviously, each and every one of us knows from our own experience that it isn't true that 'sticks and stones may break my bones, but words will never hurt me.' Words used against us do hurt. But the problem isn't just that words are used to convey negative messages. The *lack* of words to express a positive message is also part of the problem. Those individuals unable to fit within their assigned gender box face issues both of how to express their personal identity positively and how to form satisfying relationships with others who only have at hand a host of bad words. Trapped and frustrated by our limited vocabulary and inflexible way of using it, gender variant people can suffer greatly.

Creative Solutions

Some gender variant people have responded to the problem very creatively. Three principal responses have developed. The first accommodates society but does so by trying to find the least objectionable words to use. The second focuses on the existence of negative taunts used against them. The third response addresses the lack of positive words. Let's look at each.

Solution 1: Accept the Least Objectionable Words

An early response by gender variant people in our society, and one still often used, is to *adopt the least objectionable words* that can be found. Primary examples of this come from the practice of using words coined within science. The idea is that such words are more objective, and hopefully less hurtful. Terms like 'transvestite' and 'transsexual' exemplify this approach. Gender variant people who adopt them accept them as labels, but often draw comfort from the knowledge that the labels belong to groups of people. In other words, the power of the label comes from the realization of the individual that, 'There are others like *me!*'

At the same time, because these labels have been attached within the medical and psychiatric communities with mental illness, the effect of not feeling so isolated is mitigated by the realization of a judgment about their mental health. Increasingly, gender variant people have rejected such a designation. That has meant the acceptability of such words has greatly diminished. But some still search for least objectionable words embraced by the wider social community. For example, 'crossdresser' has become a popular alternative to 'transvestite.'

Solution 2: Transform Bad Words

A more aggressive approach has been to *confront the negative slang* gender people hear. An innovative solution in this regard has been to do what the first followers of Christ did. They were mocked as 'little messiahs,' folk who thought themselves anointed to save the world—'little Christs,' or 'Christians.' These early believers took what was meant as a badge of shame and began to proudly bear it as a distinctive marker of identity. In a similar fashion, some gender variant people have taken words meant as hurtful, like 'queer,' and embraced them. By claiming it as their own term they both rob the word of its negative power and invest it with the content they want to express. But this solution only partly addresses the problem of a vocabulary for gender variant persons because the former negative use and connotations persist.

Solution 3: Coin Good Words

The limitations of the first two solutions have elicited yet another creative response. In order to address the need for a positive vocabulary some differently gendered people have undertaken *the production of new words*. There are a host of such words, like 'androgyne,' 'bigendered,' 'transgender,' 'transgenderist,' 'two-spirit' (or 'two-soul'), and 'gem' (i.e., 'gender enhanced male'). There are also phrases building on gender as the root word, such as 'gender bender,' 'gender gifted,' 'gender outlaw,' and 'gender queer.' Of all of these, 'transgender' has gained the widest acceptance and broadest usage. We shall devote more attention to it in a moment, but first we must note other important coined terms.

A problem larger than nouns is presented by pronouns. English only has three kinds: those attached to masculinity, those connected to femininity, and the gender neuter, 'it.' Author and activist Leslie Feinberg, as a self-identified transgender person, is someone for whom the traditional gender pronouns don't fit. Especially objectionable to Feinberg is the suggestion to use 'it' for anyone. Transgender people want to be gendered, not neutered. Feinberg, in the mid-1990s, noted that new pronouns were being experimented with in cyberspace. Nearer the end of that decade, in *Trans Liberation: Beyond Pink or Blue*, Feinberg put out for consideration some of these pronouns: *s/he* or *sie* (both pronounced 'sea'), or *ze* (zee), and for a possessive pronoun the term *hir* (pronounced like 'here'). These proposed forms respond to the deficiency of the language by adopting new, non-gendered, or perhaps multi-gendered, pronouns.

The Three 'T's: Transgender, Transvestite, Transsexual

When gender variant people are talked about, three words in particular are likely to be used. They all begin with '*trans*' and that can lead to confusion, especially because both people in the general public and academicians sometimes use these words in interchangeable or confusing ways. The first of these three words—'transgender'—was birthed among gender variant people. The other two—'transvestite' and 'transsexual'—were coined by scholars.

Transgender

Over the last few decades, the word *transgender* has become the most common term for those who not only do not fit comfortably within their assigned masculine or feminine gender kinds, but whose degree of nonconformity exceeds a culture's ability to reasonably fit them into either of the dominant genders. Some prefer the label *third gender* to transgender, but both terms have their limitations and the relatively greater robustness of 'transgender' has led to rather widespread adoption.

Origin and Meaning

Our word *transgender* was created by arguably the most important gender variant person in our society's history: Virginia Prince. Born male in 1912, assigned to grow up as a boy who becomes a man, the person who for some years bore the masculine name 'Charles' by the end of the 1960s had adopted the feminine name 'Virginia.' From 1968 on, Prince lived full-time as a woman, without desiring or seeking a sex change. Although Prince had adopted the label 'transvestite,' it was not accurate enough to describe either Prince's behavior or identity. In the late 1980s (1987 or 1988), Prince proposed the word 'transgender' to better describe *hir* life.

By it Prince meant a description of what *sie* had done in choosing to live full-time in a gender box different from the one assigned at birth. But the appeal of the word soon broadened its meaning and widened its application. In its simplest and most direct sense transgender means 'to cross,' so that 'cross-gender' and transgender both can mean to move from one gender to another. Since in our culture gender is so closely paired with anatomical sex, crossing gender is typically understood to mean presenting in a gender not paired by our culture with the person's anatomical sex. Thus, a female who presents as masculine is displaying *trans*gender, as is a male who presents as feminine.

The 'Trans-' in Transgender

The 'trans' in *trans*gender means different things to different people. Many draw on how 'trans-' is used when affixed to other words. Drawing on other words helps lend depth and coloration to the term. For example, consider the word '*trans*gression.' Some people view transgender as a transgression of gender rules and boundaries. On the other hand, consider the word '*trans*cend.' Some people view transgender as a transcending of too-narrow gender rules and boundaries. Other instances of how 'trans' might be construed include '*trans*late' (transgender as rendering the gender associated with a different sex into a gender paired with one's own sex, as in biological males who represent a certain language of femininity through their crossdressing), '*trans*form' (transgender as reshaping gender in distinctive ways), or '*trans*ition' (transgender as moving from one gender to another while dragging one's sex along behind, as in transsexuals who live as a gender before undergoing surgery to become anatomically the sex typically paired with that gender).

Uses of the Word

There are both wider and narrower senses for the term transgender. The word itself permits a range of applications since it simply means 'cross' (or 'across') gender. The *narrow* use is typically as one of two things—as a synonym for 'transsexual,' or as Prince intended it, as naming someone who lives full-time in a different gender than the one assigned at birth, but who remains satisfied with the birth sex and does not seek to alter that sex through surgery. Some years after introducing the word transgender, Prince coined *transgenderist*, and this is now often used to retain the original, narrow sense of 'transgender.'

The more common use of the term is in its *broad* sense. Most broadly it refers to anyone who is gender variant. Depending on whom one speaks to, this has embraced the intersex, homosexuals, gender impersonators, androgynes, bigendered people, transgenderists, transsexuals, and transvestites. Despite this wide reach, most commonly the term refers to a person belonging to one or the other of the last three groups. Since we have already described a transgenderist, we must turn to the other two groups for brief introductions to them. Here our focus is on the meaning of the terms. Later we will learn more about the people.

Transsexuals

Easily the transgender group that most interests the wider public is that labeled *transsexual.* The word was coined by the famous early German sexologist Magnus Hirschfeld in the 1920s. The *trans* modifies *sexual,* and that is the essence of the word: a transsexual desires to change the sexual body to a different sex. Gender triumphs over sex, since it is not gender the transsexual is troubled by. The quest to change sex ultimately may mean *sex reassignment surgery* (SRS), which alters body appearance to match the desired sex. Transsexuals before SRS are termed 'preoperative'; afterwards they are termed 'postoperative.' Males desiring to become females are called male-to-female (MtF) transsexuals; females desiring to become males are called female- to-male (FtM) transsexuals.

Transvestites

The word *transvestite* means, quite literally, 'crossdresser.' This word also originated with Magnus Hirschfeld, whose research demonstrated that such individuals are typically heterosexual, though the idea of them being homosexual has been quite persistent. The extent of crossdressing is very varied across this group, and can be even within an individual over the course of life. Though today the label is almost exclusively attached to males, crossdressing is well-documented across history and around the world in both males and females. As with transsexuals, gender variance generally begins in childhood, often before age five. But also like transsexualism, transvestism can emerge at any time.

A Final Note: Words as Clubs or Banners

Essentialists tend to approach words as objective labels that name stable things; the best labels capture the essence of the thing named. Social Constructionists tend to regard words as social tools that provisionally and relatively label things that are always subject to change; the best labels catch the social thrust of the moment. However we might debate which theory offers the better way to understand words, in popular culture we readily see that words serve as clubs or banners. As clubs, words are wielded like weapons to intimidate and coerce. They are instruments of oppressive power, used to maintain power by those who have it at the expense of those who don't. As banners, words are waved like declarations of independence. They, too, are powerful, but in a noncoercive way. Banners invite recognition and celebration. In today's gender conversations, words are being used both as clubs and as banners. One way to look at what gender variant people and their supporters are attempting today is to draw upon a biblical metaphor: they are pounding clubs into paper, upon which they proclaim a day of liberation from the oppression of a too narrow gender scheme. We can stand with them, cheering them on, or against them, trying to shout them down. What is increasingly difficult to do is staying silent on the sidelines.

3.

Identities & Silhouettes

Recall that gender is about the decision how to sort people into kinds based on some important difference among them. When Western culture decided to sort according to apparent sex it faced an immediate difficulty. Citizens of Western societies do not parade around nude, and thus the difference that defines how they were put in a gender box is hidden from sight. If what they use to cover themselves looks the same, how is one to tell what gender they are?

This poses an awkward situation since people do not differ as markedly in bodies as our stereotypes like to suggest. Some males are short, and some have very visible breasts; some females are tall, and some have hardly noticeable breasts. Either sex can grow their hair long or cut it short. Children, in particular, lack easy identifiers. Before puberty their upper bodies look much the same, their voices sound much the same, and their faces are equally hairless. Especially from any distance telling male and female apart can be challenging.

There are various ways this fundamental problem has been addressed. One way has been to encourage beards. For the most part, that is an effective differentiator among adult males and females. But it is at best a partial solution and so one or another element of dress, whether *ornamentation* (e.g., jewelry, tattoos, or body paint), or *clothing*, is relied upon more heavily. Through much of history, there was much less variation in clothing than has become true of our contemporary world. Nevertheless, as far back as we can go there seems to have been at least some degree of gender differentiation in clothes.

Gender's Visible Difference

A difference that goes unobserved is not much use. *Dress*—which includes both clothing and ornamentation—is socially intended in our society to make the difference gender relies on obvious. The use of dress solves the major practical problem of how to display gender. We have seen how necessary this is: gender is used to divide, arrange, and direct people. It is encouraged as basic to personal identity and relied upon for critical social relations, especially the family. Clearly there is a pronounced social need to be able to readily recognize another person's gender. Dress provides a principal way. However, in so doing a number of interesting consequences have emerged.

One of these consequences is that dress can be manipulated in all sorts of interesting ways to affect gender. One way that gets much attention is called *crossdressing*. All the word means is that someone is perceived as wearing clothing associated with a gender other than the one assigned to the wearer. Of course, because of our society's gender hierarchy, not all crossdressing is equal. Males wearing feminine clothing get far more attention than do other crossdressers. Many of us see such behavior as not just incomprehensible, but reprehensible, because someone higher in social status is dressing down—gender slumming as it were. Females dressing like men makes more sense because it is socially upwardly mobile—truly 'dressing *up*.'

For a time we will look at two other consequences. First, that dress can *express* gender. Second, that dress can facilitate an *experience* of gender. The former of these clearly addresses the social need to make the difference gender is based on obvious, but the latter aspect also is very relevant. In examining both of these we shall focus on clothing rather than ornamentation.

Dress Expresses Gender

When it comes to gender, dress takes something that might be hidden and makes it visible. But this is hardly a straightforward proposition.

Display vs. Expression

All clothing needs to do with respect to gender is merely to *display* it. In other words, at a minimum all that is required from dress is a simple symbolic sign: the wearer is masculine; the wearer is feminine. Probably the easiest way to accomplish this goal is to require or encourage one gender to wear something the other gender is prohibited to wear, such as a bow in the hair, a ring in an ear, a certain color, or so forth. Interestingly, even though there are some elements of dress that are socially strongly associated with one gender or the other, in a society like our own it can be difficult to point to one-and-only-one reliable marker like this.

One reason for this state of affairs is that we don't use dress merely as gender display, but more robustly as gender *expression*. In other words, with respect to gender, we tend to do more than declare what gender we are. We also describe that gender as it belongs to us at a particular moment in time. We construct a gender presentation meant to convey something about how we exist as a gendered person—our gender *experience* as presented publicly.

The difference between mere display and gender expression means dress can be manipulated to construct gender experience. For example, feminine clothing such as a dress changes the range of activities the wearer can do and remain socially approved. Wearing a dress means not doing a cartwheel, riding a bicycle, or any number of other physical activities approved when wearing pants. To put a female body into such clothing restricts some experiences and helps reinforce a cultural stereotype of girls and women as 'the weaker sex.' In fact, by and large feminine dress not only sends the message, but constructs an experience of femininity as not as strong, not as fast, not as capable as masculinity. Or to put it in our stereotype of femininity: girls and women are 'delicate,' if not incompetent. Their subordinate gender status is thus affirmed as deserved.

Faking Gender

The ability of dress to express gender also means we can construct that expression in a calculated manner, regardless of our genuine gender experience. In short, we can *fake* a gender experience we don't have and maybe never have had. This ability is especially useful for those of us who are gender variant but wish to pass inspection as either a member of the gender we have been assigned, or a gender we feel better suits us. Yet all of us, even those of us most comfortable with our gender assignment, can use this ability to pretend to express through dress the nature of the gender we think someone else wants to see. For example, a woman who tends to be less feminine than the stereotype in her actual gender experience might 'dress up' in very feminine apparel to satisfy someone's expectation in a given context (e.g., an important interview, a dinner party, or a sexual encounter).

Because gender itself is a decision, so too is our participation in it, at least to some extent. We may not have a choice about the gender we are assigned to at birth, but throughout life we face choices as to what to do about that assignment. The easiest and most immediately apparent way we can do something is by manipulating our dress. Small children grasp this when, at a certain age, they express the belief that by changing clothes they can change genders. Turns out they were more correct than their parents thought.

Five Ways to Manipulate Gender Through Dress

Our ability to construct expressions of gender through clothing and ornamentation typically follows one or another of these five paths:
- o *Be gender*—the use of dress to enact a gender as a property of being.
- o *Borrow gender*—the use of dress to occupy another gender temporarily.
- o *Blend gender*—the use of androgynous dress or mixed gender elements to minimize or eliminate the gender divide.
- o *Blur gender*—the use of dress to make gender uncertain.
- o *Bend gender*—the use of dress to change or challenge the perception of gender.

Let's explore each a little.

Be Gender

Most of us, most of the time, practice the first pattern. We dress as though the gender we are expressing is an innate property that belongs to us. We *are* a girl, or a boy, a woman, or a man, says our dress. Most of us dress congruently with our assigned gender and no fuss is raised. Our goal is clear and so is the process: we aim to present a calculated match between our assigned gender and apparent, designated body sex. We try to follow as best we can culturally sanctioned rules governing the use of gender-differentiated clothing.

Ironically, we rarely grasp that others of us we see as crossdressing may be doing exactly the same thing we are. A preoperative MtF transsexual, for example, may select feminine dress to express an internal conviction of *being* a woman. There is a good fit between gender experience and expression, even if others are put off by the lack of congruence between gender and body sex. But dressing to *be* a gender does not require a matching sex. All it needs is the belief that dress should express the gender one experiences the self to be.

Borrow Gender

Borrowing gender occurs far more frequently than we might imagine—and it doesn't require crossdressing. We all do it imaginatively whenever we try to place ourselves in the situation of someone of a different gender. Such is an advisable strategy in the effort to understand and get along with members of another gender. Yet, in terms of dress behavior it also happens more commonly than we might guess. Even those of us who would be horrified to be called a crossdresser may occasionally 'borrow' another gender in dress.

Dressing as a way of borrowing gender happens in a variety of casual settings. In schools often a day is set aside for students (and sometimes faculty and staff) to dress as if they belonged to a different gender. Technically 'crossdressing,' such play escapes most social censure because everyone in the context knows the rules of the game and all the players participate in ways such that their assigned gender remains obvious by their talk or other behavior. Especially for festivities, many people indulge in dress meant to represent a gender other than their own, but in such a way that there is no possibility of passing for that gender. In short, the persons borrowing gender mean for others to know that what they are wearing does *not* represent or express their *real* gender identity or ordinary gender role. Though it may be playful, it is hardly immature play; borrowing a gender at least hypothetically means putting on all the things associated with it—no light or laughing matter.

Blend Gender

We do not have to be gender variant to be bothered by the gender divide and stratification. We see how a gender hierarchy inherently disadvantages girls and women—and harms everyone. Boys and men also are trapped within their gender status and because of masculine privilege find themselves confined within narrow but weighty expectations. Gender variant people experience even more profound problems. So ways of easing the pressure generated by our gender system may be sought through minimizing or eliminating the gender divide.

Androgynous dress offers a balancing through blending of characteristics associated with both genders. The expression moves the individual to somewhere more comfortable between the two gender poles. This gender choice is often seen among professional women, who must be more like men while remaining identifiable members of their assigned gender. Those who blend gender can do so in one of two ways: they can *reduce* the gender differentiated elements in dress that society relies on, or they can *equalize* these elements such that neither masculine nor feminine elements predominate.

Blur Gender

Some of us aim to blur gender so that those who observe us are left guessing as to our gender. Motivations for blurring gender vary. Some of us may do so because we object to the artificiality of socially constructed lines drawn based on sex and gender. Others of us may do so because of a sense of personal uncertainty, confusion, or disturbance about our gender identity and status. Some of us enjoy the confusion. Some of us use the uncertainty to make a point or seek some otherwise unlikely opportunity. Regardless of our motivation, the net effect is uncertainty over our gender—and the sex it is supposed to be paired with. That uncertainty of expression may mirror a gender uncertainty inside, but it need not be assumed that is the case. Either gender conforming or gender variant persons might choose to blur gender for one reason or another.

Bend Gender

Finally, dress can be used to bend (or even bash) gender. While all ways of expressing gender are political to some degree, this avenue is most likely to be seen as such. After all, it is the use of dress to change or challenge the perception of gender itself. In other words, it is dressing to call attention to the artificiality of gender and the fact that it can be manipulated. Perhaps it is the intentionality of the manipulation that makes bending gender in dress so likely to be noticed and to startle observers. Most of us, most of the time, think little about matters such as whether gender is natural or artificial, reasonable or irrational, absolute or arbitrary. Dress that bends gender intends observers to know that the sex of the body is different from the gender of the dress, but it is the gender of the dress that is being championed. This expression often accompanies the borrowing of gender by dress. Most of the time when we borrow gender in dress we make sure to also bend it so that all observers are clear we are enacting a gender farce.

The Seriousness of It All.

That we have so many different ways we *can* express gender does not mean most of us *do* express it in all of them. Nor does it mean that expressing gender is an arbitrary artifice. Quite the opposite is true. Because gender matters so much to both personal identity and social relating, the way we construct our gender expression through dress is a very serious matter, even if we do it day to day in a casual, thoughtless manner. Strong, if generally unconscious forces are guiding us.

What is especially interesting is that as we dress to express gender the way we dress impacts our experience of gender. In truth, gender *expression* through dress cannot be separated from gender *experience* through dress. Even when we are faking a gender sense we don't possess, we are affecting our experience of gender. Dress is a very powerful instrument with respect to gender.

Dress Facilitates the Experience of Gender

Clothing has been called a 'second skin,' because like our skin it creates a boundary that both protects us from the environment and mediates our interaction with it. Resting against our natural skin, this second skin is the most immediate, constant, and perhaps significant aspect of our environment on a moment by moment basis. It would be incredible not to conclude that clothing affects our experience. Because it is meant, in part, to connect us to gender, clothing affects our experience of gender. Since gender is so basic to our personal identity, our clothing impacts our very sense of self. Dress—especially clothing—affords us daily occasions of important self-experience, which may be self-exploration as we try on new garments, self-reassurance in the comfort of familiar clothes, or any number of other experiences that hinge on wearing something.

Let's dwell a moment on what dress does. Let's consider both the physical aspect and a psychological dimension. Materially, clothes provide sensory stimulation. They offer something tangible, but with traits that embody symbolic meanings. The physical reality generates psychological reality. In putting apparel on we create a physical and psychological boundary that extends us into the world while also protecting us. We incorporate in our self the physical sensations provided by our dress, and we simultaneously appropriate any symbolic meanings associated with it. Simply said, the physical and symbolic properties of dress impact our experience of our self.

The Impact of Clothing Physiologically and Psychologically

Interestingly, the 'skin' we put on with clothes interacts with our natural skin producing physiological and psychological effects that vary with the composition of the apparel. As in music, where it is not only the notes, but the spaces between them that matter, so in apparel it is both contact with skin and space away from the skin that matter. To fully understand the importance of dress for gender we must spend some time considering *how* it affects us.

Gender Comfort

Much of the time our attention to clothing is limited to our perceived *comfort*. Factors such as pressure on the skin, the dryness or dampness of the material, its smoothness or roughness, the way it conducts or retards heat transfer, its fit, and so forth, all contribute to our assessment of comfort. Clearly, 'comfort' is subjective, a matter of psychology as much as physicality. The comfort we experience with our dress extends to *gender comfort*—the degree to which what we wear fits our sense of gender at a particular time. We all know what it means to have to wear something that doesn't fit our sense of who we are as a gendered person. We can readily think of the tomboy made to wear a dress, or a man made to wear a 'monkey suit': two instances of discomfort because the clothes don't fit the sense of gender the person desires and normally expresses through other dress choices.

The gender variant among us often struggle with the issue of gender comfort. When forced to wear dress at odds with our sense of gender, there is personal discomfort even if there is social approval. The reward of winning a sense of gender comfort through clothing choice may outweigh the social censure that comes from a judgment of 'crossdressing.' Like the rest of us, gender variant people want to be dressed comfortably in all ways, including a sense of gender.

Interoception and the Impact of Clothing Fibers

Interoception is the entire body's sense of its physiological condition. This includes the psychological motivation that comes from feelings aroused by this sense. Clothing provides sensations taken into account by interoception. So, what we wear contributes to our sense of our overall condition and thereby contributes to the feelings that motivate our behavior. Dress that physically pleases us elicits positive feelings that can move us to perform better or to feel less anxiety at whatever we are doing.

If that sounds far-fetched, consider the attention athletes give to what they wear for a competition. They directly attribute a measure of their performance to what they are wearing. For example, a study published in 1994 by Chinese researchers Li Chu Wang, Sze Su Soong, and Jin Jong Chen examined 880 senior physical education students in Taiwan with reference to their relation to an item of sportswear—the T-shirts worn daily. Both physiological and psychological aspects were investigated. The students endorsed a connection between these two aspects by reporting their belief that functional and comfort attributes of sportswear contribute to better athletic performance.

As to the latter point, consider a study reported in 1980 in the journal *Personality and Individual Differences* by researchers Chris Gosselin and Sybil B. Eysenck, using the Eysenck Personality Inventory (EPI). They found that their transgender subjects, when crossdressed, scored significantly lower on the Neuroticism scale, lower on the Psychoticism scale, and higher on the Extraversion scale—results that together demonstrate these subjects felt less anxiety and were more at ease and outgoing when dressed in a manner that felt right.

Here's how it presumably works: putting on clothes alters our body's largest sensory organ, the skin, as new sensory information is provided. Receptors in the skin transmit information to the brain about the stimuli provided by the clothes. Some of these nerve signals relay information to the brain's somatosensory cortex about the contact and pressure of the garments. Other signals travel to the insula (insular cortex), a part of the brain's limbic system. The insula processes information in order to provide an emotional context for the sensory experience (i.e., it helps interpret the felt experience of the clothing). Thus mediated in the brain, the signals sent by our clothes stimulate various body processes. These processes not only relate to matters such as the comfort felt in certain apparel, but also contribute to health.

In 2004, Polish researchers Malgorzata Zimniewska and Ryszard Kozlowski reported a variety of studies conducted on physiological changes attributable to *fibers* used in clothing. Across a number of different studies they consistently found that natural fibers (e.g., cotton, linen, or hemp), by producing physiological changes conducive to health, prompt psychological changes such as feelings of being more rested, comfortable, vigorous, and so forth. Other research indicates that physical properties of fabric can be reliably correlated to touch sensations; varying the fabric will predictably change the descriptors used by people handling it. In general, people express preference for fabrics that are smooth rather than rough. In sum, clothing interacts with our skin to produce sensations our brains interpret and fit in a psychological context of pleasure or displeasure, mood maintenance or changes, and so forth.

The Sight and Sound of What We Wear

Human beings tend to value sight most strongly of the senses and the visual appeal of garments is instrumental in their selection. Clearly the sensory input provided by the eyes matters as psychological judgments are being formed. *Color* is one important factor. Frank Mahnke, perhaps the world's foremost expert on color, says that our reaction to color can be both psychological and physiological. Further, he tells us that while we may have individual associations with particular colors, many of our psychological reactions to colors seem to be inherited as part of an evolutionary adaptation. Certainly, some responses are culturally conditioned, as in our association of pink with femininity and blue with masculinity.

Our eyes also register *style*, the overall fashion look of a garment. Combining elements of fabric, color, and so forth, styles offer varying appeal. Some styles are clearly meant to convey a sense of femininity, while others intend masculinity. A style pleasing to the eye likely does so in part because of the congruence it has with a certain gender sense. Although fashion styles regularly change, the elements that suggest one gender or the other remain relatively constant for long periods of time. We shall consider these a bit later.

Finally, the *sound* a garment makes elicits both physiological and psychological responses. In 2005, researchers Jayoung Cho, Chunjeong Kim, and Jiyoung Ha conducted one study that demonstrates this. They measured the physiological response of women to the sound different fabrics make. They found both that rustling sounds elicit physical sensations, and that these are psychologically judged as pleasant (e.g., the rustling sound of double denbigh) or unpleasant (e.g., sharkskin). Our own memories likely provide examples of the kind of sounds associated with dress that we find pleasing, such as the swish of a skirt. These sounds are aspects of the gender experience of dress.

The Experience of Clothing and Transgender Experience

To understand the experience of those who are gender variant, we must connect it to our own. We all know firsthand (even if we haven't thought much about it), how different clothes feel, look, and sound. We understand clothes' comfort and we know we feel better in some apparel than others. We all make choices to maximize what we want from dress, and we all take into account the role of gender. Why would we think the situation different for transgender people? Gender variant folk also experience the physiological and psychological effects of how fibers feel, what colors signify, and so forth. A gender variant male, for example, finds the look, feel, and symbolism of feminine dress psychologically 'fits' better, provides more comfort and is more desirable than masculine clothing. The dress we choose facilitates our experience of our gender.

The Key Difference

But this experience for those of us who are transgender is complicated by the social gender system. We face unique challenges in dress. The chief problem is that *there is no gender differentiated dress for folk who aren't straightforwardly masculine or feminine*. This poses problems of two different kinds, depending on the nature of the particular gender sense we may have as a transgender person.

Different Transgender Experiences, Different Solutions

Some among us who are transgender feel comfortable in a conventional gender—it just isn't the one assigned at birth. The problems faced in this case don't concern a lack of clothes. Instead, they involve figuring out how to work with apparel intended for a different kind of body. These issues can be as minor as figuring out a dress or shirt size, to as substantial as modifying the body to better fit the clothing. Other issues can include more minor problems—like an awkwardness in shopping for clothes—and major issues, such as the constant anxiety of being discovered in dress that others view as inappropriate.

Those of us who see ourselves as a 'third gender,' neither a man nor a woman, remain in our society forced to choose how to use dress gendered just for women and men. How are we to express and experience our gender through such dress? There is more than one possible solution. Some of us may opt for an androgynous look. Others of us may find it more satisfactory to balance our apparent body sex with clothing associated with a different body sex. Either way, the goal is to find what best fits our gender sense in a system that refuses to recognize that gender sense.

41

Gender Differentiated Dress

We need to backtrack for a moment. We began this discussion by contending that dress makes visible the difference that gender in our society relies upon. Since that difference is the apparent sex of a person's body, we must see how dress makes sex apparent. Obviously, it isn't typically through making what is present between the legs more evident—though it can be, as exemplified by the codpiece of merry old England in earlier times, or the starched skirt men of ancient Egypt wore that was designed to display a constantly aroused virility.

In fact, all that is needed in a society like our own is any reliable manner of separating the genders by dress because our culture *assumes* the presentation of gender matches an appearance of sex beneath the clothes. This assumption is critical to those of us who are transgender for successfully passing as members of a different gender. We rely on observers presuming there is a match between gender and sex. Of course, when a discrepancy is discovered, trouble becomes much more likely—a matter we will discuss at a later point.

Masculine Dress Sets the Standard

But let's keep our attention for now on how dress is *gender differentiated*—which simply means how gender difference is marked in dress. For much of history masculinity set the dress standard. The distinctive markers in dress were all aimed at men. In fact, virtually everything that today is distinctive about feminine dress began as an aspect of masculine dress. Consider these items of dress:

o   *Blouse*—this derivation from the masculine shirt, named by the French in the early 19th century, first referred to a short blue, loose garment made of silk or cotton and worn by workmen; similar terms for similar masculine garments are found in other languages.

o   *Buttons*—an item with a long history, their prominence in clothing was predominantly among men's styles; the persistent gender distinction of which side buttons appear on does not seem to have been well established before the 19th century, and buttons at the back of a garment became a distinctively feminine feature.

o   *Corset*—perhaps the item most often seen as thoroughly feminine, its European origin c. 1500 as an iron corset cover was for men, and padded with silk underneath.

o   *Hosiery*—men's legs got the early attention and even silk hosiery was made first for men. Today both silk and hosiery are seen as feminine.

o   *Lace*—beginning in medieval Europe, lace was first and foremost an aspect of masculine fashion.

o   *Pajamas*—brought to the West from India in the 19th century, these were made for men and replaced the earlier nightshirt (a long, unbifurcated garment), another article of clothing made in masculine fashion.

- o *Pants*—pride of place in the gender divide is commonly awarded to pants, here used generically for the long history of bifurcated garments reserved for men, but today seen as a unisex article of clothing.
- o *Petticoats*—originally made for men, approximating to the waistcoat.
- o *Pockets*—pockets sewn into garments had replaced pouches for fashionable men by the end of the 17th century; by the 19th century they constituted a significant gender distinction in dress in English society.
- o *T-shirt*—now a ubiquitous unisex garment, the T-shirt originated in the 20th century as an item for men, adopted from European soldiers who used cotton undershirts in their uniform attire.
- o *Underwear*—the construction of modern bifurcated undergarments focused first on men; 'panties' are derivative from underpants for men.
- o *Zippers*—though invented in the 19th century, the use of zippers in clothing really began with their adoption by the U.S. army in World War I. The next big boost came in the 1920s-1930s when zippers were added to men's trousers. Now they are truly a unisex feature.

Such a list should only reinforce our awareness of how gender is socially constructed. With the gradual but significant rise of women across the last two centuries, feminine dress has become more and more important. Even so, as the list shows, basic elements of today's feminine dress began in yesterday's masculine dress. Fashion history shows a definite 'trickle down' effect.

Beyond merely being interesting, changes in emphasis from masculinity to femininity may have implications for understanding crossdressing. When the masculine standard in dress reigned supreme, female crossdressing was the far greater social concern. Today, when femininity gets most of the fashion attention, so also does male crossdressing. The gains women have made have not gone unnoticed by men—and may be influencing masculine fashion to pursue feminine fashion. Italian sociologist Francesco Alberoni suggests the success of women has now won the admiration and attraction of men, who are taking on feminine traits. Masculine dress is increasingly influenced by feminine elements.

Gender Differences in Fabric and Fiber Use

Our list of items has only offered us hints at how gender differentiation in clothing exists today. We can get more specific notions by returning to our earlier consideration of fibers and fabrics. Clothing scholar Mary Lou Rosencranz, in the early 1970s, reported studies on gender associations with fibers. On one end of the spectrum, wool was judged the least feminine; on the other end, lace and especially silk were judged the most feminine. Given the properties of these fibers the symbolic connection is unsurprising. Softness, sensuous luster and luxuriousness—all qualities silk has in abundance—are associated with femininity. The far greater range of clothing choices for women finds parallel in the wider use of alternative fibers and fabrics. Synthetic fibers are more likely to find their way into feminine apparel; in blended fabrics feminine clothing is likely to have a higher percentage of synthetic fibers. Individual items made entirely of synthetic fibers are also more likely to be gender-differentiated as feminine. Practically, this means a greater sensory range in how clothes feel for girls and women than for boys and men. Masculine wear, on average, feels rougher.

Even with natural fibers like cotton, used widely in both masculine and feminine clothing, there is a degree of gender differentiation. For example, boy's clothing is far more likely to be 100% cotton than is girl's clothing. The greatest use of synthetic fibers is found in girls' apparel, particularly skirts. By the time boys become young men (ages 25-34) it is little surprise to find they have the strongest preference for natural fibers. Women and girls, on the other hand, show a keener interest in the fiber composition of clothing, an interest fueled by many factors, but not least the greater range of choices open to them and their greater experience growing up with the feel of different fabrics.

Markers of Gender Differentiated Dress

These remarks may still leave us unsatisfied as to the question whether there are any general features that even with the long lens of history reliably differentiate genders in clothing. The most likely candidates are these:

o   *Angularity* vs. *curves*—masculine garments accent angles while feminine garments accent curves.

o   *Verticality* vs. *horizontality*—by and large, masculine garments claim vertical space while feminine garments are more expansive into horizontal space (as exemplified, for instance, by the use of fringes and expanders such as the bustle or dress hoops).

o   *Free* vs. *restricted motion*: typically, masculine clothing has provided a greater range of motion—and thus activity—than feminine clothing.

o   *Short* vs. *long*: feminine garments have customarily been longer than masculine ones; women's legs have been more likely to be covered.

o   *Rich colors* vs. *muted colors*—relatively speaking, feminine ornamentation has been more brightly (and lightly) colored, even when masculine clothing is vibrantly (though more darkly) colored. Far more often than not, masculine colors are muted and solid, with black particularly favored.

o   *Durable* vs. *soft* fabrics—masculine clothing traditionally has been aimed at the practical necessities of the workplace, while feminine clothing has accented softer, less durable but more sensuous tactile properties.

o   *Heavy* vs. *light* fabrics—not only the texture but the weight also tends to differentiate gendered clothing, with feminine clothes being lighter.

o   *Bifurcated* vs. *unbifurcated*—unbifurcated garments embracing both the whole garment (i.e., not divided at the waist), or just the legs (i.e., not divided below the waist), have been almost exclusively feminine. Bifurcated garments were typically regarded as masculine in Western societies until their thorough appropriation by women in the 20th century, but they still retain a mild masculine association.

Clearly, gender differentiated dress is a complex matter. But perhaps focusing on individual elements misses the most important point.

The Crux of Crossdressing: The Silhouette

Psychologically, separate properties such as color, fabric, fit, and style, together with their associated symbolic significance, create a *Gestalt*—a perceptual whole—which we experience directly through our senses and mediate meaningfully through our thoughts and feelings. The individual elements may emerge to the foreground of consciousness in any given situational moment, then recede into the background, but it is the *Gestalt* from moment to moment that constitutes the experiential skin of dress. Putting it on alters our experience of the self. Neither the physical properties of the apparel nor the meanings associated with them can be meaningfully separated; the *Gestalt* holistically integrates all. As a result, our experience is robust because any dress ensemble is replete with physical and psychological properties we temporarily incorporate into our self.

Silhouette and Identity: The Imagined Self

One partial manifestation of this *Gestalt* is the *silhouette*. The silhouette is like a shadow on a wall. It casts an illusion representative of more than the sum of its parts. Like a shadow, the silhouette suffers from too close inspection; it has its most power at a distance or by a casual glance. Also like a shadow, the silhouette can be manipulated, making it ideal for gender conformists and gender variant alike to accomplish some semblance of the effect sought in dress. *The silhouette is a physical projection of an imagined self.* We *all* have imagined selves.

The silhouette offers us a way to craft a self we desire, using dress to mask body imperfections and shape a sense of gender best suited to us in the moment. Dress can thus unite gender and sex in the silhouette. But in so doing, social expectations remain a potent influence—and standard. These various facts open new possibilities, and hazards, for a crossdresser.

Crossdressing Silhouettes

Although the silhouette presumably represents body sex, the *actual* body of the dressed person is often not what generates the silhouette. Instead it may be the apparel itself, or undergarments. Male crossdressers know that a female bust line can be simulated with the artful use of a bra and inserts. The affect on the silhouette shifts the body representation away from male and toward female.

The silhouette cast by crossdressing potentially makes possible passing as a member of a different sex as well as gender. While this is highly desirable for some transgender people, it can be hazardous for all who attempt it. In cultures where the gender divide helps protect a separation of the sexes, crossing the former successfully bridges the latter, too. But regardless of whether we believe gender can be altered through dress, sex clearly cannot. If the apparent sex is revealed as an illusion, disillusionment followed by unpleasant, punitive consequences is highly likely to follow. People do not like being fooled about this.

On the other hand, *not* passing can be equally dangerous. The silhouette that fails to create an apparent match between gender and sex raises suspicion at the very least. If observers conclude that a masquerade is being intended for deception in order to pass as a different sex, the general reflex is not to ask why but to respond harshly. The crossdressing silhouette matters. Given the potential for undesirable repercussions, why would anyone risk creating a cross-dressed silhouette? The answer resides in what we just said: silhouettes *matter.*

The silhouette has power in expression *and* for experience. Various commentators on crossdressing have remarked that crossdressers may seem narcissistic in their use of mirrors when crossdressed. Yet if we accept that one goal of crossdressing for some is the experience of a differently sexed body then the gazing at a silhouette does not seem odd. Coupled with the feel of the clothing, which affects posture and movement in ways meant to identify a certain sexed body, the sight of the silhouette offers an important experience. Thus, for example, a crossdressed male who wears a bra relies on it both for the feel of it (which includes its affect on posture and movement), and for the contribution it makes to the look of the silhouette. Both expression and experience are at play.

The silhouette matters as well to those not trying to match a sex type. Transgender people who experience themselves as between masculinity and femininity may crossdress in such a manner as to create an androgynous silhouette. For example, a male may put on a blouse and skirt but forego a bra and so retain a male-appearing chest. The silhouette thus formed might be jarring to an observer, but satisfying to the crossdresser. Regardless of whether a transgender person seeks to use dress to be, borrow, blend, blur, or bend gender, the silhouette constitutes an important aspect.

Crossdressing as a Hallmark of Gender Variance

Perhaps now the importance of crossdressing for gender variance is more apparent. We all rely on dress to both express gender and to experience it. Dress is arguably more important to those of us who are gender variant because crossdressing is relatively more vital to how we can experience and express ourselves. Those of us who are gender conformists have many ways offered by society to experience and express our gender. Because gender variant people have a narrower repertoire for doing so, dress becomes even more critical. Then, too, the stakes are higher because of social expectations and the severe punishments that can accompany crossdressing. Given how high those stakes can be—a crossdresser literally risks life and limb by dressing so—we might well wonder why anyone would do it. Of course, that leads us to the larger question of what might cause gender variance, a matter to which we must now turn.

4.

Recipes

The notion of transgender *realities* includes both that such realities are many and that they are varied. We already have discovered how physical realities provided by Nature interact with psychological and social realities. Gender is socially constructed; so also is transgender. But that doesn't preclude a biological connection. Nowhere are the many different realities of transgender more evident or more important than in talking about what *causes* gender variance. Science depends on a language of cause and effect, but our observations of complex human experiences make determining causation much more difficult than explaining that apples fall from trees because of gravity. Inevitably, our talk becomes speculative musing, often short on evidence and far short of proof.

Given that state of affairs we might wonder why we should bother. Two comments can be made in that regard: first, if we give up the task because it is complicated, difficult, and uncertain we might as well close up shop for all the social sciences. We don't because even imperfect answers can prove useful. Second, we genuinely want to know about causation because it both helps us understand and because we decide the appropriateness of moral judgments based on whether some behavior or condition is 'natural' or 'selected.' Right now we will attend to the desire to comprehend transgender with respect to how it originates; later we will address the matter of moral judgments.

One of the enduring debates about transgender realities is whether ultimately they derive from biological origins (Nature) or environmental ones (Nurture). To manage the materials for our discussion we will consider first what contributions, if any, that Nature might make. Then we will attend to Nurture. Of course, today most investigators suspect that somehow both are involved, but that doesn't end the debating because which side exerts the greater influence still matters. Let us begin, then, with biological factors.

Natural Ingredients

If we embrace the notion of *Natura non facit salut* ('Nature makes no leaps'), then gradations between male and female are expectable and acceptable, as are those between genders paired with the various sexes. Such a notion presupposes a biological foundation generating diversity across a range of natural realities which in turn are paired with genders. Certainly, the sheer persistence of transgender realities through history and their appearance across cultures suggests a biological component, perhaps even origin. Otherwise we should expect a more significant variation in incidence and display across cultures and across time than we actually encounter, as well as a sizable number of cultures where transgender realities are absent. Such does not appear to be true.

In our own society, we who identify as transgender possess a common sense that our experiential reality, which we typically become aware of at an early age, is natural and rooted in biology. Anthropologist Jason Cromwell said it well in remarking that even when gender variant people do not identify themselves as 'transgender,' they "are always aware of their transness—an awareness situated in their bodies." This makes we who are transgender no different from those of us who identify as having grown naturally from girls to women or boys to men. *All* of us tend to regard what we have always known as 'natural' and since we experience it in our bodies it seems incredible not to think there are biological factors involved. Biology may help shape gender identity and the behaviors meant to express it, behaviors like crossdressing or body alteration.

Since crossdressing is such a prominent behavior marking transgender, much of what we consider concerns it. Yet even before we examine individual biological elements, there is an important matter that needs contemplating. When we call something 'natural' we typically mean that it occurs regularly in Nature. We usually also assume that it serves some purpose. So we might ask first if there is any counterpart to human transgender realities found among animals. That there is helps buttress the contention that transgender is 'natural.'

Crossdressing Animals (Sexual Mimicry)

The idea of crossdressing animals probably seems absurd on the face of it. Unless clothed by human beings, animals do not wear clothes. But if crossdressing in humans involves one sex taking on the appearance of the other, then 'crossdressing' does occur in nature. *Sexual mimicry* in other species is well documented and occasionally referred to as 'crossdressing' or 'transvestism.' Biologist Bruce Bagemihl, who remarks that animal transvestism is widespread in the animal kingdom, divides it into two kinds: *physical* (or morphological) and *behavioral.* In morphological, or physical transvestism, Bagemihl says mimicry may vary from almost total physical resemblance between males and females, to the mimicry of only certain primary or secondary sexual characteristics. When it comes to behavioral transvestism, he observes, an animal of one sex acts in a way characteristic of members of the opposite sex of that species.

Among 'crossdressing' insects are sweat bees, butterflies, beetles, and fruit flies. The phenomenon has been observed in fish, birds, reptiles, and mammals. Mimicry of the opposite sex fulfils important purposes, advantaging the individual who practices it. For example, among the red-sided garter snakes (*Thamnophis sirtalis parietalis*) some males emit a pheromone that leads other males into perceiving them as females. They don't do this for mating purposes (in which they actually prove more successful with females than do other males), but apparently for survival when they emerge after winter hibernation. The attention they attract from other males, who swarm around them, offers both warmth and protection from predators.

If snakes seem a far cry from human beings, then consider primates. More than 30 years ago, zoologist John Hurrell Crook noted that just as male mimicry of female genitalia can be found among Old World monkeys (*Cercopithecoidea*), so female mimicry of male genitalia can be found among some New World monkeys (*Ceboids*). Primatologist Andreas Paul lists female mimicry as an alternative mating tactic in mate competition. And ethologist Wolfgang Wickler observes that among primates both sexes may utilize sexual signals 'emancipated' from their original context and now used for social greeting.

In sum, animal transvestism, or sexual mimicry, serves more than one purpose. It can aid survival, provide an advantage in sexual competition, or facilitate social behavior (as it does, for example, among hyenas). If such mimicry among other species can fulfill different purposes, then perhaps it is not so far fetched to think something similar is happening among human beings. For example, there may be a reproductive advantage for some crossdressing males who thereby gain access to women's company in social environments where the sexes are sharply segregated. Or, there may be a reproductive advantage gained in cultures like our own where men hide their crossdressing from prospective mates, yet demonstrate transgender behavior that diminishes their aggression and enhances their sensitivity such that some women are more drawn to them than to aggressive males. Or, the gain may come from lowering the aggression of other male competitors, who do not see the 'feminine' male as a threat.

There also may be advantages only indirectly related to reproductive advantage, if at all. For example, crossdressing females may find the behavior allows them to escape the aggression of males if they can successfully 'pass' as male. Or crossdressing by either sex may serve as one of nature's ways to keep the sexes from too great a distance from each other; nature prefers to move incrementally and hedge her bets for survival through diversity. In this case, the advantage to the individual lies in finding a particular environment where there is a good fit between self-expression and social acceptance. Some cultures reserve a place of tolerance, even esteem, for the transgendered, such as in work niches (e.g. entertainment, religious roles, or the sex trade), or in geographical places (e.g., large cities). In sum, a number of possible advantages can be conceived for sex/gender mimicry among humans, of which crossdressing occupies an instrumental but not exclusive place.

Attachment Biology

The British originator of 'attachment psychology,' John Bowlby, was inspired by ethology to look for similar biology among humans. He argued that we all possess an attachment biology that drives us to seek attainment and maintenance of closeness to those we perceive as more capable than ourselves in one or more important respects. Infants depend on attachment for survival, but the biology remains with us all our life and may help explain things like romantic love. This biology may also play a part in crossdressing.

There are instances where crossdressing apparently has developed in response to the loss or absence of a loved one. The donning of the loved one's clothes seems to function for some adults as a symbolic substitute for a significant other. There have been anecdotal reports of elderly men crossdressing in the spouse's clothes after her death. Literature also reports instances where women have donned an absent lover's clothing as a way of feeling close. Perhaps in some way crossdressing engages attachment biology and for some people reduces the distress caused by absence or loss. Attachment biology may also play a part in small children crossdressing to gain greater closeness with a parent. In time, fueled by the biological, psychological, and social rewards of this behavior the child may develop a transgender identity.

Biologically Predisposed Response (Temperament)

There may also be a role played by *temperament*—the biologically based predispositions that serve as a foundation to the development of personality. One such factor is *sensitivity to stimuli*. An exaggerated sensitivity to touch stimuli (hypersensitive tactile responsiveness), such as experienced by some among us to various fabrics, may produce negative feelings and reactions when we are exposed to certain touch sensations that others manage without a second thought. Perhaps a contributing factor in some male children preferring feminine articles of clothing is a biological predisposition toward their softer textures coupled with an aversion to the harsher touch of masculine apparel. If this sounds far-fetched, Sidney Chu, a specialist on so-called 'tactile defensiveness' in children notes specifically that some children may avoid rough textures in clothing and at the same time express an unusual preference for softer styles and textures. Perhaps some children initially gravitate toward crossdressing because of a biologically-rooted preference for the softer tactile stimulation of feminine apparel. This material may also add warm, comforting feelings associated with the maternal presence they symbolically represent.

Two lines of evidence support this speculation. First, tactile defensiveness is a behavioral response associated with autism and reference to gender crossing behavior among autistic children is not uncommon in the scientific literature. This is not to suggest either that autism causes gender variance or that all transgender kids are autistic. Instead, it may mean that the kind of tactile sensitivity found in autism might also be a factor in some cases of crossdressing. Second, research with crossdressers finds a tendency toward behavioral patterns that may be rooted at least in part by a temperamentally driven avoidance of overstimulation from the environment. A highly reactive central nervous system and/or hypersensitive tactile responsiveness may contribute to the pattern of choices that produce crossdressing behavior in some individuals.

Genetics

As a general precept, all behavior involves some genetic contribution, but such a statement by itself says little. More than a half century ago, psychiatrist George Wiedeman warned that no specific genotype can be assumed to produce a behavior such as crossdressing. The caution is as applicable today. Demonstrating a genetic contribution to gender variance is difficult, but there are some findings suggestive of such a role.

We already have discussed genetics in connection with intersex people. Some speculation exists of possible ties between intersexed conditions and some instances of transgender, especially transsexualism. For example, congenital adrenal hyperplasia (CAH), the most common cause of intersexed conditions among those bearing XX chromosomes, results in the adrenal glands producing an androgen precursor rather than cortisone. This then leads to virilization anatomically (e.g., a large clitoris and/or labia that resemble scrotum), and behaviorally (e.g., tomboy behavior). CAH has in some instances been linked to female-to-male (FtM) transsexualism.

Familial incidence is used in testing ideas about whether a genetic component exists. The larger role of genetics is glimpsed in finding conditions appearing frequently in families and across generational lines. The secrecy accompanying gender variance makes this especially difficult to investigate yet there is some evidence to report. Prominent gender researcher Richard Green, writing in *Archives of Sexual Behavior*, noted that using the prevalence rates typically cited for transsexualism (1-in-10,000 males; 1-in-30,000 females), we should expect the odds for two family members both being transsexual to be about 1-in-a-million if due to random choice. Yet his 2000 article reported a study of 1500 individuals that included 10 pairs of transsexuals in families—an incidence far greater than chance suggests possible. These included same sex and opposite sex pairings of parent-child or siblings. There are also case studies. For instance, researcher Neil Buhrich tells of a case involving a father and son, both heterosexual, and each engaged in crossdressing. But imitation could be ruled out as the son was unaware of his father's behavior; Buhrich could find no environmental factors to explain the crossdressing. Other case studies have reported a 13-year old transsexual male with two maternal gender variant uncles, and a case of two transsexual sisters. In sum, the notion of a genetic component is reasonable.

Human Brain Anatomy Studies

Are the brains of transsexuals anatomically different? The question is intriguing, but not easy to investigate. To do the kind of close inspection desirable requires post mortem examination. In the mid-1990s, a team of Dutch researchers reported such a study in the pages of the prestigious journal *Nature*.

Their groundbreaking work looked closely at an area in the brain—the central subdivision of the *bed nucleus of the stria terminalis* (BSTc) in the hypothalamus—known to be essential for sexual behavior. The volume of this area is larger in men than in women; in male-to-female (MtF) transsexuals this area is female-sized. The researchers concluded their study supports the hypothesis that gender identity develops as a result of an interaction between the developing brain and sex hormones. In investigating possible explanations for what they observed, they concluded that the small size of the BSTc in MtF transsexuals cannot be explained by differences in adult sex hormone levels. Rather, it appears this area's volume is established by the effect of sex hormones during prenatal development, meaning *before* environmental influences and learning.

Research reported in 2000 in *The Journal of Clinical Endocrinology & Metabolism* also investigated the neural organization of the transsexual brain. Neurons are brain nerve cells that communicate messages by means of chemical messengers. In this work the focus was on *somatostatin (SOM)-releasing neurons* found in the same region of the hypothalamus as studied in the earlier research—the BSTc. The study found the number of SOM neurons in MtF transsexuals similar to heterosexual females while being significantly less than in either heterosexual or homosexual males. Pointing to other studies, the researchers suggested the influence of perinatal exposure to androgens (male sex hormones) seems instrumental in the organizing of the development of the BSTc and its SOM neurons.

Hormonal Factors

The studies we have been reviewing highlight the critical role *hormones* may play in transgender realities like transsexualism. This idea has been around a long time. In the 1950s endocrinologist Harry Benjamin—the most famous early researcher of transsexualism—speculated on biological factors, and in his 1966 landmark book *The Transsexual Phenomenon* implicated both genetics and hormones. In 1980, prominent sexologist John Money remarked that androgenic influences on the prenatal brain might be directly involved in any number of things, including transvestism and transsexualism. He probably had in mind studies like that of the late 1960s and beyond that showed depriving the male fetus of normal androgen levels leads in adulthood to expressions of femininity.

Both androgens (so-called 'male' hormones) and estrogens (so-called 'female' hormones) may play critical roles in the development of one form or another of gender variance. In a review published in *Psychoneuroendocrinology* of 19 studies on the behavioral effects of prenatal exposure to hormones, a team led by June Reinisch (former director of the Kinsey Institute) found that such exposure can play a profound role. Concentrating on individuals whose prenatal hormonal environments were atypical, it is clear that various hormones have specific effects. For example, prenatal exposure to an androgen-based synthetic hormone exerts a masculinizing and/or defeminizing influence on behavioral development. On the other hand, prenatal exposure to progesterone (a naturally occurring female hormone), or progestin (a synthetic female hormone) has a feminizing and/or demasculinizing influence.

One hormone of particular interest has been *luteinizing hormone* (LH). A 1982 report in *Archives of Sexual Behavior* looked at the possible relation between LH and transsexualism. The data collected found suggests that transsexualism may be related to a difference in the way LH is secreted. The following year, a team of researchers reported that MtF transsexuals, after estrogen stimulation, show a rise in LH—just as do genetic females. In 1995 in the *Journal of Endocrinological Investigation* another examination of LH, this time in 9 MtF transsexuals, discovered that a *decrease* in LH pulse frequency may be a marker for transsexualism.

In light of what the research shows, and responding to some of Money's ideas, researchers Richard Pillard and James Weinrich in the *Journal of Sex Research* proposed a "periodic table model" for gender transpositions. Their sociobiological model gives prominence to the role played by both prenatal and perinatal hormonal fluctuations. As others have, they noted the importance of critical periods during development when such hormonal fluctuations may play a dramatic role in altering brain formation from the normative evolutionary pattern. Together with genetic and environmental contributions the resulting variations constitute degrees of masculinization and/or defeminization of the brain. The consequence is a range of sex and gender differences among human beings. However, these differences fall into one or another of four broad groups depending on the masculizing or defeminizing that occurs. Thus, the quadrants of their model contain those who are "masculinized and defeminized" (e.g., typical heterosexual males), those who are "unmasculinized and undefeminized" (e.g., typical heterosexual females), those who are "unmasculinized and defeminized" (e.g., male-to-female transsexuals), and those who are "masculinized and defeminized" (e.g., most homosexuals).

Environmental Stirring

There is much more involved in biological studies of gender variance than this brief review covers, especially with respect to hormones. But what we have examined is sufficient to support as highly reasonable that Nature is at work in much, perhaps all, gender variance. Yet there remain environmental factors to examine. A number of hypotheses have been proposed to explain transgender realities in terms of the environment. At present the weight of evidence has led most researchers to give greater prominence to biology, but that does not mean the environment is inconsequential for the development of gender variance. Let us look at some proposed environmental influences that suggest gender variance is *learned.* Sources of such learning may be culture, parents or experience.

Cultural Beliefs

An aspect of learning related to transgender may be *the personal incorporation of a cultural belief.* For example, in 1977 a case was reported in *The Journal of Nerv-*

ous and *Mental Disease* of a girl presenting with apparent gender disturbance who claimed to remember a previous life as a male. Because she hailed from Southeast Asia where belief in reincarnation is common, her situation was interpreted in a cultural context where such belief is not pathological. Such instances can be multiplied. In 2001 another case study, in the *Journal of Clinical Psychology & Human Sexuality*, reported on a male child in Thailand who displayed transgender behavior reflecting his parents' belief that he is the reincarnation of his maternal grandmother—an idea echoed in the boy's own claims as he grew older. A birthmark on the child prompted this belief. The belief that *karma* accrued in one life produces effects in the next is not infrequently appealed to by transgender individuals in Eastern societies as an explanation for why they are as they are; such an explanation holds no power in our Christian-dominated society, for Christianity has no similar belief.

Disturbed Parental Patterns

The influential psychoanalyst Robert Stoller, like many of his colleagues in the 20th century, thought *disturbed family patterns* can elicit gender variance. This basic idea has been developed in several ways.

Dominant Mother/Distant or Absent Father

In particular, the combination of a dominant mother and a distant, or absent father has been speculated as instrumental. A 1971 study reported in the *Archives of Sexual Behavior* of 18 crossdressing adolescent males found that two-thirds of them had fathers who were distant and passive, while the mother encouraged feminine behaviors like crossdressing either openly or subtly. In these families there were also a sister who was seen as the mother's favored child. The crossdressing boys appeared to be engaging in their crossdressing less for sexual arousal than as part of their desire to appear feminine. Stoller himself in 1979 reported 9 boys with significant feminine behavior whose fathers did not fill a normal role. In the mid-1980s a larger study, which included 77 male transvestites, used the Parent Characteristics Questionnaire (PCQ) to assess subjects' perceptions of their parents. The results found that non-normative parent sex-role traits were significantly different for the study's lesbians and transvestites than for the heterosexual and male homosexual participants.

These findings, however, have not been supported by other research. Overall, the psychoanalytic hypothesis of the influence posed by a father's absence has not been upheld. More systematic research reported in 1985 failed to confirm it. A comparative study involving over 200 men (65 transvestites, 33 male-to-female (MtF) transsexuals, 57 homosexuals, and 61 men whose sexual orientation remained unidentified), found no support for this idea. For all three groups—transvestites, transsexuals, and homosexuals—absent fathers proved no more common than in the general population. Self-reports from most crossdressing males also do not seem to support this hypothesis. A classic 1972 survey of 504 adult male crossdressers by Virginia Prince and psychologist Peter Bentler in *Psychological Reports* found that more than half (51%) of their subjects identified their father as the dominant parent. Moreover, nearly three-quarters (72%) affirmed that their father provided a good masculine image for them. A survey study reported by Richard Docter and Prince in *Archives of Sexual Behavior* a generation later (1997), patterned on the 1972 survey, found similar numbers: a little more than three-quarters (76%) reared by both parents through age 18 and a like number (76%) reporting their father provided a good masculine image. The psychoanalytic hypothesis has not enjoyed much acceptance outside psychoanalytic circles.

Parental Wish for an Opposite Sex Child

Psychoanalysts also have speculated that a parent's wish—especially the mother's—for a child of the sex opposite of the actual one of a child is a factor in the development of gender variance. That the mother would play a critical role if she held such a wish seems obvious—she typically provides the primary care, including the selection of clothes and dressing of the child. Sociologist Gregory Stone, in 1965, wrote of this fact that it means a child's first reflected glimpse of the self is provided by a woman—and some women see their male offspring as girls, and dress them accordingly. How widespread such a practice might be is unknown, and not a lot of research has been done on how common is a wish for an opposite sex child or how it affects dress behavior.

But the Kinsey Institute's *Sex and Morality in the U.S.* (1989) offers some intriguing evidence. Questions were asked of study participants concerning any sign while growing up that either parent would have preferred the respondent to have been born the opposite sex. When it came to the behavior of fathers, four times as many females (1.5%) as males (0.4%) affirmed that such a sign included his preference in how he wanted his child to dress. Yet when it came to the behavior of mothers, more than twice as many males (1.6%) as females (0.7%) affirmed that a sign included her preference in how she wanted her child to dress. For those answering affirmatively in either scenario, significant percentages of both males and females report this continued at least into adolescence.

In his 1974 review in *Archives of Sexual Behavior* of 80 cases of female-to-male transsexuals reported between 1922-1970, Ira Pauly found nearly two-thirds (62%; N-16) of the subjects in cases where the question came up remembered their mothers as having preferred a boy instead of a girl. The commonly reported finding that transgender folk remember having wanted as children to be members of the opposite gender may occasionally reflect parent-child dynamics. Perhaps for some gender variant individuals the development of their gender identity flows from a response to the parental wish and the rewards they receive for transgender behavior like crossdressing.

Escape from Gender Role Pressure

Anthropologists in the past often explained male crossdressing as a vehicle of *escape from gender role expectations*. Males, unable to meet the demands of masculine gender as set forth in their society, may seek relief or escape from such demands by affiliating with femininity. In many societies this move is a sanctioned one with the transgender male coming to occupy a new gender role with its own set of expectations. This model has received some empirical testing. In the late 1970s, the anthropologist and psychologist team of Robert and Ruth Munroe examined 73 societies for which ratings exist both with respect to male transvestism and the sexual division of labor in subsistence activities. They found in every society where male transvestism was documented, males had the greater role in subsistence activities. Males unable to cope with the social gender expectation are provided in many societies a sanctioned escape through their transvestism—which may be a motivation for developing gender variance. Our own society does not sanction male gender variance, yet the gender role pressure males experience may still be a factor in transgender development.

Learning Factors

The conviction that gender variance is learned elicits a number of notions as to exactly how the learning proceeds. Three psychological learning theories—classical conditioning, operant conditioning, and social cognitive learning—may be useful in understanding at least some transgender displays. The first two can be grouped as 'behavioral conditioning' and treated together.

Behavioral Conditioning

A few theorists have stressed learning in the sense of *behavioral conditioning* (either classical conditioning or operant conditioning). A general statement of this idea is found in the eminent American sexologist Alfred Kinsey, who tried to explain crossdressing in his 1953 volume *Sexual Behavior in the Human Female*. Noting that crossdressing occurs in both males and females, but is far more common among males, he argued the explanation lies in a sex-based difference in learning, with males more prone to conditioning by psychological stimuli. As Kinsey's remark might suggest, behavioral conditioning has been used especially to explain male transvestism. Classical conditioning suggests a small boy might pair the sight of feminine clothing with a pleasurable experience such as being bathed and substitute the neutral stimulus of the apparel for the natural stimulus of the bath so that the clothing becomes a conditioned stimulus offering pleasurable body sensations when seen or worn. Operant conditioning places an emphasis on the reinforcing nature of a pleasurable experience from crossdressing regardless of why it was initially undertaken. Such explanations to date have received little empirical support even for male transvestism, let alone realities like transsexualism, and are not widely embraced.

56

Social Cognitive Learning

Psychologist Albert Bandura broadened learning theory by his studies demonstrating the importance of 'vicarious learning'—learning accomplished by the imitation of a model. Naturally, this has been speculated upon as a factor in at least some gender variance. In the late 1970s, psychiatrist David Krueger presented the situation of a crossdressing father and three crossdressing sons. All three sons began their crossdressing in early adolescence. Krueger thought that the father's role modeling played a significant part in the behavior exhibited by the sons. However, while this theory has established the power of observation and imitation of models in learning, including gender learning, this hypothesis with respect to the development of transgender people has not received much support. Abundant examples exist of families in which the same-sex offspring are aware of the parent's crossdressing but show no inclination to imitate it.

Different Mixings, Different People

Virtually all of us who investigate transgender realities ultimately conclude that Nature and the environment interact in such a way that each makes some contribution to the particular gender variance found in a given individual. There are many ways that can be looked at. We shall use one as an example.

Male Crossdressing: How Different Factors May Interact

Logically, if a boy—for whatever reason, constitutionally or environmentally—is exposed to feminine apparel and finds the resulting experience richly satisfying, because the feel and look of the clothes prompts changes physiological and psychological associated with pleasure, then the boy will seek to repeat such experience. The initial experience may be largely independent of either consciousness of gender differentiation in dress or concern about gender differentiation. In short, the initial experience may have little or nothing to do with gender *per se*. The child may not be seeking to express anything; the experience is satisfying in and of itself because the clothes in their independent reality offer a venue for pleasurable sensation. This child's body interacts with the physicality of these clothes such as to produce a pleasing experience. The experience is not one of crossdressing so much as simply an experience of dressing.

Because society insists on labeling such behavior as crossdressing and investing it with gender associations the child inevitably must connect the dress behavior with one or another conclusion about his gender. For some children this means translating the pleasurable feeling in sexual terms, over time developing into what mental health professionals term 'transvestic fetishism.' For other children whatever sexual component might be present becomes secondary to the relief and generalized pleasure associated with temporary affiliation with another gender through periodic practice of crossdressing. These kids may be identified eventually as transvestites or transgendered (in the narrow sense of that word) individuals. For yet other children the experience of gender differentiated clothes resonates with a sense of gender identity to such an extent the body itself feels wrong and the child becomes someone identified as transsexual.

The point is this: comprehending the influence of dress on physiology and psychology offers a plausible hypothesis for a common ground underlying the multiple developmental pathways of transgender connected to crossdressing. For at least some crossdressers, early experience of clothing associated with each gender may have produced significantly varying results. A preference for the experience accompanying dress assigned to the other gender presents then a psychological challenge to the individual. The different ways in which the individual solves this challenge leads to one or another transgender identification. As long as dress remains gender differentiated any continuing experience of dress associated with a gender other than the one assigned at birth will necessitate some personal reckoning of gender that makes some transgender identity likely, if not inevitable.

3 Broad Conclusions

The material we have considered may leave us feeling bewildered and convinced that since no one explanation has carried the day we might as well believe whatever we want because we have as much chance of being right as the next guy. But that response is unwarranted. Though we may not have a satisfactory general explanation for what causes gender variance we do have some reasonably solid lines of evidence that permit some broad conclusions that fit most, if not all, transgender people.

First, it seems uncontestable that Nature has a hand. In fact, the passing of time and the development of ever more sophisticated instruments to examine this role has only granted it a greater weight. More attention seems to be given today to the role of biology than to environmental factors to explain the origin of transgender realities. In sum, biology seems to have the greatest influence.

Second, it seems equally uncontestable that environmental factors help shape the particular course of gender variance development. If biology provides the seeds, the environment nurtures their development. The relatively greater weight of Nature, though, seems evident in how even in hostile environments we who are transgender find ways to experience and express our gender. It may be that we need to learn from this better ways to shape environments supportive of Nature and conducive to the health and well being of all of us.

Finally, it appears inarguable that the individual also contributes a distinctive element. The sheer variability in transgender experience and expression make this perhaps the most certain point of all. In fact, given this notion it is not surprising to find those of us who find transgender realities objectionable arguing that such realities are deviant *choices*, for which the individual must be held morally accountable. How we judge transgender reflects at least in part how we view causation and is the matter to which we must now turn.

5.

Staking the Moral High Ground, or Transphobia?

In considering what causes gender variance we ended by acknowledging that alongside Nature and the environment there is an individual contribution to each person's gender. In short, we all contribute to our gender identity and role, if only by accepting and abiding by the gender assignment made for us at birth. Those of us who conform to social expectations often have trouble understanding why anyone wouldn't. Nonconformists in anything tend to be regarded as people who are nonconforming by *choice*. This is certainly the case with gender. In our society gender variance is often made a moral issue by focusing on the perceived degree of choice made by transgender persons. This issue tends to move to discussions of causation because we sense that things not chosen are things we cannot be held responsible for. That idea is where we must begin.

Choice and Moral Judgment

Let's wax philosophical for a moment. The language of science is cause and effect; the language of morality is choice and responsibility. But despite the different character of these languages, science is not without ethics and moral decision-making should be constrained by reason and evidence. Many of us struggle with messages we have received from institutions of culture such as the Church or parents about the morality or immorality of transgender realities. To get at the complexities of moral reasoning, which we tend to seldom examine, we need to consider a number of things. We can begin by a brief return to the two opposing camps of Essentialism and Social Constructionism.

Essentialists think that they have uncovered an objective reality, rooted in Nature, that makes gender a given of the human condition. If gender exists as a fixed and universal standard, based on body sex, then deviations from the pairings between sex and gender (masculine male or feminine female) *must* represent either errors in Nature or human perversion. Determining which is the case permits an Essentialist to make, or refrain from making, a moral judgment.

Social Constructionists regard gender as rooted in social needs and processes. Though related to Nature, gender is neither fixed nor everywhere the same. Different societies construct gender in various ways—and thus the moral judgments made within each society reflect to great degree the social standards for gender. However, this variability also should occasion reflection on whether the individual or the society is the party in error when moral judgments are made. We err if we automatically assume an individual is morally wrong when in conflict with society.

Whether we feel the Essentialists or the Social Constructionists have the better case, for most of us the key issue resolves down to one matter. Fortunately, it is one science helps understand: *choice*. On that point both camps agree: science offers pertinent observations that may help explain why things occur. Such explanations can assist us in weighing the element of choice. Are those of us who are gender variant transgender persons by choice? Or is it a matter set perhaps before birth, or shaped by an environment over which we had little if any control? For most of us, such questions matter in moral conversation.

Do We Choose to be Transgender?

The legitimacy of a moral judgment depends on the reasonableness of seeing a behavior as freely chosen. Virtually all of us are very uncomfortable with the notion we might be held accountable for a behavior we did not choose. For instance, if we ingest food we purchase at a restaurant and have a violent reaction to it, vomiting all over the table, we would not expect to be censored for it. People around us would understand we did not choose to be sick, even if we chose to buy the food. Of course, if they concluded we knew we would be sick if we ate the food, then our choice will likely result in a judgment by others that we acted immorally. Clearly, we decide how accountable people are for what they do based on the degree of control and choice they have in the matter.

So how much choice is involved in being transgender?

Should We Be Held Morally Accountable for Our Biology?

We have talked about a number of factors that might be involved in producing transgender realities. Many of these come from Nature and are biological forces at work even before birth. If what our society calls gender variance is the result largely of such forces, it seems unconscionable to call it an immoral choice, since no choosing was involved. After all, we don't proclaim that the gender conformity we attribute to Nature is a matter of moral choice; it just *is*. Essentialists might believe gender variance stems from an error in Nature, but that is not the same thing as saying it is immoral. In fact, to the degree that Essentialists believe gender flows naturally from biology, all gender is morally neutral since no gender results from choice.

Social Constructionists look at the issue differently but can come to a similar conclusion. If gender is socially constructed the choices involved belong to all of us collectively. What can—and should—be morally weighed are the choices of our *society*. Do they promote the well-being of all of us? Are some of us harmed by the way gender is constructed in our society? What are we going to do about our society's problematic choices? These are the critical moral judgments we might be spending time considering.

The weight of the available evidence today strongly implicates biological factors although few would use language as strong as saying the case is 'proven' for a biological origin to transgender. Unfortunately, a few of us use this uncertainty as an excuse to simply ignore the evidence. Not liking gender nonconformity we simply condemn it as a matter of personal choice created by 'preference' for a certain 'lifestyle.' This way of talking is irresponsible in light of the facts and we ought to challenge it as lazy thinking at best and transphobia—an irrational, negative emotional response—at worst. But we will deal with this sort of thing later. For now let us assume the vast majority of us genuinely desire to be sensible and righteous in our moral thinking.

Should We Be Held Morally Accountable for Our Environment's Forces?

Let us return to science. If contemporary science offers sound grounds for seeing transgender realities as natural, there still remains the possibility that environmental factors may be important, too. Maybe being transgender is something that either always requires an environmental trigger, or is sometimes caused by environmental factors. In either case, the question remains, to what degree should the transgender person be held accountable? If we, for example, are crossdressed by a parent from an early age because that parent desired us to be a member of the opposite sex, how can we be held accountable for the behavior? The key here is *causation*. If the environment causes transgender, then how can those of us who are transgender be said to be any more morally responsible for being gender variant than are those of us whom the environment causes to be gender conforming?

Essentialists tend to see the environment as responsible for reinforcing Nature through gender socialization and an orderly society reflecting the proper differences and separations associated with gender. In this light, any environmental forces that would lead Nature astray, such as parents promoting gender variance, would be censored. But the person thus victimized by the choices of others cannot logically be held morally accountable. The only time an Essentialist can conclude a transgender person is morally culpable for gender variance is when that person, made fully aware of how the environment has acted wrongly, then chooses to endorse that error personally. But that situation we must look at a bit later.

Social Constructionists think the environment of the individual is a microcosm of the society. Cultural values and the pressures they generate are filtered down in various ways and degrees to the individual. If environmental forces cause transgender realities, or if such forces merely trigger biological potential to be transgender, then these environmental factors do so in relation to the social construction of gender. If gender variance occurs and is prompted in some manner by the environment, that suggests the social construction of gender has mechanisms that permit it (e.g., socially approved crossdressing at festivals, for entertainment, etc.), or is somehow flawed so that such occurrences must happen and thereby indict the society's construction of gender. The former possibility means that the system must allow some room for gender variance to vent the pressure created by strong gender expectations and intense socialization. With respect to the latter possibility, gender variance should be welcomed as a signal that the social construction needs change—change we are *all* morally responsible for. In either instance, the transgender individual is faultless.

What Weight Should Personal Choice Be Given?

In sum, the above moral reasoning adheres to the basic rubric that where individual choice is absent or minimal, moral accountability should not be assigned. But we still have to account for the third causal factor—*individual* contributions to being transgender. If we are gender variant largely or entirely by choice, then moral accountability for that choice ensues. Essentialists, for whom gender reflects an inner essence, in practice are more prone to make this judgment despite the greater difficulty of reasoning the possibility within the principles of their position. This strange situation largely stems from the fundamental attribution error, which we shall consider in a moment.

First, let us ask how a Social Constructionist might view the matter. Since gender is socially constructed, and all of us are parts of society, there always exists an element of choice about how much we ratify our society's constructions or challenge them. So a Social Constructionist has no trouble seeing how an individual can make choices about personal gender that place the person in conflict with society. However, from the Social Constructionist perspective moral reasoning about this must not be confined to assessing the individual alone. It is at least as valid to judge the society as the individual. For example, in our society we champion social dissidents in communist countries; we judge the social construction of communism as immoral, not the individual who opposes it. If we conclude that our society's gender construction is the problem, then gender variance can hardly be assumed to be immoral.

But let us consider how individual choice might interact with both biology and the environment. Perhaps gender variance is like alcoholism, an inherited tendency that never develops unless a person chooses it through specific behavior. Although the person cannot be held morally liable for inheriting the tendency, or for living in a society where alcohol is legal and readily available, the person can be held accountable for choosing to drink if possessing the knowledge of what that might result in. This is the way some of us reason about homosexuality; the inherent condition is not wrong, but acting on it through same-sex sexual behavior is. Some of us apply similar reasoning to transgender. Being gender variant *inside* may be something that can't be helped, but showing it *outside* through behaviors like crossdressing is something we can control by choice.

There are choices involved in things like crossdressing. How we estimate the power of those choices will influence how we view those of us who cross-dress. Yet, to acknowledge that choices are made says surprisingly little in itself. The crux remains to what degree even our personal choices are constrained by other factors, such as those driven by biology or elicited by the environment. We might do well to ask ourselves honestly whether our judgment of the morality of what a person does is really driven by our reasoned conclusion of the causal forces involved or merely an objection to a behavior we find personally distasteful. Put another way, are we assessing the moral choice of the person, or applying a predetermined judgment based on the behavior, so that no matter why one does that behavior it is wrong because the behavior is wrong.

Religious Sentiment and Moral Judgment

While perhaps all of us would agree that where there is no free will there is no moral culpability, most of us would also cling to the idea that there is *always* free will. Many of us want to hold a person morally responsible for any behavior we find objectionable based on the conviction that what matters is that the person was free not to do it. In essence, many moral judgments focus less on the person than on the objectionable act. The moral reasoning is this: *anyone who does an immoral act is morally wrong because the person always has the choice not to do that act.* In deciding what acts are wrong in themselves, many of us look to religion.

Moral judgments are often accompanied by religious sentiments. Some of us object to anyone being transgender as against God's intention. We might argue that God created a man and a woman, not a man, a woman, and a transgender person. We might also say that there can only be two genders because there are only two sexes. Therefore, we may reason, behaviors like crossdressing or seeking to change the body to appear like a different sex are morally wrong in and of themselves, standing outside of God's intention and creation. We may also add they are wrong because God intends order and such things by their deceptive nature create confusion and disorder.

This line of reasoning prompts important questions. Are those of us who are transgender weak-willed or willfully sinful? Those are certainly possible explanations, *if* we assume being transgender is inherently evil, or *if* we believe transgender behavior is *always* wrong no matter why it is done, and *if* we conclude that the mere existence of freewill sets aside all other causal factors. We may, for example, believe that those of us viewed as crossdressing chose to start the behavior and can choose to stop. We may believe that failed efforts to stop reflect a weak will, one corrupted by the sin we chose. We may believe that those of us who actively persist in things like crossdressing—and enjoy it— suffer from a seared conscience.

An Unexamined Assumption

In all of this there may rest an unexamined assumption: that the element of personal volition is more pertinent than biological or environmental factors as a causal factor. If we conclude that crossdressing is immoral behavior that results from individual choice, and that it can be stopped by the same act of will once transformed by moral change, then we are likely to brush aside all talk about other possible causal factors, whether biological or environmental. In essence, we make of them inconsequential forces. We reduce causality to choice, a conclusion that leads to speedy moral verdicts—but at a steep price.

While the simplicity and clarity of such thinking may seem irresistibly desirable to some of us, we have reason to hesitate before endorsing it. The end of such 'logic' is to reduce scientific investigations to irrelevancy and leave all of us prey to the moral values and judgments of those few who hold real power to enforce their will. That path historically leads to oppression rather than liberty, divides rather than unites, and harms rather than helps. The language of science—an appeal to reason and evidence open to evaluation by all—is a language of discourse on a level field where personal feelings and subjective convictions are subordinated to rational testing and facts. This does not displace religion, but it does protect *all* of us from the beliefs of *some* of us.

Prejudice

The definition of *prejudice* is that it is 'pre-judging' others. Whenever we conclude that any act is inherently wrong we prejudge the person who does it. We are well-advised to avoid such a course. Even in the matter of one person killing another, we refrain from pre-judging the person as immoral pending full investigation of the forces prompting such an act. When the evidence is in we may conclude the person was morally justified because it was self-defense, or morally culpable because it was murder. To set aside any causal factors in favor of only one, or to place all the weight of our moral judgment on a decision made beforehand about the act itself is very dangerous ethically.

If we are honest, we may need to confess that it is our other choices—about religion, morality, social values, personal feelings and so forth—that really shape our judgments toward those of us who are transgender. The attractiveness of science lies in it offering common ground where we can all speak the language of reason and evidence in an effort to understand behavior. We don't have to set aside moral or religious convictions, but we *suspend our certainty* that we know enough to pass life-altering judgments on matters where reason and evidence provide pause. In short, we need not choose between science and religion when there are so many advantages to employing both in being human.

'Prejudice,' of course, is a strong word—one most of don't want to hear applied to ourselves. We need to contemplate how we may make ourselves vulnerable to such a charge. To do so we might consider how errors in thinking may happen. Let us examine three among many possibilities.

Three Paths to Poor Judgments

The three elements we may look at here are emotional thinking, the fundamental attribution error, and stereotyping.

Emotional Thinking

Trusting our feelings is valuable. But practiced indiscriminately it can lead to trouble. Feelings provide important information, but they are only *one* source of information. Moreover, mere strength of feeling is no guide to assessing the accuracy of the information conveyed. So while we can trust our feelings, what that means is understanding the nature of the information they relay and how it can contribute to our reasoning.

Feelings tell us how we *are* responding to something, not how we *ought* to respond. When our feelings motivate us to act based on them we call that emotion—a movement of feeling outward through behavior. Merely justifying any behavior as the result of feeling is clearly irresponsible. All the feeling does is tell us how we are responding internally; no feeling dictates how or even if we should act behaviorally.

Emotional thinking is drawing conclusions based on believing that how we feel tells us how we ought to reason and behave. In this manner, we justify our thoughts and acts based solely on feeling, with the stronger the feeling the greater the justification for how we think and behave. People who commit crimes of passion may feel justified in their violence because of the strength of their feeling. Such 'logic' fails to persuade others not similarly moved by feeling. Unfortunately, when groups of people share strong feelings and couple this with emotional thinking the results can be devastating.

Gender variance, for some of us, elicits strong feelings. If we understand that those feelings are only telling us what is actually going on inside us, and not telling us what we should think or do, then we might be able to act rationally. In *rational thinking conclusions are drawn based on assessing evidence concerning why we are having such feelings.* We may find our feelings are a reflection of how we have been taught to respond to certain things. We may discover our feelings reflect our own values, which may not be shared by others. There are numerous possibilities, depending on the available evidence, but the end is always the same: rather than *act out* the feeling as a kind of imperative, we *act on* the feeling by treating it as information about what is going on inside us and worthy of reflection. Only after sober reflection do we then decide what, if any, behavior is called for.

Fundamental Attribution Error

Let's next consider an error in thinking that stems from the different way we evaluate our own acts compared to how we judge others' acts. We tend to explain what *we* do as the result of many forces and influences, not all of which are of our choosing or under our control. At the same time we tend to be impatient with others who do the same, rejecting their explanations as excuse-making and insisting they take more responsibility for their behavior. We interpret their acts as reflections of personal traits or internal dispositions. What is curious about our doing this is how much we do it toward others, yet how little we do it to ourselves! This imbalanced process is known formally as committing the *fundamental attribution error*. For ourselves we may explain behavior by elements in the environment (situational attribution); for others we tend to assume an internal factor, one that is stable and reflects the self.

We don't commit this error just with isolated acts but with ways of being. We explain the way we are as a complex result of many forces, including our choices, but also the choices of others and things like biology over which we have no choice at all. Yet we easily grow irritated at others who do so when they are explaining being the kind of person we don't like. This process is very much alive when it comes to evaluations of gender. Because we at least tacitly recognize that gender variance is highly individualistic, we are prone to attribute to others a fundamental responsibility for the way they *are* in their gender. If we don't think they have the gender they should have, we assume this is because of something inside them that they can (and should) change. Of course, our own gender we reason to be natural and beyond our control.

Stereotyping

Most, if not all of what influences our notions about how others ought to be with respect to gender comes from our society. But it comes largely in a manner exaggerated by attention to the alleged differences between the genders. Thus gender at the poles of masculinity and femininity becomes caricatured by *stereotypes*. The word derives from a late 18th century printing process that created a solid plate that could be used over and over again. That is what stereotypes provide—a preformed template that can be continually used without change. Stereotypes give us ready packages of qualities we assume show us best what femininity or masculinity truly is. These packages probably arose out of the need to buttress and justify the gendering division of people by explaining that the sorting into groups makes sense because of the many differences between the genders.

For example, in his 1984 book *Adolescent Sex Roles and Social Change*, sociologist Lloyd Lueptow offered a review of studies reported between 1957-1980. He found the traits most often endorsed for men were dominant, aggressive, competitive, independent, ambitious, self-confident, adventurous, and decisive; those for women were affectionate, submissive, emotional, sympathetic, talkative, and gentle. At the end of the century Lueptow and colleagues did a review of some 30 studies, as well as examining data from surveys involving more than 4,000 respondents, to see if changes in this regard had transpired over the span between 1974-1997. Reporting their work in 2001 in the journal *Social Forces*, they found great stability; our gender stereotypes and the 'sex typing' practiced in our society has remained remarkably consistent. Even as we may acknowledge that no one fully embodies gender stereotypes they persistently provide for us standards against which we are always measuring ourselves and others.

Writing in 1990 in the *Journal of Personality & Social Psychology*, psychologists Curt Hoffman and Nancy Hurst argued that gender stereotypes do not stem from real sex differences in personality; they flow from our rationalizations rather than from valid perceptions. We generate stereotypes to explain why men and women sort into different roles—and our rationalizing includes the notion that gender personality differences make one gender better suited to certain roles than the other. It is not fact derived from observation that creates our belief in gender-based personality differences, but our need to explain the obvious social separation into masculine and feminine roles.

Steeped as we are in the process though a life of gender socialization, we can justly call ourselves experts at stereotyping. Now imagine that along comes a male in a dress. Though the image presented does not fit our stereotype for gendered dress, we still stereotype. Like a knee jerk reflex, this mental tool flings itself out of our mind's toolbox to fix the jarring discrepancy we find before us. In fact, psychologists Neil Macrae, Alan Milne, and Galen Bodenhausen found in their research, reported in the *Journal of Personality & Social Psychology* in 1994, that we actually depend *more* on stereotypes when our social perception occurs under taxing conditions such as our example. In this instance the likely template we draw upon is the stereotype of a gay man. Lacking any other evidence than wearing a dress, the person is stereotyped as a homosexual in drag. As Macrae and colleagues point out about stereotyping in general, it costs *us* little to apply one, though the other person to whom it is applied may find the cost high.

It is that greater price—one consequence of moral judgments that may come from errors in thinking—that we must examine if we are to better grasp how practically important our judgments can be for others among us.

Stigmatizing

Stereotyping may collude with the fundamental attribution error and emotional thinking and produce *stigmatizing*. A stigma is some mark borne by another person we perceive as warning us to stay away. The sociologist Erving Goffman described the cost paid by those we stigmatize, which begins with our judgment that the stigma makes the person somehow less than, or not quite human. "On this assumption," Goffman wrote in his book *Stigma: Notes on the Management of Spoiled Identity*, "we exercise varieties of discrimination, through which we effectively, if often unthinkingly, reduce his life chances."

Goffman observed we engage in forming theories to explain why the stigma-bearer is inferior and poses a danger to us. We apply metaphoric labels to disparage the person. We add imagined defects to the stigma we know. Curiously, we also may add notice of some quality generally desirable, such as the notion that the one with a stigma is supernaturally gifted with special understanding or insight—though we ourselves have no wish to obtain such a gift at the cost it carries. And then, when we witness how such a person reacts defensively toward us, we see in it a justification for our attitudes and behaviors—the person has, after all, deserved it.

All of these observations pertain to how those of us who are transgender are too often regarded by those of us who aren't. Some of us are branded; those of us who wield the brand blame the mark it leaves on the bearer. Transgender people are often in various cultures regarded as special in possessing gifts that in another person would be treasured. Some societies still treasure them and by virtue of them make places of respect for transgender people. But most societies in today's world, under the pressure of Western culture, have learned to regard transgender as stigmatized—and so the gifts such folk possess go unwanted and unused by the society.

No wonder, then, as Goffman found, those of us stigmatized may respond by making every effort to change so as to escape the stigma. Some of us use the stigma as an excuse for our lack of success due to other causes. And some of us bear the stigma but are neither impressed nor repentant because of it. What is important to acknowledge, is that those of us burdened with a stigma *must* respond somehow. A common path for those of us at risk is to act preemptively by limiting what is known about us so others won't brand us. We live secret lives—another fact often used against us if we are discovered. Goffman says that stigma groups have two kinds of members: those who are "discreditable," who hide a stigma that may be discovered and who must always be on guard to protect their secret, and those who are "discredited," bearing a stigma either visible or otherwise known to others, and who thereby are confronted by the stresses arising from how so-called 'normal' people interact with 'abnormal' people. Those who bear a social stigma constantly must reconcile their self-image with the very different one reflected by others.

How high is the price we insist others pay for moral judgments we make so easily and swiftly!

A Final Note

The matter of moral judgments is too important for us to leave at one sitting. We shall return to it later. For example, we will look more closely at the role of religion. We shall give attention to responses made by others in society, including family and friends. At all times our task will be not only to assess our reasoning but to soberly consider the consequences for real people who spend their lives as we all do—hoping and praying for acceptance, daring to dream of finding those who will move beyond tolerance to celebration of their lives.

6.

Between the Divine and Humanity

Religion provides ways for us to explore and connect to transcendent realities or to the wholeness of the universe. Because most of us believe there are realities both greater than our own limited existence and to some extent removed from us, many of us turn to religion for a bridge to such realities. But bridges reach both ways. Even as we may seek what lies on the other side, whatever is there may be reaching out toward us. Thus religion is a two-way avenue with our portion involving both giving and receiving sacred actions.

On our side, the task is complicated by certain factors such as our relative inability to see or understand realms beyond our own world, or unities greater than our own individuality. We draw upon things in our own finite realm to comprehend and represent divine realities. Because we have gender, we rely on the concept as a tool to comprehend divine beings, and this act generates questions: Do deities have bodies? Are they sexed and gendered? What roles do sex and gender play in transactions between mortals and immortals? But the questions cut both ways. We often find ourselves questioning our own nature and seeking answers by looking to the Divine nature. More questions arise: Is our gendered nature in the image of God? Is a gender hierarchy divinely ordained? Can we manipulate gender like our deities appear to?

The complexity of gender in our world, coupled with the mysteries of the sacred, make for nearly endless possibilities in the questions asked and the answers determined. Not surprisingly, then, we find cultural variety in conceptions of sex and gender—particularly the latter. Many people across history and around the globe have sought an understanding of gender by looking to divine figures—an effort we ourselves will take some time doing, with a focus on the religion dominant in our own society, Christianity. In so doing we may find new resources for comprehending transgender people.

Gender variant people have a long history of occupying an important place in the religious struggle to understand ourselves, divinity, and how the two may meet. Because we who are transgender people live outside the cultural norms for gender—however that is understood in a particular society—we tend to be perceived as in a unique position. Often this means seeing us as well-suited to mediate between the conventional genders and to stand as mediators between all people and the Divine.

But even we who are gender conforming people can participate in gender crossings for sacred purposes. Transgender realities like crossdressing can be entered into by anyone. Sometimes such a reality is engaged to lift us out of our ordinary world in order to glimpse a different way of being—even a divine way of being. By virtue of the power of transgender realities to enact sacred crossings, some people find themselves permanently embodying a religious role such as priest or shaman for the benefit of the entire community. The reason gender crossings have such power resides in the nature of gender itself. Whenever gender is seen as a fundamental sorting that divides people, gender crossing offers the hope this divide can be breached. If that can happen among people, perhaps it may also occur between human beings and divine figures.

Sacred Gender Crossings

Sacred gender crossings reflect violation of normal gender boundaries for sacred reasons or by deities for their own reasons, whatever those may be. Our world has numerous instances of such divine crossings. In general, these fall into one or the other of the following broad categories: divine or other sacred nonhuman beings appearing in unexpected gender manifestations; human beings pursuing sacred roles or tasks through a gender performance different from the gender identity and role assigned at birth; and, sacred festivals, where divine and human interact, and where an aspect of that interaction involves gender crossing.

The key element in sacred gender crossings is not the gender crossing itself. It is that it is *sacred*. The gender crossing is an act set apart from ordinary acts. Things become holy by being removed from mundane occurrence or use, and in sacred gender crossing it is gender thus removed. The individual—whether divine, semi-divine, or human—sets apart (or aside) 'normal' gender presentation (and perhaps experience) for the express purpose of some kind of interaction. Just as food becomes holy and wholly different by being offered to a deity, so gender becomes holy and wholly different in sacred gender crossings.

Divine gender crossings exist in various forms. A principal form concerns the manifestation of deities in gender-manipulating ways. Another resides in the gender acts of characters found within the pantheon of non-human religious figures (e.g., demons and demigods). Though best known in the West through stories coming down from the ancients, divine gender crossings persist in religious traditions kept alive today in various parts of the world. Such crossings are familiar in many, many societies of both East and West.

Divine manifestations that confuse or confound gender expectations may be divided generally into three kinds:
  o   Deities appearing as *ambiguous* in gender (i.e., neither clearly masculine nor feminine, usually because they are absent gender);

o   Deities appearing as *androgynous* (i.e., with both male and female characteristics), such as hermaphroditic deities; and,

o   Deities appearing as an *altered* gender, one different from the one they are traditionally assigned (e.g., a female deity appearing in male guise), and thus engaged—from the human standpoint—as emasculated, masculinized, or in a gender masquerade.

Each of these merits a quick examination.

Ambiguous Gender

Many deities, especially the greatest figures, are conceived as possessing no inherent gender—and perhaps no body either. Such beings can, however, assume any gender shape they wish. Even if they do not do so, their followers can (and usually do) use gender language to metaphorically speak about them. Such divine figures are found around the globe, both in major world religions and in smaller indigenous ones. In some instances the emphasis is on divine unity (e.g., 'G-d' in Judaism, Allah in Islam, Cghene of the Isoko people of Nigeria, and perhaps Tlaltecuhtli and Tlaloc of the Aztecs. In other cases, the genderless supreme being is viewed as 'One-as-Many,' like Brahman of Hinduism, or of dual gender, such as Ometechutli of the Aztecs. What all of these deities have in common is that gender with respect to them is *ambiguous* in some manner.

The God of Christianity has no inherent gender, though the masculine pronoun is most often used in referring to 'him.' This usage reflects the patriarchal structure of the societies in which Christianity has been dominant, both in the past and presently. God is always associated with power and status. Though masculine pronouns, attributes, and metaphors abound, feminine ones are not unknown. Thus, for example, the Hebrew Bible has the prophet Isaiah's utterance from God that pictures a woman in childbirth: "Now I will cry out like a woman in travail, I will gasp and pant" (Isaiah 42: 14, RSV). Or the same prophet's message from God wherein the deity compares self with motherhood: "As one whom his mother comforts, so I will comfort you" (Isaiah 66:13, RSV). A sense of the feminine in God has been kept alive in Christianity's mystical tradition. For example, Mother Julian, a Christian mystic of the early 15th century wrote in her *Showings* (chapter 52) that God both enjoys being Father, and also being Mother. The truth of the Trinity is 'father,' but the wisdom of the Trinity is 'mother' (chapter 54). Even Christ can be depicted as mother, in whom the believer is endlessly born (chapter 57). In fact, the second person of the Trinity is especially singled out for use of metaphors of the feminine (see chapters 58-62). Such usage is entirely appropriate because God has no gender.

Androgynous Gender

Another group of divine figures express more than one gender simultaneously—another way of solving the problem posed by the limitations of dichotomous gender. Androgyny in divine figures is explained by religion scholar

Mircea Eliade in his *Patterns in Comparative Religion* as existing "to express—in biological terms—the coexistence of contraries, of cosmological principles (male and female) within the heart of the divinity." Examples are numerous and include some who, despite being assigned a gender, have managed to defy the cultural conventions in their behavior, dress, or reception by devotees. Among them are Aphrodite, Artemis, Athena, and Dionysus of Classical Greek religion; Inanna of ancient Sumeria; Shiva in Hinduism; and Jesus in Christianity.

Jesus

The last name on this list may come as a surprise. For those of us raised in Western societies where the ambiguous deity is the norm, the idea of an androgynous deity can be challenging. Jesus, though revered as the Son of God, in orthodox Christology has been 'officially' viewed as both wholly divine and wholly human (cf. the Definition of Chalcedon, 451 C.E.). The key in this formulation is *wholly*. Gender experience is intrinsic to humanity as we know it, and gender markers are used in speaking of God. How can the gender differentiation of masculine and feminine be applied to understanding Jesus as *wholly* divine and human? As we might expect, more than one answer is possible, but whatever the precise nature of the response it must acknowledge in some fashion the femininity of Jesus.

Hildegard of Bingen, in the 12th century, stood the whole problem on its head. She offered that we are reflections of Christ: men represent his deity, women his humanity. Other approaches have looked for expressions of Jesus' femininity to balance our patriarchal emphasis on the higher status of masculinity. In this respect, attention to Jesus' Passion, where the traditionally feminine role of passive victim is played, offers one way to redress the imbalance.

There is a long history of talking about femininity in connection with Jesus. Christian New Testament and Early Christian History scholar Stephen Davis, writing in 2002 in the *Journal of Early Christian Studies*, tells us that, "among different early Christian communities, Christ was viewed as an androgynous or gender-ambiguous figure: he was variously identified as the incarnation of the female, divine Wisdom, pictured in eschatological visions as a woman, and depicted in early Christian art in the form of Orpheus, the androgynous figure of Greek myth."

As early as the 2nd century Clement of Alexandria referred to Christ as 'mother,' drawing an analogy between Christ's giving of his blood in the Eucharist and a mother nursing her infant. Historian and late medieval period expert Caroline Walker Bynum, in her 1987 book *Holy Feast and Holy Fast: The Religious Significance of Food to Medieval Women*, observes other writers followed this approach across the centuries. Later male writers when they depicted the motherhood of God sometimes used the imagery of the soul suckling at Christ's breast. Moreover, both men and women (like Catherine of Siena) employ the image of drinking from Christ's breast—an image sometimes found in religious visions.

The medieval saint Mother Julian of Norwich (1342-c. 1417), among the most famous of mystics, depicted Jesus as 'Mother' in her famous *Showings*. She ascribes to Jesus such attributes as childbearing and nurturance. Julian pictures Christ as a pregnant woman who, after sustaining Christians in his womb, brings them forth safely through the travails of childbirth. Julian sustains the idea of the maternal Jesus as she depicts Christ as a mother raising a child.

Meister Eckhart's disciple Henry Suso, a Dominican friar and 14th century mystic, was famed in his own time for his devotion to the suffering Jesus and his ministry to women. He extolled the figure of Christ/Sophia ('Wisdom'). Religion and Classics scholar Barbara Newman, writing in the journal *Spiritus* in 2002, comments that in his *Horologium Sapientiae* (*Wisdom's Watch Upon the Hours*), Suso plays with gender—both human and divine—referring to himself at times as a feminine soul longing for Christ the Bridegroom, and at other times imagining himself as a masculine disciple in love with Christ the goddess. Similarly, Jesus is imaged both as male and female, as an excerpt from his autobiographical *Life of the Servant* makes clear in talking about his beloved Eternal Wisdom: "The minute he thought her to be a beautiful young lady, he immediately found a proud young man before him." In his use of gender Suso offered male believers a way to spiritually embrace a heterosexual marriage to God, with the added benefit of retaining their own masculinity. Newman quotes Suso's depiction in the *Horologium* of coming from the royal wedding where "the supreme King and divine Emperor himself has given me his only beloved daughter, Eternal Wisdom, as a bride." Far from proving scandalous and resulting in Suso's rejection as a heretic, his work was warmly embraced; the *Horologium* was one of the most widely read devotional works of the Medieval period.

The depiction of Jesus in terms of feminine gender does not emasculate. Rather, the juxtaposition of such imagery with more familiar masculinity creates androgyny in the strong sense—as a figure embracing the best of both men and women. Jesus is not neutered but balanced. The androgynous Christ is a figure as fully feminine as masculine because Jesus is *wholly* human. This inclination to re-envision the gender of Jesus persists, showing up sporadically in Christian expressions, especially artistic ones, right down to our current era. Contemporaneously, some theologians key on episodes in the Gospels which portray Jesus as transgressing the boundaries which separate men from women and episodes showing Jesus performing functions more commonly associated with women (e.g., serving food, washing feet, ministering to the sick). Theologian Eleanor McLaughlin, in a 1998 essay in the volume *Reconstructing the Christ Symbol*, has gone so far as to suggest the notion of a transvestic Jesus—Jesus the cross-dresser, a "destroyer of dualities." She is not arguing for an effeminate Jesus but an appreciation of a Jesus who is "like a 'cross-dresser,' one not 'caught' by the categories" but free to express feminine ways of love, sacrifice, and forgiveness.

Other Androgynous Paths

Many of the deities we might classify as 'androgynous' are so in ways different from being assigned a gender and rising above that gender assignment. Some are what we might call *'either gender' beings*. They include Agni in Hinduism; Asgaya Gigagei of the Cherokee Nation; Atutahi of Polynesia; Nyame of Ghana; and perhaps Atum of ancient Egypt. More familiar to most of us are so-called *'hermaphroditic' deities*, who combine genders, or sexes. They include Agdistis and Hermaphroditus in Classical Greek religion; Ardhanari and Ayyappan in Hinduism; and Inle of the Yoruba people of West Africa.

Altered Gender

Gender altering deities can be found in at least three distinct forms. There are the so-called *'emasculated gods'* such as Mahadeva in Hinduism; Odin of old Norse religion; Quetzalcoatl of the Aztecs; Ra of ancient Egypt; Uranus in Classical Greek religion; and Amaterasu in Japanese Shintoism. As the name suggests, these deities at some point undergo a change in gender status, from masculine to feminine. Some gender altering occurs by calculated disguise and among *'masquerading deities'* are Athena and Zeus of Classical Greek religion, and Vishnu in Hinduism. The masquerade might be for any number of reasons but often happens to facilitate a sexual liaison. Finally, there are the *'trickster' deities* whose gender altering has a more peculiar and particular flavor than mere masquerade. Such deities include Hermes in Classical Greek religion, and especially Loki of ancient Norse religion. Tricksters show the capriciousness of gender.

Sex and Gender in Religious Life

In addition to figuring out the nature of divine figures and how best to relate to them, we also have to determine the role of sex and gender in our own lives, and how these fit into the religious sphere. Answers differ radically. Some of us view sex and gender as those aspects of human experience most directly relevant to religion, particularly because they involve relationships and the renewal of life. Others of us think human sex and gender are those parts of human existence that most interfere with connecting to the divine because they are distracting and deluding powers. In fact, some of us regard humanity's division into male and female as a fall from an original androgynous state. Many others of us take one or another position in-between the extremes, finding a place for sex and gender without making it central or excluding it as evil.

Different perspectives help generate different judgments as well as varying behaviors. The very same gender crossing seen by some of us as a blessed way to meet the divine is viewed by others of us as intrinsically wrong. But before we dare engage again the issue of moral judgments we would be advised to see how diverse are the perspectives and practices found among religious people around the world. Among the more notable avenues for transcending gender—

or at least crossing culturally dominant gender conventions—in a religious context are serving as a shaman, as a priest or priestess, as a disciple, or as a eunuch.

Four Traditional Religious Roles for Transgender People

Shamanism is a phenomenon found around the world, albeit in various forms and under different names. The *shaman* is a religious figure who bridges the mundane and sacred spheres. Mircea Eliade calls shamans an example of 'ritual androgyny.' They unite, or 'reconcile,' opposing principles such as masculinity and femininity. A sign of this is their crossdressing—a very common feature of shamanism. In gender crossing they are able to access the power in both genders, bridge and unite them, and offer healing. Religiously, they also serve as a bridge, or as gatekeepers. They not only offer a way to approach the divine, but for the divine to reach through them to the community.

Priests and/or priestesses, holders of a sacred office whose purpose is the linking of people with the divine, serve a similar function. They also are often involved in sacred gender crossings and crossdressing. At the dawn of literature, in ancient Sumeria, we find references to crossdressing priests called the *kurĝara*, whom may have been a template for later gender crossing priests, such as the effeminate male *assinnu* of Ishtar, or the male prostitutes referred to in the Jewish and Christian sacred literature (1 Kings 12:24). We might count among their figurative descendants the 'Galli,' priests of Cybele, famed throughout the classical world. They not only crossdressed, but sometimes castrated themselves. These acts represented their imitation of a revered figure (Attis) and constituted a transformative action whereby the priests became acceptable to the deity they served. Examples abound around the world. Even in the modern West a remnant of the gender crossing nature of priests is glimpsed in the perception that Catholic priests' garb appears feminine by cultural standards for dress.

Disciples or *devotees* are similar to priests/priestesses, though without the specific role and duties of that office. A sign of their devotion is the adoption of the Master's gender. Thus some early Christian women sought to masculinize themselves—to become men—as a sign of their devotion. The so-called 'crossdressing saints' were women who became like men to enter a discipleship ordinarily closed to them. In other religions, some males feminize themselves, becoming women devotees. Some worshippers of Krishna in Hinduism have followed this path of devotion.

Eunuchs occupied a unique and often privileged place in many ancient societies. Their infertility made them a logical choice for sensitive positions, such as service among the women of a ruler's harem. Many of these eunuchs were intersex individuals—eunuchs 'made by nature.' Others were eunuchs 'made by man,' sometimes voluntarily, often by the choice of another. However they arrived at this state, it was generally viewed as placing them in a border state between sexes. The eunuch's position *between* sexes and gender statuses also was ideal for religions. Religion scholar Richard Gordon, writing in the *Oxford Classi-*

cal Dictionary, observes that castration placed an individual 'between worlds' and was parallel to other acts of devotion such as voluntary poverty or homelessness. Some way was needed to mark out such persons and acts like crossdressing served this purpose. Religious eunuchs were known in both East and West.

Transgender People and Religious Roles Today

Although in other places transgender people may have a vital role in one or another of these traditional religious roles, this seems pretty much confined to smaller indigenous groups—religious communities many of us in our Western hubris call 'primitive.' In our supposedly more enlightened societies religions like Christianity not only generally resist transgender people in offices of ministry, but often marginalize them in the wider life of the spiritual community. Perhaps the most vocally transphobic voices in our society come from Christian leaders who confuse their Essentialist philosophy with sound biblical thinking. Their noise, coupled with the silence of too many of us who have a gentler spirit and fairer mind, complicate life enormously for those of us who are transgender Christians.

We transgender Christians face all of the same issues as nontransgender believers, as well as issues related to our unique reality, especially the way in which other believers respond to us. As counselors Suzanne Lease, Sharon Horne and Nicole Noffsinger-Frazier, writing in the *Journal of Counseling* in 2005, observe there persists a common perception that people with sexual orientations other than heterosexual cannot have a religious identity. This same assumption is often extended to all of us who are gender variant. By virtue of the misunderstanding and prejudice we may receive from other Christians, we become more likely to avoid the forms and institutions of formal religion. Instead, many of us favor cultivating a personal spirituality.

However, no one should assume that such a step means we simply choose to believe whatever suits us. Rather, like a great many people who are nontransgender we find more meaning in a personal relationship with God than in the observance of religious rituals or attendance at Church. A majority of contemporary Americans draw a distinction between *religion*—the institution of the Church and activities associated with it—and *spirituality* as a personal, individualized relationship with God. Sociologist of religion and gender studies scholar Melissa Wilcox reports in a 2002 article in the journal *Sociology of Religion* that her research with transgender women shows they may craft a religiosity of their own through one or more of at least six distinct ways: leaving their religious tradition before coming out; staying in their tradition as they come out; switching to another congregation or denomination; struggling with a homophobic, bi-phobic or transphobic tradition; seeking a new religiosity among alternative or new religious movements; and/or relying on divine assistance. For those of us who find ourselves unwelcome in too many churches, cultivating a personal spirituality is a reasonable response. At least God welcomes us.

In truth, though, an increasing number of churches and Christian organizations do as well. While there are Christians who believe transgender realities reflect a broken Nature and a sinful humanity, there are others who regard transgender as a gift of grace, loved and accepted by God, and worthy of the same response from God's people. Some congregations have styled themselves as 'Welcoming' congregations and formally declared that transgender people will be accepted—not merely tolerated. Welcoming congregations can be found among Baptists, Methodists, Mennonites, Roman Catholics, Presbyterians, Disciples of Christ, Lutherans, United Church of Christ, and other denominations.

Sacred Festivals for Sacred Gender Crossings

Religions around the world mark special times for the enactment of sacred festivals. These may vary in purpose and duration, but key to them is the sense that in these sacred festivals divine figures interact with human ones. Frequently this interaction is a solicited *meeting* of the parties. Often this is construed as a passive act on the part of the deity, who may merely hear a prayer or accept an offering. But in some instances the deity takes a more active part, typically through a representative human figure, perhaps a priest (or priestess) or a figure masquerading as the deity, or serving as a conduit for the divine presence, perhaps through spirit possession.

Reasons for Gender Crossing

In sacred festivals the meetings between divine and human beings may entail one or both parties engaging in gender crossing. The deity may do so for any number of reasons, including putting the worshippers to the test, seducing a person, or mixing among the faithful. A human may also gender cross, perhaps because such is suitable for the worship of the divine being, or in imitation of the divine nature, or even because the human is attempting a subterfuge to trick the deity for some reason. In this last named situation, human participation in the festivities sometimes may involve actions to *avoid* a divine, semi-divine, or demonic figure. In such cases the person may cross gender as a way to deceive a wrathful deity or a malevolent one. Through successful deception the person escapes harm until the danger is past. Rarely, the divine figure also might be portrayed as gender crossing to avoid being met by human pursuers. In such a case the idea is to use a disguise in order not to have to yield some benefit.

While the above ideas are not exclusive to sacred festivals (i.e., they can occur in individual experience outside any religious structure), they take on special meaning in a festival. The occasion of the festival adds regularity and fixes the contextual form and process for the gender crossing. It has a sacred character by virtue of being set apart from ordinary action. The gender crossing is *not* typical of ordinary, mundane experience. Instead, it exists in a special time and place for a concrete and sanctioned reason.

The Role of Crossdressing

The easiest way to convey a gender crossing is through dress. It is not the only way, however. Dramatic and extreme steps might also be taken, as among eunuch priests who self-castrate and undertake a life of gender crossing that sets them apart from others. Obviously, for the majority of the faithful this is not a course that will be taken. Festivals offer a way to do something similar, though limited in time and extent. We shall consider them in a moment.

We should note that both male and female crossdressing is known in religious contexts of the ancient world and our own. Since crossdressing inherently represents a significant change, it often was connected to *rites of transition*. For example, in many societies initiatory rituals involve the initiate crossdressing to signify a transformation into the other gender, or to create a state of androgyny. In other cases—such as in what has been term 'ritual transvestism'—crossdressing can represent either a *temporary gender role reversal* for a sacred act or event, or (more rarely) a *permanent gender role change*, as in the acquisition of a new status or sacred role. The symbolic power of crossdressing makes it useful in a variety of situations for religions.

Examples of Christian Festivals with Sacred Gender Crossings

Sometimes this power becomes available to anyone, as in sanctioned occasions to crossdress at festivals. Throughout Church history there have been festive occasions where crossdressing has been common and unremarkable. Two illustrate this connection well. They are Carnival and Halloween. Both still enjoy widespread acceptance. Remarkably, at times these festivals even have seen crossdressing activities involving the clergy.

Carnival

'Carnival' (Mardi Gras in the United States), is a festival celebrated around the world. It derives its name from the Italian *carnevale* (itself from the Latin *carnelevarium*), referring to the 'removing of meat' characteristic of the Lenten period. It was known by this form—'Carnival'—as early as the 13th century, but centuries earlier as "Carne Levale." In 1091 C.E., the Synod of Benevento formally established Ash Wednesday at the conclusion of Carnival, thus joining the festival to Lent. Christian missions spread the festival everywhere Catholicism prospered so that it became a fixture in many cultures, from Brazil to Trinidad to the United States. Carnival customs include feasting, games, parades, costumes—and crossdressing. Role reversal is a fixture of Carnival practice, including gender reversal through crossdressing. Such practice is *sanctioned*.

Halloween (All Hallows Eve)

For most Christians in the United States, Halloween (All Hallows Eve) is the best known Christian festival where crossdressing may occur. While this is completely unremarkable when small children are dressed in costumes so that young boys might become witches and small girls Harry Potter, it draws little comment even when it is adolescents or adults crossdressing. Halloween offers a rare and limited period where public crossdressing is sanctioned because it is not going to be taken as a serious statement about gender.

Donning costumes is a popular aspect of Halloween. While the most often chosen reflect the theme of departed souls and the supernatural, adults especially may select costumes that satirize one or another aspect of culture—like gender distinctions. In our society Halloween has almost entirely lost its religious connection and so the crossdressing occurs in a secular rather than sacred context. However, the Jewish holiday of Purim, similar in many respects to Halloween, preserves a Western sacred holiday where crossdressing may still happen in a religious context. Given our current cultural rigidity with respect to gender the practice of crossdressing during Purim is controversial, with some Jews regarding it as inappropriate and others not troubled by it at all.

Christian Controversy over Transgender Realities

Despite the growth of other religions in our society, Christianity remains the dominant cultural force. It seems fitting, then, to conclude our brief examination of the relation between religion and transgender realities by focusing on the controversy within American Christianity over gender variance.

The Essentialist Theological Argument

Some of us who oppose transsexualism believe that someone who seeks to modify the body God gave them is thereby sinning. One common theological argument we alluded to earlier when we discussed moral judgments. It is an Essentialist argument that God created two sexes divinely intended to be reliably paired with two genders. Anything such as crossdressing or body altering is an intentional confusion of gender differences, an acting as though such differences are inconsequential. One advocate of this way of thinking, Baptist ethicist Daniel Heimbach, in his book *True Sexual Morality* argues that while behavior like crossdressing does not necessarily involve sexual relations with someone else it inevitably stirs up sexual thoughts and desires in the direction of homosexuality. In other words, preventing gender crossing preserves the heterosexuality that he regards as the primary concern. This linking of transgender to homosexuality is a common tactic that displays the earmarks of stigmatizing, making both guilty by association with the other.

As for the argument itself, that God intends only two genders and that gender variance means a confusion of the differences God established, it is less a biblical argument than an Essentialist one. The biblical texts themselves provide no limitation to the number of genders, show little interest in spelling out gender differences, and offer exactly one succinct comment on crossdressing.

The Biblical Text on Crossdressing

That text—Deuteronomy 22:5—reads, "A woman shall not wear a man's apparel (*keli*), nor shall a man put on a woman's garment (*simlah*); for whoever does such things is abhorrent to the Lord your God" (NRSV, with key Hebrew words in italics added). It seems more straightforward in English than it actually is in Hebrew, as consultation of any number of commentaries would reveal. The word *keli* (כְּלִי) is a very versatile term, capable of being translated as 'accessory,' 'armor,' 'bag,' 'clothing,' 'jewelry,' 'weapons' and various other words. But its ordinary use is of 'implements,' such as weapons of war. *Simlah* (שִׂמְלָה) has a more limited range, but can be translated as 'cloak,' 'clothes,' or 'garment.' The use of two different terms suggests they are not meant to be understood as synonyms. So how do they stand in relation to one another? That is debated. Interestingly, though, the ancient Jewish rabbis of the Talmud (*Nazir* 59a) reasoned this text cannot be simply understood as a general prohibition of men wearing women's clothes or vice versa, because the Torah is talking about something that is an 'abomination' and such behavior does not qualify! So the easy assertion that the Bible is talking about 'crossdressing' as practiced by transgender people today is by no means certain.

The 'Love the Sinner, Hate the Sin' Argument

A much more common kind of theological position is succinctly expressed in the sentiment: 'love the sinner, but hate the sin.' This position may consciously build on an argument like the one we just reviewed, but quite often it merely *presumes* transgender is a sin and adopts this argument as to how best to deal with it. That makes it an argument of a different kind—one after the fact, the conclusion already having been drawn on some other grounds.

Some of us as Christians characterize this formula as the heart of what we call 'tough love,' an exercise of Christian charity that wields a stick for the punished one's own good. We might claim a parallel between this and the discipline administered by parents in rearing righteous children. Or we might appeal to the notion that one's eternal state is more consequential than their temporary state in this world, and thus acts designed to secure a favorable eternal state justify harsh warnings and even punitive acts in this present life. Our thinking is not arbitrary; it rests on an old intellectual tradition.

The Crux of the Argument

The idea of 'love the sinner, hate the sin' relies on a basic philosophical distinction between personal identity and behavior. *Who* one is must be distinguished from *what* one does. Where the former is relatively stable, consistent, and enduring, the latter is highly variable. The dualistic split between act and identity relies on the older division between body (external source of acts) and soul (internal source of being), or to put it more pertinently, between imperishable spirit and perishable flesh. The soul is prized above the body (e.g., Matthew

80

10:28; Luke 12:4), so that it seems truly gracious to some of us to secure the destiny of the soul even if that requires the sacrifice of the flesh (cf. Matthew 5:29-30), as was the logic in the Inquisition.

Of course, few of us among today's Christians favor anything remotely approaching the tactics of the Inquisition. Yet we might agree that Christian love mandates doing what one can to secure another's eternal well-being. We may believe that just as God disciplines those he loves (Hebrews 12:5-11), the Church has a responsibility both to discipline those who would be part of the community of faith (cf. Colossians 1:28), and to warn those outside the faith of their need to repent and be saved (Mark 16:15-16). In this light, warnings to turn away from transgender behavior (e.g., crossdressing, sex changes, or homosexual acts) place the soul (or identity) above flesh (or transitory actions). Christians, we might remind others, are called to hate sin (Romans 13:9), and calling sin what it is can hardly be construed as hateful. Although this phrasing is nowhere found within the Bible, it makes sense to many of us and seems to us to fit ideas that are found within Scripture.

Problem #1 with the Argument: Can We Actually Make Such a Separation?

However, this logic often vexes those of us who are gender variant. It can leave us wondering whether we are truly loved or actually hated, since in our personal reality it seems impossible to distinguish between *who* we are and *what* we do. A significant problem many of us find with the formula 'love the sinner, hate the sin,' is that it is not all that easy to separate act and identity. In a world where, as Jesus himself declares, 'You will know them by their fruits' (Matthew 7:15-20), how can what one *does* be separated from who one *is*?

Women's studies scholar Janet Jakobsen and religious studies scholar Ann Pellegrini, in their book *Love the Sin: Sexual Regulation and the Limits of Religious Tolerance*, wonder if it is truly possible to 'love the sinner, but hate the sin.' They ask whether the so-called 'compassion' and 'tolerance' espoused by holders of this position feels like that to those on the receiving end. "Does it really feel any different from contempt or exclusion?" they ask. In the final analysis, they contend, court cases such as *Bowers v. Hardwick* (1986) and *Romer v. Evans* (1996) show that the sinner-sin distinction is no distinction at all. In fact, the line fixed between *whom* we are supposed to love, and *what* we are supposed to hate proves not to be fixed at all; it moves in baffling and even contradictory ways. Jakobsen and Pellegrini remind us that tolerance, though an improvement over outright hate, is not the same as freedom. Rather than proving a sign of openness, this kind of tolerance proves hierarchical, exclusionary, and undemocratic.

It certainly feels that way to those of us who are transgender. Is it just us, or do such people really hate us? In an online essay, Disciples of Christ minister Rev. Kenneth Collins remarks knowing many who invoke the formula's principle, but finds that none of them are able to maintain the fine distinction; they inevitably wind up hating the sinner. "In fact," Collins writes, "I have never met a person who sighed soulfully, 'That minister hates my sin, but I know he really loves me.'" In Collins' estimation, this rationale is a Satanic tool that ends up chasing off the very people the Church should minister to. He asks why Christians would waste time hating sin when there are sinners who need to be loved.

Problem #2 with the Argument: Is Being Transgender a Sin?

Of course, we who are transgender Christians have objections to being characterized as sinners simply for being gender variant. The real problem is the conclusion that being transgender is a sin—an idea that seems to us rooted in cultural prejudice rather than sound theology. We argue that before you can use the formula it must be determined if it is applicable. Simply assuming something is sinful does not make it so, no matter how personally offensive one might find it. After all, a good many folk find proselytizing Christians offensive! We might point out that nowhere does the Bible explicitly condemn gender variance—and may not even address it all. We may also argue that it seems just as logical to view transgender people as made in God's image as anyone else, especially in light of all the evidence that biology is the principal force in making us the way we are. We may object to the idea that God makes mistakes—*all* people are okay just the way they are made. And to the idea that sin has corrupted the world so that transgender is a consequence of a broken created order, we merely need respond that such a contention places the burden of proof on those who claim it, not the rest of us. In short, there are at least as many and as plausible reasons for rejecting the idea being transgender is a sin as there are to endorse it. How then can some Christians feel so secure in their condemnation?

More Responses By Transgender Christians

Many of us who are transgender, and a good number of us who aren't, who object to this formula try to address it in the same terms as its advocates—by appealing to the Bible and using theological reasoning. Most often this takes the form of another popular formula, 'God tells us not to judge others, but to love everyone.' In support of the former clause we may cite Jesus' words, 'Judge not, lest you be judged' (Matthew 7:1; cf. James 2:13). In support of the latter clause we might appeal to Jesus' words both to 'love your brother' (John 13:34-35) and to 'love your enemies' (Matthew 5:43-48). We can also point out that not only does Jesus not make the distinction between hating the sin and loving the sinner, but instead boldly tells his followers to focus on their *own* behavior (Matthew 7:1-5)! Jesus warns us to avoid being angry with others or insulting them (Matthew 5:21-22), and instead to seek out anyone who has something against us, not to confront them, but to be reconciled (Matthew 5:23-26). We argue that the tenor of the New Testament favors words of loving-kindness over those of condemnation, reconciliation over estrangement, and good deeds over punitive ones. In sum, we reject the formula 'love the sinner, hate the sin' as true neither to Scripture or to Christian love.

7.

Across Time & Space

One important consideration for those of us living in our society, wondering how best to understand transgender realities, is to try to obtain a wider perspective. If we can at least glimpse such realities across history and around our globe, perhaps we will be able to more easily see transgender as an enduring, widespread, and thoroughly human condition. Though the name 'transgender' may be recent, the underlying gender variance from the dominant forms of gender in a society is neither recent nor confined to Western societies. What is different in many cases is the legitimacy granted in some societies to being a 'third gender.' Let us begin with history and then look at a few examples today.

Transgender Realities Throughout History

We begin with a problem. Some key obstacles beset the historical study of gender, transgender, and crossdressing. First, the conception of gender has not been static. Even in our own time fierce debates exist over exactly what gender is, and such debates—albeit in different forms—have marked previous eras. Second, the concept of transgender as such is relatively recent and still somewhat unformed. To apply today's incomplete and sometimes controversial labels and concepts to people of the past may help make them feel accessible to us but it comes at a cost: in their own context such labels were not used and the meaning today attached to them may or may not have existed then.

We might also note that the study of transgender realities across history is largely the study of crossdressing. This also has its problems. Crossdressing, too, has been subject to changing conceptions and preoccupations. Exactly what constitutes crossdressing is not as straightforward a matter as it may superficially appear. Through much of history the principal fascination of the general public seems to have been over crossdressing females rather than crossdressing males. This means in one era our knowledge of a particular sex's gender-crossing behavior may be much richer, only to find a much different situation in studying another era. This complicates drawing any general observations applicable across the span of history.

Transgender Realities in the Ancient World

Crossdressing likely is as old as the practice of dressing. While we cannot know with certainty either when or where crossdressing began, we do know the practice dates back at least 3500 years to the Egyptian ruler Ma'at-ka-Ra Hatshepsut. Some of history's most famous mythic figures crossdressed, such as Achilles, Heracles (Hercules), and Odysseus of Western culture, and Krishna, Amba, Arjuna, and Bhima of the East. Notably, the greatest warriors of both East and West were prone to crossdress. While the many commoners who embraced transgender realities are often lost to history, their more famous counterparts, notably rulers, have been remembered, such as several Roman emperors and many Christian crossdressing saints.

We possess references to crossdressing and gender transformations in ancient plays, novels, and poems. For example, In the West Ovid's *Metamorphoses*, whose very name reflects transformations, has many stories where gender crossing occurs, sometimes as cross-dressing (e.g., Achilles and Heracles), sometimes more radically (e.g., Caeneus and Iphis). The sacred literature of the world's great religions know of it, such as the Bible, the *Qu'ran* of Islam, the *Mahabharata* of Hinduism, the *Lotus Sutra* of Buddhism, and the *Kogoshui* of Shinto. In sum, we have no lack of materials on gender variance or gender change.

Ancient societies held no uniform view on transgender realities. At various times and in various places they drew a range of responses from sanction for sacred purposes, to indifference, to mild disapproval, to restrictions to limit or discourage such practices as crossdressing (at least among certain portions of the populace). The response to gender variance has differed by time and place.

In the West, as we have discussed, gender has been tied to sorting people by kind based on origin. The question of an original human nature crops up in Plato's famous *Symposium*, where Aristophanes argues that originally human nature meant three genders: man, woman, and "the union of the two." These genders reflect dominant forces in Nature: the sun, earth, and moon. Man is the child of the sun, woman of the earth, and 'the man-woman' of the moon, because that body is made of sun and earth. Aristophanes elucidates a number of characteristics flowing from this original reality, including matters often placed today under the umbrella of transgender.

It is clear the ancient Greeks were aware of such 'third gender' people in their world, like eunuchs, hermaphrodites, and even culturally specific groups like the all female Amazons and the all male Enarees, a group found among the Scythians. The Greeks themselves sanctioned crossdressing in the theater, and used it in religious festivals such as the festival of Cotyttia in Athens, where males dressed as females when they danced. At the festivals honoring Aphrodite at Argos (called the 'Hysteria'), both sexes crossdressed. Gender crossing was also important in the male rite of transference from youth to adult citizen in the festival of Ekdusia ('Festival of Disrobing') celebrated at Phaistos. There was no shortage of transgender realities the ancient Greeks knew about, and this also was true for the ancient Romans and other peoples of both West and East.

Transgender Realities in Europe's Medieval Period

The Middle Ages in Europe (roughly the 5th century to the Renaissance) were marked by a greater sense of gender fluidity than we retain today in the West. Historian Joan Cadden, in her *Meanings of Sex Difference in the Middle Ages*, argues that while Medieval Europe may have maintained a binary system of the human sexes, the gender continuum was anything but static. Instead, both a range of body physiognomies and gender behaviors were acknowledged. Medieval writers avoided a narrow dependence on medicine. They tried to explain what they observed by drawing variously on Christian scripture, philosophy (especially Plato and Aristotle), science and history, as well as medical speculation.

One of the more prominent Catholic philosophers of the 12th century, the Scholastic theologian William of Conches (c. 1080-c. 1154), is illustrative of how reasoning out of these matters proceeded. Basing his thinking on Plato's *Timaeus*, he reworked the Platonic notion of reincarnation to make his own statement about gendered souls. In William's view the soul itself does not contain anything pertaining to either sex within it; gender transformation occurs according to *behaviors*. He explained the phrasing on reincarnation in the *Timaeus* to show that transformation happens not in essence but in "resemblance of manners." Because William located such a transformation after fifteen years of age, it became a 'second birth' that literature scholar James Cain, writing in the journal *Essays in Medieval Studies*, believes William associated with the age of puberty. In Cain's view, this Neo-Platonic model allows for gender change from what was assigned at birth through sheer persistence of habit. A person can become the gender they imitate.

This openness to gender fluidity seems rather widespread and corresponds to a similar, if more limited openness about the sexed body. Writing in the journal *History of Political Thought*, historian James Blythe remarks, "Medieval medical and scientific views of sex and gender were complex and not fully determinate, resisting binary categorization and making possible various combinations of masculine and feminine traits." With regard to gender, for example, Blythe refers to the mid-14th century medical professor Jacopo da Flori at the University of Sienna, who formulated three indices of gender: complexion, disposition, and physique. Any individual can be gender-mixed along these indices; for example, feminine on one, masculine on another, and even indeterminate with regard to the third.

Certainly, Europeans of this period were familiar with what we call transgender realities. Heroic figures like Hervör, the heroine of the Hervarar Saga, illustrated the bravery of countless female warriors in armies throughout Europe's wars. Literary pieces like the 13th century poetic novel *Le Roman de Silence* (*Romance of Silence*), by Heldris de Cornuälle, raised intriguing and important questions about identity and gender. So, too, did Church plays of the period, often performed by all male casts. One example is the 13th century French drama *Miracle de la fille d'un roy*, in which the maiden Ysabel, to avoid pressure from her father to assume the role of her dead mother, disguises herself as a knight. The 14th century French play *Miracle de Théodore* presents another such story, that of a crossdressing saint. Such plays depict struggles and dilemmas their audience was acquainted with in real life.

Transgender realities were something seen among both males and females, though the latter received the bulk of attention. Incentives to crossdress included seeking access to the privileges or activities typically reserved for another gender, or to hide a forbidden relationship. It is clear issues of gender identity also played a role for some. Although no one used the term 'transsexual' in the Middle Ages, it seems certain the reality existed. For example, the trial of Katherina Hetzeldorfer in 1477 indicates a likely instance of a female-to-male transsexual. Female crossdressing was common enough that there were efforts to regulate it by local ordinances. In sum, the West in the Middle Ages wrestled with the nature of human sex and gender, and struggled how best to comprehend and respond to gender variance. Their efforts reflect a greater openness to natural variability than our own, but like the later West also a resistance to strong challenges of the gender hierarchy.

Western Transgender Since the Middle Ages

Since the 14th century the West has continued to witness transgender realities and to debate their proper nature and place. Like our predecessors, we continue to find gender variant people at every level of society. Prior to our own day, European royalty like Queen Christina of Sweden and King Henry III of France required reckoning with behaviors like crossdressing. There remained crossdressing saints, the most famous of whom is St. Jeanne La Pucelle of the 15th century, better known as Joan of Arc. In fact, crossdressing females remained the primary focus of attention as they posed the greater threat to the reining gender hierarchy in Western societies. Efforts like the sumptuary regulations of England in the 14th-15th centuries attempted to protect social status lines by regulating dress behavior. They failed.

Ideas about gender continued to be debated between the end of the Middle Ages and the triumph of the medicalization of sex in the 19th –20th centuries. Culture historian Thomas Laqueur, in his *Making Sex: Body and Gender from the Greeks to Freud*, marks a decisive turning point in the late 18th century when, he says, Europeans moved from a 'one-sex' model (i.e., male and female are variations on a common type) to our modern 'two-sex' model where the sexes are set opposite one another on a horizontal axis. No matter where one dates the shift, a study of literature across this time supports the thesis that a significant conceptual shift—or narrowing—does indeed occur. Its consequences mark our own day and this turning merits special attention.

The Medicalization of Sex

Our own time is characterized by a medical view of sex, sexuality, and gender. The so-called *medicalization of sex* has had a profound impact on our contemporary social perceptions. The phrase refers to the rise to prominence of a way of understanding and talking about human sexuality that especially developed from the latter half of the 19th century to become dominant by the middle of the 20th century. Previous to this new way of looking at things, social focus had been on sexual *behaviors* rather than about the inherent dispositions and psychological states said to produce them.

Why did things change? The 19th century in Europe and the United States was marked by lively conversation about sex and gender. Appeals to science were common. Medical science, in particular, emerged as the most prominent voice in talking about sex and sexuality; linked to gender this made medicine an authority on it as well. Medical researchers possessed an understandable desire to scientifically classify and categorize human behavior related to health—including sexual health and mental health. Words like 'homosexual' and 'heterosexual' began to emerge as behaviors and people were categorized. The variants of human sexual behavior were being labeled—and sometimes linked to gender (e.g., 'hysteria' as a woman's mental disorder), or gender variance. Behaviors like crossdressing—already discouraged by various laws—became 'officially' linked to mental disorders. One outgrowth of this process was modern psychiatry's diagnostic model, set out in the successive volumes of the *Diagnostic and Statistical Manual of Mental Disorders* (DSM model), which we shall examine later.

Ostensibly this new medical language of sex, sexuality, and gender is scientific, rooted in an objective discernment of natural reality. But as historian Angus McLaren points out in his history of 20th century sexuality, medical professionals solidly ensconced in the middle class proved oblivious to the efforts of their own social class to impose their values about sexuality and gender on everyone else. Like others of their class, these medical professionals accepted certain social conventions about behavior, especially about masculine sexuality. Masculine men obviously don't go out in feminine apparel! Masculine men are heterosexual! The temptation to merge 'deviancies' is irresistible: if men aren't dressing like men, they must be emasculating themselves, which isn't normal. Since dress was widely theorized to exist to attract potential sexual partners, crossdressed males must be looking for men; therefore, male crossdressers are homosexual. This 'logic' was driven not by empiricism but by deductively working out unexamined presuppositions about what is 'natural' and 'normal'—presuppositions derived from culture, not Nature. It was simply Essentialism.

Much of our conversation has involved considering the price we all pay for inheriting this perspective. As our brief historical review suggests, this shift was by no means inevitable nor does it reflect complete continuity with the past. We must now turn our gaze to our contemporary world, where we shall see this modern perspective also does not define the entire globe.

Transgender Realities Around the World

Let's begin with the most obvious transgender reality: crossdressing. Today a number of facts seem established beyond reasonable doubt. First, clothing to mark gender appears to be a universal cultural characteristic. Second, wherever gender distinctions in clothing exist, there is a distinct possibility for crossdressing; in such situations some crossdressing almost invariably has been documented. Third, crossdressing is not confined to one sex. Females as well as males may crossdress. Fourth, crossdressing is not limited to one particular purpose, nor motivated by a singular desire or need. Indeed, the uses served by crossdressing are many. Finally, while there are some commonalities across many cultures with regard to crossdressing, many also know distinct and unique crossdressing groups. In short, crossdressing reflects in microcosm the diversity of human experience and expression as shaped within cultural contexts.

We should, in fairness, ask if the label 'crossdressing' really serves us well in looking at other cultures. What appears to us—bound as we are by thinking dichotomously—as crossdressing may not be so seen by others. A consistent use of logic suggests we judge crossdressing by gender rather than sex. Thus, a male body in feminine dress is *not* crossdressing *if* the behavior reflects a distinct gender sense that puts the person in a recognizable gender group. The same pertains to a female body in masculine dress when the gender sense experienced and expressed is consistent with the gender type of the dress. So, though we use the word 'crossdressing' we must remember we are using it as a referent within our own cultural myopia, and we would do well to develop better vision.

Transgender Realities in the East

Although transgender realities are found throughout the East, they have been most studied and discussed in India and Southeast Asia. The picture in other places is clouded by various factors, notably political realities. Mainland China, for example, denies, minimizes or tries to explain away transgender realities. While Chinese history makes plain that crossdressing has long happened in the land, mainland Chinese officialdom apparently prefers to regard most instances of Chinese transgenderism as evidence of Western decadence. This, for example, is the judgment about transsexualism presented by the nation's media. At any rate, we cannot hope to cover all the lands of this region, so we must be content to briefly examine a few of the more well-known instances of what we Westerners call transgender.

The Hijra of India and Pakistan

Indian languages recognize the possibility of gender beyond the dichotomy of 'man' and 'woman.' The *Kama Sutra* speaks of *tritiya prakriti* (a 'third nature'). The Sanskrit *napunsaka* and the Urdu *namard* are terms used to cover members of various groups that our term 'transgender' is often applied to: homosexuals, transvestites, transsexuals—all kinds of crossdressers. There are gender variant females as well as males, such as the *sadhin* of northern India, who renunciate sexual relations, or the *basivis* of Madras, who crossdress. Other females engage in same-sex relationships. Today, colloquial terms are used for female same-sex relationships (*sakhi*) and for those among boys (*masti*). Effeminate (uncastrated) males with a homosexual orientation, who crossdress and take the passive, receptive role in sexual interactions are known locally as *Jankhas* (or *Jhankhas*), or *Zenanas*, or *Kothis*.

Throughout the nation, but especially in northern India (and Pakistan) the most famous of the region's transgendered people are found: the *Hijras*. They are regarded as neither 'male' nor 'female'—but a 'third' sex and gender. Nevertheless, a linguistic distinction can be made between those whose bodies are male (*Hijras*) and those whose bodies are female (*Hijrin*). *Hijra*, living together in communities (*hijra gharanas*), may divide by ritual categories into those preparing for castration (*akwa*) and those castrated (*nirwaan*). The *nirwaan* ceremony confers status as irrevocably a 'real' *Hijra*. But while some voluntarily become eunuchs (often seen as the root meaning of '*Hijra*'), and some may be sexually ambiguous by birth (true or pseudo-hermaphrodites), many *Hijras* are neither. They do not easily fit any Western categories, though Western scholars have likened them, variously, to homosexual or heterosexual crossdressers, or to transsexuals. The Indian National AIDS Control Organization (NACO), influenced by Western categorization, specifies four distinct subgroups: transvestites, transsexuals, hermaphrodites, and drag queens/*Satia Kothi*. We do best, though, to leave them as themselves—a distinct and unique group. *Hijras* are called 'crossdressers' only because from a Western standpoint they typically are biological males who appear in the dress and gender role of biological females.

Found principally in India's larger cities, like Bombay and Delhi, the number of *Hijras* have not been kept by official census data and estimates range widely; anthropologist Laurent reports unofficial estimates from a half million to 5 million. They belong to a distinct community, with its own order, rules, and customs. Adolescents leave their birth families to join a new household—one of seven lineages preserved by the *Hijras*—organized in communes where at least five *chelas* ('disciples') are led by a *guru* ('spiritual master'). In this new family they take a feminine name, refer to one another by feminine pronouns, put on feminine clothing, and adopt feminine mannerisms. They receive training in *Hijra* traditions and activities such as the ritual performances by which they will earn income. They may have sex with males, typically assuming a passive-receptive role in anal intercourse. Their sexual activity may be motivated by personal desire or as an act of prostitution to help support their *Hijra* community.

Thailand's Kathoey

Perhaps no other country in the world is more famous for its crossdressers than Thailand, in Southeast Asia. Historically, says researcher Peter Jackson, an expert on gender in Thai culture, three distinct gendered groups have been recognized: masculine (*chai*), feminine (*ying*), and transgendered (*thang ying thang chai*—'both feminine and masculine'; or, *ying pra-phayt song*—'women of the second kind'; or *Kathoey*—variously understood, depending on context, as 'hermaphrodite,' 'transvestite,' 'transsexual,' or 'transgender').

Contemporary Thai *Kathoey* males may be placed in one or more of several Western categories, including effeminate homosexuals, transvestites, transsexuals, or transgendered in the narrow sense. They are publicly accepted in Thai society, though often with a lower social standing. In rural villages they may participate in local festivities in a feminine role, such as food preparation. In more urban areas they may hold any number of professional positions but are often associated with certain occupations such as prostitute, beautician, hairdresser, florist, or fashion designer—positions identified with women. Entertainment and media also offer opportunities, though media presentations often reinforce stereotypes of the *Kathoey* as histrionic and emotionally unstable—again, like women. Much of the stereotyping applied to the *Kathoey* may be linked to many Thai people seeing all *Kathoey* as being like gay drag queens.

Transgender Realities in the Mideast

Transgender realities are no stranger to the Middle East, having existed both in ancient times and down to the present. As elsewhere in the world, there has been no uniform social response to transgendered realities. Best tolerated have been intersexed conditions; hermaphrodites are known and discussed in Islamic religious/legal traditions. The existence of transsexualism, including individuals seeking sex reassignment surgery (SRS) also has prompted Islamic response, which has varied from place to place. In a region where transgendered people are marginalized and must often fear the State, most remain hidden and those who emerge in public do so largely in barely tolerated niches such as the sex trade. However, as in other places, the most visible road to tolerance has been through public entertainment. Together, the sex trade and entertainment continue to represent the most visible means for supporting themselves open to many transgendered people.

In the Middle East the transgendered community is far more diverse—and hidden—than a few very public figures (e.g., Israeli music star Dana International) might suggest. It embraces Muslims, Jews, and Christians. Repressive laws in some nations keep many transgendered people largely invisible, while others in public view often lead precarious lives, minimally tolerated because they provide a desired but unsanctioned outlet such as through the sex trade, but harshly treated when that role draws unwelcome attention. Many more transgendered people lead lives wearing the mask of social conformity in public to avoid negative social consequences.

Perhaps the most noted special group of gender variant people are the *Xanith* of Oman, a mostly Muslim nation with a small Hindu minority, situated at the edge of Arabia, across the Gulf of Oman from Iran. *Xanith* are, in Western terms, transgendered males. Norwegian social anthropologist Unni Wikan, whose fieldwork was among the Arabs of Oman's city of Sohar on the northeastern coast, concluded in the mid-1970s that these distinctive folk constitute perhaps 2% of the adult males of Sohar. Wikan noted they speak in a falsetto voice and present in distinctive dress that lies intermediate to the appearance of men and women. For example, while men and *Xanith* both wear ankle-length tunics, those of the *Xanith* are cinched at the waist like a woman's dress. Where a man wears white and a woman wears bright colors in patterned cloth, the *Xanith* wear unpatterned colors. Men keep their hair short, women wear theirs long, and the *Xanith* have hair whose length is in-between masculine and feminine styles.

The *Xanith*, observed Wikan, occupy a distinctive role in Sohar. Unlike other males, they are free to move among women, who may show their face to them. However, if they marry a woman they then lose this privilege and are treated like other males. *Xanith* sing at weddings, and perform other social tasks, but are perhaps best known for their involvement as prostitutes. Both the Euro-American terms of 'transvestite' and 'transsexual' have been applied to the *Xanith*, though they may also be considered an example of a third gender.

Transgender Realities in the West

Obviously, much of our conversation has been about the transgender people among us in our own Western society. We employ labels like 'transvestite,' 'transsexual' and 'transgender.' But rather than reiterate what we discuss elsewhere, let us pause a moment to recognize that there are distinctive gender expressions in Western societies that do not fit simply in the categories we seek to create by such labels. We can only look at a few, so we shall do so by selecting one example from each region in a journey back toward the United States. We shall begin across the Atlantic with Europe, then move to the Western Hemisphere and move from the South northward.

Europe: Sworn Albanian Virgins

In Europe, a notable gender variance is found in Albania among the so-called 'sworn Albanian virgins.' These *virgjinesha* ('sworn virgins') are genetic females who by their manner of dress as males signal a male gender identity, assume a male gender role, are accorded status as males, but remain celibate. This unusual situation is found principally in northern Albania among families who adhere to the Kanun, a code governing gender and marital relations. As a part of this code, gender is clearly marked by dress. But unlike many societies, where biological sex governs perception of gender regardless of dress, under

Kanun one's gender is as one presents it. A female may become a man by swearing a vow, so long as certain conditions are met. One such is that the girl's family has no sons to inherit, thus threatening the loss of the family's wealth (because all wealth is transmitted from generation to generation through the males). Since a sworn virgin is treated as a man—right down to being referred to as 'he'—this provides a male heir. In this social setting there is no shame in crossdressing; the sworn virgin is an honored part of society.

South America: The Machi of Chile

Among the indigenous Mapuche people of Southern Chile are two groups of individuals who would be termed transgender in contemporary Western terms. Both historically enjoyed positive status. One is comprised of intersexed people, physical hermaphrodites called *alkadomo* ('male-female'), who traditionally have been seen as co-gendered. The other group is comprised of anatomical males, whom anthropologist Ana Mariella Bacigalupo says have been culturally defined as co-gendered, meaning they may become either masculine or feminine, or both. This ability opens up important avenues to function as mediators in this world, and between this world and the realm of spirits. Like women, they can open themselves to possession by spirits. Persons who perform this and other shamanistic functions are called *Machi*.

Most *Machi* are female; male shamans (*Machi weye*) are transgendered people. Such males may dress and act like women. The *Machi*, honored among the Mapuche, do not enjoy the same esteem from other Chileans. The *Machi weye* are even further separated from the majority population and if their dual status as Mapuche and *Machi* were not enough, their transgender characteristics further complicate their reception within the larger society. Bacigalupo writes of one individual among modern *Machi weye* who was falsely accused of a crime and jailed without trial while public characterizations were made that the individual was 'a sexual deviant' and 'dangerous uncivilized Indian.'

Caribbean Islands: the Machi-embra of the Dominican Republic

Sexologists Paul Abramson and Steven Pinkerton regard the Dominican Republic as one of only two nations (Papua New Guinea being the other) where a three-gender system is clearly established as socially embraced. In addition to 'masculine' (men) and 'feminine' (women) there is a generic 'other'—which fits particularly the intersexed. In this regard, reporter Zachary Nataf points to the *machi-embra* ('male-female'), popularly known among the locals as *Guevedoche* ('balls at twelve')—intersex individuals assigned femininity at birth and raised as girls who at puberty become boys. Their condition has a biological basis—a hormonal deficiency that causes these genetic males to be mistaken as biological females at birth. At puberty, however, they begin developing male secondary sex characteristics. Not all *Guevedoche* transition to the masculine gender, however; some prefer to remain in the gender in which they were raised.

The Muxe of Mexico

In Oaxaca, a region of Mexico near the Tehuantepec Isthmus, are found individuals known locally as *Muxe* ('like a woman'; pronounced *Moo-shey*). Biological males, they seem to be regarded as a third gender. The general public there views them as joining characteristics found in women and men, while occasionally showing special intellectual and artistic gifts. They are regarded as born *Muxe*, not made, and though some families have difficulty accepting them as such, they have a distinct place within Oaxacan society. They tend generally to occupy jobs traditionally associated with women and to perform traditional feminine tasks such as cooking, housecleaning, childcare, and elder care. As adults they occupy a sexual role like that assigned females—as passive, receptive partners. Men who pair with them are known as *Mayate* and are not seen as homosexual. No one knows how many there are, but they seem common enough that most everyone knows one, perhaps even among their extended family.

The Berdache of the United States and Canada

Among the most famous transgender expressions found around the world are those among the indigenous peoples of the Americas: the so-called *berdaches*. A modern alternative to this label is 'two-souled' or 'two-spirit' people. While such individuals are known from North, Central, and South America, most attention until fairly recently focused on North America. In this area alone more than 150 tribes have been identified as recording transgender realities. Transgender Native Americans might be either genetically male or female, though the former are more common. They are probably best understood as occupying within indigenous culture a distinct social group that might also be characterized as a 'third gender.' They typically play important and distinctive social roles.

Outsiders first applied the label *berdaches*, a term derogatory in nature as it is derived from an Arabic term meaning 'sex slave boy.' The Spanish, encountering these native people, attempted to suppress the apparent crossdressing, and enlisted the power of the Christian missions to help reform the natives. The term *berdaches* soon became especially associated with Indian males in female dress and role, despite the fact that some women occupied a male gender role. Today, *berdaches* is defined in a scholarly manner using general and in-offensive terms, though some still object to its use, preferring instead 'two spirit.' If we follow scholarly convention, we shall speak of the *berdaches*, but there is no need to argue with any who prefer 'two-spirit.'

In contemporary Western culture's terms, the *berdaches* are transgender people in the broad sense. As such, they exhibit a range of distinctive characteristics. While some are intersexed individuals, most are not. Some are chosen to this identity/role/status by others, some choose themselves, and some claim to be born to it. Various tribal societies differ in whether they call all their transgender people by the same name or by different ones. For example, the Acoma refer to 'women-men' as *Mujerado* ('womaned'), *Qo-Qoy-Mo* ('effeminate person'),

93

or *Kokwina* (translation uncertain). The Omaha people distinguish the intersexed from other transgendered individuals, using different terms with varying social regard. On the other hand, the Navajo use a single term, without distinction. The translation into English of a particular word can be fraught with difficulties. For instance, the Cree term for people whom those outside the tribe might call *berdaches* is *Ayekkwew*, which can be understood either as 'both man and woman,' or as 'neither man nor woman'—a conceptual distance of some significance. By whatever name, these people hold a distinct gender status.

Indian societies traditionally often granted them a socially adaptive place. Will Roscoe, in his history of these people entitled *Changing Ones: Third and Fourth Genders in Native North America*, writes that, "in this land, the original America, men who wore women's clothes and did women's work became artists, innovators, ambassadors, and religious leaders, and women sometimes became warriors, hunters, and chiefs." Because they inhabit a space between masculine males and feminine females such individuals are often looked to as mediators between men and women. However, the idea of mediating often extends beyond being a go-between in only one respect. Often perceived as mixing masculine and feminine characteristics they may also be thought uniquely able to 'see' better than either gender and so be called upon as 'seers' whose visions bridge this mundane reality to the spiritual realm. Accordingly, in some tribal societies they become shamans. In sum, when accorded the legitimacy of a separate gender, such people are able to hold a firm place in society and contribute in unique and distinctive ways.

Seeing Better

As we mentioned earlier, we tend to suffer from cultural myopia, a condition exacerbated by the power our culture, and especially our own society, wields in the world. We may confuse economic and military might with legitimacy of cultural values. We tend, in fact, to endorse the exporting of our values, and to insist other societies see things as we do. Such thinking should be challenged if we are to create a world where there is room for all of us to live in peace. Perhaps in light of the amazing diversity found throughout history and around the world we might discover there is no harm in letting others be as they are; we may even be advantaged by what different ways of being tell us about being human. Perhaps, too, we may now better see our own time and place. With that hope we next turn our attention to the transgender people among us in our own society.

8.

Profiling

There is an abundance of information about those of us who are transgender people in our society. This material encompasses personal anecdotes, historical accounts, anthropological and sociological observations and analyses, and psychological research. For a while, let us focus on the empirical research with regard to demographic and personality characteristics of transgender persons. This research offers a somewhat mixed bag of findings, but generally it supports the conclusion that we who are gender variant are folk pretty much like we who aren't. Whether speaking of personality, mental health, or sexuality, transgender people are not as different from gender conformists as many of the latter think. Especially with regard to overall mental health, major reviews conclude that those of us who are transgender are no more liable to mental disorders than any of the rest of us.

But as we consider this material we must be mindful of some important limitations. First, most of us transgender people continue to hide in plain sight; we are not obvious to others as gender variant in any unmistakable fashion. Second, those of us who provide information to researchers may either come from a group who are in treatment for one or another problem, or from a self-identified group who are more public than most transgender people. Either way, those who are subjects of such research may not be representative of the general transgender population. Yet we must work with what data we have.

General Research Findings

Research gathered over the last few decades consistently challenges many of the stereotypes our society presents of transgender individuals. Particularly revealing have been studies built around personality testing of gender variant individuals. Other research has investigated the sexual attitudes and behaviors of transgender people. Yet other studies have focused on the gender identities of these individuals. For the most part, reflecting our culture's anxiety over the gender hierarchy, the research has centered on males, especially White males.

What does the research reveal? The overall picture highlights two broad conclusions. First, those of us who are transgender males are more like members of the general population than we are unlike them. Second, in the ways that we gender variant persons, as a group, are different from general population norms, the differences are generally not significant, nor clinically meaningful. They do not, for example, suggest personality traits indicative of greater risk for mental illness—a matter we will explore further at a later point. These conclusions pertain to the personalities of transgender individuals, and may be surprising to some of us, whether we are transgender or not. But even more surprising might be that studies of sexuality yield similar results. In this aspect of living, we who are transgender are also more like than unlike the general population in sexual functioning. In fact, one team of researchers characterizes the situation as being that crossdressers are virtually indistinguishable from noncrossdressers in both personality and sexual functioning.

The one area where we who are transgender males display a consistent difference from others is exactly where it might be expected, in showing a greater feminine gender affiliation. Yet, even here the findings might surprise those of us who are not gender variant. Not all transgender males show the same degree of affiliation with feminine gender. Transsexuals, for example, differ from transvestites in this respect. It is simply impossible to put a 'one size fits all' judgment on us—and that truth also makes us like everyone else.

Personality Traits

Although gender variant and gender conforming individuals, as groups, do not significantly differ overall in personality, there may be certain personality traits or patterns that are often associated with gender variant persons. Again, most of the research in this regard pertains to males. We can organize our approach to this material in two ways: first, by the kind of personality test used (projective or self-report inventory), and second, chronologically. The terminology used in different studies varies, but typically the subjects were identified by virtue of engaging in what others see as crossdressing, so 'crossdressers' is the term we shall often use in talking about this research.

Projective Tests

A number of different projective personality tests have been used to compare gender variant people to others. *Projective tests* assume that an individual's personality will be projected outward as they interact with ambiguous stimuli (e.g., inkblots or pictures). Some well-known projective tests are the Rorschach and the Holtzman Ink Blot tests, and the Thematic Apperception Test (TAT). We cannot look at all the studies that have been done, but we can look at some.

Study 1: Holtzman Ink Blot Test (1970)

One early study reported in the *Journal of Clinical Psychology*, conducted by Peter Bentler, Richard Sherman and Charles 'Virginia' Prince, dates from 1970. In it, 25 male crossdressers not in therapy were administered the Holtzman Ink

Blot Test. This projective test consists of a set of 45 inkblots presented to the individual sequentially, with only one response per card permitted. The results obtained are then compared to norms for the general population. Crossdressers, this research found, tend to respond more to the form of the inkblots than to their color or shading, a response style associated with relative rigidity of personality—which we might think a guardedness against our culture's judgments. Although crossdressers exhibit some greater preoccupation with the body, and elevated levels of anxiety and hostility, overall they do not differ significantly from the general population. The researchers concluded that "the scores for transvestites seem to indicate generally organized and intellectually adequate thought processes."

Study 2: Rorschach (1982)

Transsexuals, specifically, also have been administered projective measures. In a 1982 study in the *Journal of Clinical Psychology* by Michael Fleming and colleagues, the Rorschach inkblot test was used. This test is the most widely used projective instrument. A series of 10 bilaterally symmetrical ink blots, on 5"-by-9" cards, are presented in order. The subject is asked to describe fully what is seen in each. In this study, 20 transsexuals (10 male-to-female (MtF) and 10 female-to-male (FtM)) were administered the Rorschach both before and after sex reassignment surgery (SRS). The results of these tests were then compared to norms drawn from subjects in the general population. The researchers found "a lack of obvious difference from norms for the general population." Apparently, seeking SRS—as crazy as it may seem to some of us—is not an indication of disturbed personality. Nor does SRS seem to make one disturbed in personality.

Of course, while clinicians often use projective tests, many in the wider scientific community question their validity. We shall return to their role in the assessment of gender identity. For now let us concentrate on the kind of personality tests often called 'objective,' which enjoy high confidence by scholars.

Self-Report Inventories ('Objective' Personality Tests)

There are many personality tests that are not projective. These so-called 'objective' tests rely on *self-report* and have been more often used in assessing gender variant individuals. Let's look at several, but this time with an eye particularly to any differences we might find from the general population.

Study 1: Maudsley Personality Inventory (1965)

In 1965, a report by F. S. Morgenstern and colleagues was published in *Behavior Research and Therapy*. It contained the results of tests performed on 19 adult male transvestites. On one instrument, the Maudsley Personality Inventory's Extraversion Scale, these males averaged one standard deviation below the norm (-1 SD), meaning they were significantly less extraverted (hence, more introverted). On the other hand, a +1 SD average was found on the Neuroticism Scale, indicating greater than average anxiety—a finding affirmed by scores on the Willoughby Anxiety Scale. Finally, gender testing revealed scores that, on average, indicated greater femininity than found in most males.

Study 2: Personality Research Form (1969)

Peter Bentler and Virginia Prince did a major comparative study reported in 1969 in the *Journal of Abnormal Psychology*. It involved 181 adult male crossdressers, 1,029 norm subjects, and 62 control subjects. The crossdressers were not clients in clinical treatment. The research examined variables on the Personality Research Form (PRF), Form BB, an instrument used to measure normal personality traits. A total of 22 traits are assessed through the 440 items of the test. The results showed crossdressers are "clearly more controlled in their impulses" as reflected in these traits:
- o a tendency to avoid risks of bodily harm alongside a dislike of exciting, but potentially dangerous activities;
- o a concern to maintain neat and organized personal surroundings;
- o a preference for routine over new and different experiences;
- o a tendency toward deliberate rather than spontaneous acts; and,
- o a reluctance to express feelings and wishes.

Another set of differences between these subjects and those they were compared to concerned their "degree and nature of interpersonal orientation." The subjects exhibited the following traits:
- o being relatively withdrawn socially;
- o tendencies toward introversion;
- o a preference not to be the center of attention;
- o less nurturing (e.g., in doing favors or offering sympathy);
- o less concern for approval from others;
- o less likelihood of seeking roles of dominance—or enjoying them;
- o a dislike of arguments and conflict, and,
- o being relatively more self-reliant and autonomous.

Such characteristics hardly indicate pathology!

Study 3: Multi-trait Analysis (1976)

In 1976, writing in the *Archives of Sexual Behavior*, researcher and theoretician Peter Bentler offered a rough and preliminary list of 32 factors involved in the development in males of gender variant identities. Some of his factors indicate personality traits, like an emphasis on independence, together with an absence of same-sex affiliative behavior. Transsexualism and transvestism he associated with training in impulse control, harm avoidance, and behavioral inhibition. For transvestism alone he also found an emphasis on intellectual success. Interestingly, Bentler hypothesized involvement both of biological (hormonal) and environmental factors in the development of gender variance. In fact, he thought the differences observed among the subgroups of gender variant males might reflect an underlying difference in either or both of these forces.

Studies 4-5: Eysenck Personality Inventory (1980)

In a 1980 report by Chris Gosselin and Sybil B. Eysenck in the journal *Personality and Individual Differences*, 13 crossdressing males were administered the Eysenck Personality Inventory (EPI). What makes this study particularly noteworthy, though, is that the subjects were tested both while crossdressed and when not crossdressed. Results showed that the men, while crossdressed, scored significantly lower on the Neuroticism scale. They also scored lower on Psychoticism, but higher on Extraversion. In sum, these men demonstrated less anxiety and were more at ease and outgoing when crossdressed.

This study provides an interesting counterpoint to other research reported in the same year and journal by Gosselin and Glen Wilson, also using the Eysenck Personality Questionnaire (EPQ), among other instruments. Based on data obtained from 269 adult male crossdressers who were not in treatment, the researchers reported that crossdressers rank higher in introversion and neuroticism compared to norms from other adult males.

If we put the studies together, perhaps, as crossdressers themselves claim and their partners often endorse, being crossdressed produces notable changes in psychological functioning toward less anxiety and greater sociability.

Studies 6-7: NEO Personality Inventory (1991, 1996)

Thus far, the research we have examined has involved subjects who were *not* receiving therapy and had not been diagnosed with a disorder. But what does research show about those who do receive a diagnosis and receive treatment? Though they may not be representative of a nonclinical population, they still merit consideration. A team in 1991 looked at just such a group. Their article in *The Journal of Nervous and Mental Disease* reported a study of 24 men diagnosed with transvestic fetishism and receiving treatment. They were interviewed in addition to being administered two psychological tests. Personality traits were measured by Costa and McRae's NEO Personality Inventory (NEO-PI). This instrument is a 181-item questionnaire based on the well-regarded five-factor model (OCEAN) of personality. Sexual functioning was assessed using the Derogatis Sexual Functioning Inventory (DSFI). It employs 255 items to measure 10 dimensions.

The data obtained from these instruments was then compared to data from 26 men diagnosed with other sexual paraphilias. The researchers' analysis of the comparison led them to conclude the two groups were more alike than dissimilar on most dimensions of the NEO-PI and the DSFI. Both groups were higher than general population norms in N ("Neuroticism"), and lower in A ("Agreeableness"). Among key findings concerning the male transvestites in treatment in comparison to the general male population were these:

o   Relatively high levels of neuroticism (a personality trait associated with tendencies toward anxiety, depression, self-consciousness and vulnerability to stress) were common.
o   Relatively high levels of hostility also were found.
o   Relatively high levels of role identity with femininity prevailed.
o   Relatively low levels of agreeableness were seen.
o   Relatively low levels of emotional intimacy (whether because of need or capacity) also were observed.

Of course, this kind of study raises an inevitable question: how do transgender persons *in* therapy compare to others *outside* of treatment?

A study done by George Brown and associates, reported in 1996 in *The Journal of Nervous and Mental Disorders*, offered a glimpse at the answer to this question in a major study. The research involved 188 subjects classified in one or another of three conditions: 83 transvestites (44% of the subjects); 44 transsexuals (23%); and 61 transgendered (33%; a group equivalent to what other researchers term the 'marginal transvestites'). They were further differentiated by whether they had received treatment or not into four groups: 'no treatment' (81 subjects; 43%); 'treated for psychological problems' (49 subjects; 26%); 'treated for transvestism' (41 subjects; 22%); and, 'treated for gender change' (17 subjects; 9%). The study examined these subjects both with reference to personality characteristics and for sexual functioning. Personality traits were measured by the NEO-PI; sexual functioning is assessed using the DSFI.

With regard to personality characteristics, the researchers concluded: "Overall, the personality profile of this sample of 188 male cross-dressers did not deviate substantially from the NEO-PI normative sample of community-dwelling men." Specifically, crossdressers scored in the normal range on all personality dimensions of the NEO-PI except one. For the 'O' ('Openness') dimension, crossdressers were in the high range for Fantasy, Feelings, and Values scales. Such scores, however, are not intrinsically negative.

The researchers reached a similar conclusion about sexual functioning. The DSFI results revealed that crossdressers do not deviate dramatically from so-called 'normal' male heterosexual subjects. A modest difference was found in one respect. As a group, crossdressers' scores were lower in the area of the DSFI that indicates they are more likely to endorse a poorer body image. (However, a 1977 study reported by Ira Pauly and Thomas Lindgren of 67 transsexuals found that progression from a no treatment stage, through hormonal treatment, to SRS led to increased body satisfaction, as measured by the Body Image Scale (BI-I), which considers 30 body features evaluated along a 5 point scale.)

Brown and colleagues, then, found that at least some male crossdressers demonstrate personality and sexual functioning much like norms obtained from the general male population. They also suggested their data raises questions with regard to the adequacy of the DSM model. That is a matter we must eventually turn to, but at present let us move to another significant body of research.

Gender Identity Variance

As we have seen, the one area where those of us who are transgender differ from the rest of us is in gender identity. Formally put, transgender males exhibit more affiliation with femininity than society approves, and transgender females show more affiliation with masculinity than society accepts. However, even among those of us who are transgender there are enough differences in this respect to have led to creating separate labels for subgroups within the gender variant. In 1982, Kurt Freund and colleagues, in the *Archives of Sexual Behavior*, proposed that crossdressers—by whom they meant both transvestites and transsexuals—all experience cross-gender identity. In other words, transvestites do not differ from transsexuals in merely playing at a transgender identity, even though that identity may be somewhat different. Perhaps an important differentiation between transsexuals and transvestites is not only the *degree* of cross-gender identity, but also its *constancy*. In other words, transsexuals experience greater cross-gender identity and do so more constantly than transvestites, who may experience this cross-gender identity only when crossdressed. Thus historian Peter Ackroyd, alongside many other observers, notes that feminine gender characteristics do not predominate when the crossdresser is not crossdressed but is occupying his male gender role.

This speculation can lead to useful hypotheses. Studies can be conducted to find if there are differences among transgender subgroups, as well as documenting through testing the differences between transgender people and gender conforming folk. So, what does the research show?

Study 1: California Personality, Draw-a-Person, Franck Drawing Completion (1979)

Personality testing reveals that crossdressing males express a stronger feminine gender identity than do other males, but also differ among themselves such that two groups can be found. Researchers Neil Buhrich and Neil McConaghy reported a study in 1979 in the *Journal of Clinical Psychology* that worked with a group of 64 male crossdressers (transvestites and transsexuals). These subjects were divided into two groups based on their degree of feminine gender identity. Both groups were compared to two other groups (homosexual and heterosexual men). Four tests were administered to measure gender feelings and behavior. The tests were: the California Personality Femininity Scale (CPF-Fe), the Draw-a-Person (DAP), the Franck Drawing Completion Test, and two subtests (Information & Vocabulary) of the Wechsler Adult Intelligence Scales (WAIS).

The DAP provides the test subject with a 9½"-by-12" blank sheet of paper, plus a pencil, with instructions to draw a picture of a person. After completing it, the subject is asked to then draw a picture of a person of the opposite sex from that of the first drawing. The CPF-Fe Scale is comprised of 38 True/False items. The Franck test provides 36 simple, but incomplete line drawings to be finished by the subject. Results from the scores obtained indicated that two of the tests (CPF-Fe & DAP) support the crossdressing males' expressed degree of feminine gender identity. On the DAP, whether the subjects expressed a moderate or a high feminine gender identity, they were significantly more likely than most men to draw a female figure first. (This result parallels that found in a 1972 report in the *Journal of Personality Assessment* by Richard Green and colleagues about "feminine boys.") Both the CPF-Fe and DAP apparently measure some aspects of gender feelings and behavior in males. But the authors speculated that they measure different aspects. The CPI-Fe, for example, differentiates transvestites and transsexuals from homosexuals, but the DAP does not.

Study 2: Draw-a-Person Test (1982)

The DAP has also been employed in helping to predict successful candidates for sex reassignment surgery (SRS). A 1982 study reported by Michael Fleming and colleagues in the *Journal of Clinical Psychology* found that the DAP, used in conjunction with the Animal and Opposite-Animal Drawing Technique (AOADT), yields results indicative of which prospective candidates for SRS are most likely to undergo the surgery. The study's subjects were 9 genetic males and 10 genetic females. All were administered both the DAP and the AOADT. Results showed that MtF candidates who draw a member of the opposite sex first on the DAP are most likely to complete SRS. The AOADT provides another differentiation. Those who complete SRS draw second animals who are congruent with their biological sex significantly more often than do MtF or FtM transsexuals who have not had SRS.

Studies 3-4: Derogatis Sexual Functioning Inventory (1978, 1988)

We earlier mentioned the use of Derogatis Sexual Functioning Inventory (DSFI) in connection with another study. This instrument has been used in other research concerning transgender people. Its creator, Leonard R. Derogatis, together with colleagues Jon K. Meyer, and Noelia Vazquez, reported in 1978 in *The Journal of Mental and Nervous Disease*, that they had found a pronounced feminine gender role definition using the DSFI with 31 MtF transsexuals. The pronounced identification with the feminine gender role, even to a somewhat extreme stereotyped notion of it, was underscored by the results obtained in an earlier study reported in 1974. In that comparative study, the 17 MtF transsexuals more strongly endorsed middle class sexual conservatism (as measured on a 64 item Masculinity-Femininity Scale) than did either 17 heterosexual men or 17 heterosexual women.

In 1988, in *The Journal of Nervous and Mental Disease*, Peter Fagan and associates described a study in which they employed a different instrument in assessing 21 male "distressed transvestites" in comparison with 45 married heterosexual males. Using the DSFI, the team found that the crossdressing males endorsed a more feminine self-representation. In self-description they preferred adjectives generally associated with gender role stereotypes for women.

Studies 5-6: Bem Sex Role Inventory (1981, 1982)

A 1981 study reported by Candice Skrapec and K. R. MacKenzie in the *Archives of Sexual Behavior* described the results of a battery of tests given to 24 adult men (ages 21-35), who were placed in three matched groups: transsexual, homosexual and heterosexual. The tests include the Bem Sex Role Inventory (BSRI) and the Rosenberg Self-Esteem Scale (RSES). The BSRI uses 60 characteristics, 20 each that are designated 'masculine' or 'feminine' and 20 that are considered 'neutral.' Scores on the BSRI indicate whether someone endorses a stereotypical gender role or a more androgynous one. Androgyny has been linked with more positive psychological and social outcomes than found for those who embrace gender stereotyped roles. The RSES is perhaps the most widely used instrument for assessing self-esteem. It has 10 items commonly scored along a four point Likert scale, with response options ranging from "strongly agree" to "strongly disagree." The three groups differentiated as follows: transsexuals showed the most identification with the feminine role but scored lowest in self-esteem; homosexuals reported the most identification with the masculine role and scored the highest in self-esteem; and, heterosexuals scored as masculine to androgynous and displayed moderately high levels of self-esteem. The correlation of identification with the feminine role and lower self-esteem perhaps reflects the somber social reality for males who express as feminine in a culture where masculine males dominate.

In 1982, sociologist John Talamini in his book *Boys Will Be Girls: The Hidden World of the Heterosexual Male Transvestite* reported a study using the BSRI. In the research, matched groups of heterosexual males who don't crossdress and those who do scored differently. The crossdressing males scored significantly higher in androgyny. Perhaps the endorsing of a more feminine gender identity and/or role leads to greater androgyny among these men. Talamini expressed the belief that "cross-dressing is somehow bound up with the universal personal drive toward androgyny."

Study 7: Cross-Gender Lifestyle Inventory (1995)

Mary Hogan-Finlay, in her 1995 Ph.D. dissertation in psychology, compared a sample of 101 "non-clinical cross-gendered men" with an equal number of heterosexual controls. The comparison examined demographics, childhood experiences, psychological functioning and gender issues. With respect to demographics, there were no significant differences between the transgender subjects and the control subjects. The transgendered males were sorted into three distinguishable groups: transsexuals (27%) and two groups of transvestites (83%) differentiated by degree of "physiological fantasies" of being a woman. Hogan-Finlay found that the transsexuals displayed more "gender disturbance" than transvestites or controls—meaning they had the greatest degree of identification with femininity. Because of the incongruence between their psychological gender identity and their body sex, transsexuals showed the highest levels of "psychological distress." Unlike the other groups, the transsexual subjects scored outside the normal range in this respect. She did not find support for transvestism as a mental disorder.

Study 8: Docter & Fleming 70-Item Questionnaire (2001)

In 2001, writing in the *Archives of Sexual Behavior*, Richard Docter and James Fleming discussed transgender identity using factor analysis and as explored through 26 items of their 70-item questionnaire administered to 516 adult males (ages 19-78). Of these subjects, 88% were identified as transvestites who periodically crossdress fully as women and 12% were identified as transsexual. The 26 items have content such as "I wish I had been born a woman," "I do not enjoy functioning as a man," and "My true gender is feminine." All 26 items received some endorsement with factor loads ranging from .48 ("I daydream of being a woman at least 10 times per day") to .92 ("I would choose to live as a woman"). There was overlap between the two groups on this scale, with the mean score for transsexuals (20.9) somewhat higher than for transvestites (12.2).

So What?

Taking this time to examine specific research studies—which some of us may find tedious in the details—is important because through doing so we can be reassured that solid science lies behind the contention that gender variance does not produce serious personality disturbance. Gender variance produces gender variance—period. Not all gender variant people differ in the degree of their affiliation with a different gender. Predictably, transsexuals show greater identification than do transvestites. The evidence confirms transgender claims.

Yet we may still wonder if that one difference, by itself, remains sufficient to elicit psychopathology, or to be in itself pathological. The research we have examined suggests that gender variance does *not* create a sexuality different from that found among gender conforming people, save with respect to gender identity issues. So if there is not sexual variance, but there is gender variance, is that enough to warrant calling someone mentally disturbed?

The issue is an important one. We shall return to it later, but now we will continue our investigation into what research suggests about those of us who identify as transgender. Thus far, the evidence we have seen suggests that while some differences can be found between the gender variant and everyone else, these differences seem not to rise to a level of significance, save for the obvious matter that makes transgender people distinguishable—a different sense of gender. Still, interesting and important as these studies are, they are only part of the picture. They offer an indirect way for those of us who are transgender to speak. But there are other tools that provide more direct access to transgender self-perception. It is logical that we turn next to such instruments.

9.

Life at the Margins

A basic difficulty long hampered discussion of transgender males: the ones who were talking were not transgender people! Typically, they were psychiatrists and other health professionals. The 'subjects' they were discussing, often in case studies of one or a few individuals, were in treatment and usually in distress. In short, much of the scientific literature, especially the older literature, painted a picture distorted by the population it was drawn from. Yet it didn't seem to stop some professionals from making claims about all transgender people. Much of what we knew in the 20th century, prior to the 1970s, came from a group sharing four characteristics: they were male, heterosexual (though often seen as at least latently homosexual), receiving psychological treatment, and identified as crossdressers. A real question posed itself: do these individuals represent most transgender males?

If the first difficulty is whether a clinical population of male crossdressers adequately represents the larger group of male crossdressers, a second difficulty is whether limiting study of crossdressers to males is appropriate. Anyone familiar with the history of crossdressing is struck by the preponderance of attention given to female crossdressers prior to our contemporary scene. Yet today the attention is almost exclusively fixed upon male crossdressers. Moreover, in a third complicating difficulty, though it is known that some homosexuals also crossdress, the research focus has been on *heterosexual* males. In large part this has been because of the desire to highlight a single behavior—crossdressing—that distinguishes a group of heterosexual men from other heterosexual men. Yet this focus on heterosexual males represents a bias in data collection that inevitably distorts the overall picture. Finally, there is also the difficulty posed in too closely equating crossdressing with transgender identity. Although it is a hallmark behavior, we should resist simply identifying one with the other.

Of these difficulties, perhaps the most problematic, historically, has been an over-reliance on data collected from those crossdressers most distressed by their condition, or whose crossdressing became attached to some other circumstance (e.g., relational problems) that resulted in seeking professional help. Because so much of the data historically has been obtained from a 'clinical population'— people in treatment for some condition, whether crossdressing or not—the resulting portrayal has tended toward an extreme, especially given the interpretations put to the behavior by professionals predisposed by their own unexamined cultural biases to regard it negatively. In short, this subset of the much larger crossdressing population, most of whom never seek counseling with reference to crossdressing, may not be a representative sample and certainly often has not been studied dispassionately. Therefore, as time progressed and new perspectives on gender helped open up the research perspective on transgender, the conclusions drawn only from such research were increasingly seen as needing to be balanced against data drawn from a wider group of crossdressers and without the lens of preconceived pathology. In essence, the new task became to let crossdressers speak for themselves, in settings outside mental health facilities, and to listen without preconceptions and prejudgments of pathology.

Giving Transgender People a Voice

The desire to give crossdressing males a chance to speak for themselves led to the use of surveys, interviews, and various tests voluntarily undertaken by nonclinical groups of crossdressers. Since the early 1970s such instruments have played an increasingly important part in learning about adult male crossdressing. Through these various instruments crossdressers have a chance to describe themselves, both directly (as in interviews or through surveys), and indirectly (as through various tests). The results can then be compared and contrasted with those found with a clinical population. Unfortunately, by their very nature such studies cannot claim to include representative samples. If anything, together they are only broadly representative of those crossdressers more open to disclose their crossdressing and willing to assist in research. Yet, the results across studies are both illuminating and often compellingly consistent.

Growing Up

A number of research studies have investigated what childhood is like for male crossdressers. Much of this research is retrospective: adults remembering back.

Birth Order

Some research indicates a greater likelihood of male crossdressers being a firstborn child. The groundbreaking 1972 report by Virginia Prince and Peter Bentler, involving 504 participants in a survey whose results were published in *Psychological Reports*, found that fully half were first born. Later research has found percentages nearly as high. In 1995, writing in *Archives of Sexual Behavior*, Richard Schott found 40% of his 85 subjects were firstborn. Results published online of a 1999 survey, with 1,316 subjects responding to the question, found 41% firstborn. All of these percentages are substantially higher than national norms for families where the firstborn is male.

What do such figures mean? Various explanations are possible. With respect to biology, perhaps some hormonal factor in a first pregnancy makes transgender more likely to develop. Or perhaps some environmental factor is decisive. Psychological theorists, for example, speak of the 'dethronement' of the firstborn when a new child enters the family. Perhaps efforts to renew and reinforce affiliative ties with the mother lead some sons to adopt crossdressing as a means of identification. Adlerian theorists point to the characteristics typical of firstborns, who tend to take rules and role responsibilities very seriously, perhaps leaving them more vulnerable to gender role pressures. Other theorists note that all males in our culture are placed under heavy gender role expectations. Perhaps, then, crossdressing is adopted by some males as a way of easing away from such burdens or expressing rebellion against the artificial confines in which they find themselves. These are all speculations, of course, and no one knows what significance—if any—birth order has for crossdressing.

Relation to Parents

The family background of crossdressing males receives attention in many studies. This research is important because of efforts to explain the origin of crossdressing as a result of some kind of family dysfunction. If so, it apparently is not the result of a broken family. A study of 110 crossdressing males, reported by Richard Docter in 1988 in his book *Transvestites and Transsexuals: Toward a Theory of Cross-Gender Behavior*, shows that four-fifths (80%) of them come from intact families. But that, by itself, says nothing about the nature of the child's relationship to his parents.

We discussed earlier that a common idea has been that transvestism in males results from a dominant mother and an absent father. Yet self-reports from most crossdressing males do not seem to support this hypothesis. Prince and Bentler's 1972 survey reported that about half (51%) of their subjects identified their father as the dominant parent. Moreover, nearly three-quarters (72%) affirmed that their father provided a good masculine image for them. A survey study conducted by Docter and Prince a generation later, patterned on the 1972 survey and reported in the *Archives of Sexual Behavior*, found similar numbers among more than a thousand subjects: a little more than three-quarters (76%) were reared by both parents through age 18 and a like number (76%) reported their father provided a good masculine image.

Comparative research published in 1978 in the *Australian and New Zealand Journal of Psychiatry* by Neil Buhrich and Neil McConaghy, as well as the report in 1995 by Schott, also found no support for the hypothesis of a disturbed relationship with the mother. However, at least one study did find evidence of a parent sex-role reversal in some transvestites' parents, with the fathers appearing to their sons as more dependent and affiliative in behavior compared to the perceptions of noncrossdressing males. And Schott's 1995 report suggests that relationships with fathers may be viewed less positively than those with mothers; more than two-thirds (68%) of his subjects put the father-son relationship on the lower end of a continuum, with judgments ranging from 'neutral' (31%) through 'fairly negative' (20%) to 'very negative' (17%). Overall, however, crossdressing males appear mostly to have had stable and relatively normal relationships with their parents, with their fathers present and acting as masculine role models.

Happiness

While relatively few studies probe crossdressers' assessment of their childhoods as happy or unhappy, the results of those studies that do seem to be fairly consistent. In a 1983 study with 65 participants, long time transgender researchers Vern and Bonnie Bullough found less than a quarter (23%) reported their childhood as 'unhappy'; the remainder called it either 'mixed' (39%) or 'happy' (38). Some 15 years later, in a 1997 report of 372 subjects included in the volume *Gender Blending*, the Bulloughs and Richard Smith found an even smaller percentage (12%) calling childhood 'unhappy.' The other choices continued to be nearly even: 'mixed' (46%) and 'happy' (42%). The overall picture, as the 1997 study concluded, is one of a "more or less normal childhood."

One might suppose that crossdressing contributes to being less happy in childhood, if for no other reason than fear and the consequences of being caught. Plenty of research suggests that transgender children, especially those who crossdress, are at risk for displeasure, even rejection, from other family members. In light of the possibly disastrous consequences of the behavior we might expect a learned association between crossdressing and punishment that would help extinguish the behavior, or at least render it so fraught with anxiety as to become unpleasurable. Yet Schott's study reports that more than half (55%) of the 85 male crossdressers he surveyed recall positive emotions of enjoyment and happiness from crossdressing. Transsexuals, on the other hand, are emotionally neutral about their crossdressing since, for them, it is 'normal.' Perhaps all this says is that pleasure exists in the act for those who succeed in not being caught, or who live in supportive family environments. Or perhaps it reflects the power of crossdressing to produce congruent and positive feelings that outweigh the risks or even the punishments. In either instance, this fact alone does not speak completely to the larger question of whether childhood overall is remembered fondly as a generally happy time.

Education

Academic performance also has been investigated. Those crossdressers who participate in surveys and interviews are generally well-educated. Prince and Bentler's 1972 report, based on data collected in the late 1960s, found more than a third (37%) had a B.A. or more of college education. It is important to bear in mind the norms of the time. For instance, in the 1960s far fewer people attended or completed college than was the case in the 1990s. In Docter and

Prince's follow-up study published in 1997, nearly two-thirds (65%) reported such level of achievement. Doctor, with James Fleming, in a 2001 report in the *Archives of Sexual Behavior*, found nearly three-quarters (73%) with a B.A. or more. Clearly, being a crossdresser does not prevent educational attainment!

However, academic achievement and academic experience are different matters. Despite their attainment, many crossdressers may feel inadequate as students. The comparative study conducted by the Bulloughs and Smith with 65 male transvestites and 33 male transsexuals found that both these groups described their performance as somewhat poorer than did other groups. Still, more than a third (35%) of transvestites reported having been "excellent" students, and only 11% said they were "poor" students. The numbers for transsexuals were a bit worse: 30% "excellent," but 21% "poor." Such figures should be placed in the context of overall school experience, which is often problematic, especially if others detect gender variance in any respect.

Early Crossdressing

We saw a moment ago that many crossdressers remember childhood crossdressing as a happy experience. The vast majority of crossdressers start this behavior in childhood, typically before puberty. However, no uniform practice can be discerned after it starts. Some do it more often than others. Some do it more completely than others. Jack Croughan and associates, in a 1981 study published in the *Archives of Sexual Behavior*, found that even initial efforts vary widely: about half use only undergarments, most of the rest use some combination of under- and outer-garments, while just 10% start fully crossdressed. By adolescence, more than half are crossdressing partially or fully at least once a week, and the percentage of those so doing rises after age 30. Schott's 1995 survey found that while nearly half (45%) only crossdress infrequently in childhood, a sizeable minority (13%) do so regularly. But, as Schott also discovered, one factor does unite most childhood experiences—they are kept secret. More than three-quarters (78%) keep their crossdressing secret, with the highest percentages among nuclear transvestites (83%) and the lowest among transsexuals (69%). Of the 22% who are more public, it is because another family member encourages and supports the behavior, at least up to school age.

Adulthood

The self-testimony of transgender males seems to reveal recollections of growing up that compare favorably with the rest of us. What about adult life?

Occupational Social Status

Male crossdressers are represented in a range of occupations, some lower and others higher in social status. Prince and Bentler's 1972 report shows that among its subjects one out of six (17%) were either president of a company or business owners. But, as found with other matters, there were differences between crossdressing subgroups. Male transvestites fared better than male transsexuals in matters of occupational social status. The 1983 comparative study referenced earlier found that nearly two-thirds (64%) of transvestites ranked above the national median in occupational prestige. This compares to less than a third (31%) of transsexuals and homosexuals (30%) ranking above the national median. Transvestites were also well above the undifferentiated group they were compared to (64% to 48% above). The authors commented that the crossdressing males in their study were "heavily represented" in white collar professions like engineering, accounting, teaching, clerical and sales work. Similar findings pertain in the later studies reported in Docter's 1988 book and Docter and Prince's 1997 survey, though in the latter with relatively more representation in technical and professional groups and relatively less in unskilled positions.

Transsexuals may not fare as well as transvestites. A study published in 1971 in the *Archives of Sexual Behavior* by Jon Meyer, Norman Knorr, and Dietrich Blumer, of 599 transsexual respondents to a survey, reported, "Most respondents clustered in the lower middle-upper lower and lower socioeconomic classes. Since male respondents were drawn to employment usually considered feminine, the overall effect was to lower the socioeconomic level of that group." However, the authors of the study noted mitigating factors that might be influencing the findings, such as a reluctance by transsexuals in higher economic classes to respond to the survey.

Perhaps pertinent to this area is the research done by clinician Ingrid Sell and published in *The Psychotherapy Patient* about Americans who identify as 'third gender' people. Her study of 30 such folk, including biological males and females, with ages ranging from 29-77, found that compared to the general population a disproportionate number (43%) work in health and helping professions. They also are more likely than the general population to be engaged in highly creative and artistic endeavors; nearly half (47%) are writers, musicians, or other performers—and 17% earn a substantial portion of their income from their art. As Sell perceptively notes, these characteristics parallel cross-cultural evidence about the activities of third gender people elsewhere around the world.

Marriage and Family

A substantial number of crossdressers are married—or have been. Among crossdressing men who identify themselves as heterosexual, the majority are, or have been, married and have children. This finding has been consistent across various studies. Prince and Bentler's 1972 survey reported 78% were or had been married, with 74% having children. A range of six studies from then through 2001 found anywhere between 75% to 83% were or had been married, with 59% to 74% having children.

However, again the case may well be different for transsexual males. The 1971 study by Meyer and colleagues differs from the others we have considered in some important respects. First, its subject pool was entirely comprised of self-identified transsexuals. Second, it included both males and females (73% males). It found only 19% of the 599 subjects were or had been married. This study, however, differentiated between marriage and cohabitation, and the percentages increase to about 47% when cohabitation is included. Nevertheless, this study, though reflecting a more difficult historical period for transsexuals, may indicate that they are less likely to marry than other crossdressers.

But doesn't crossdressing make marriage a rocky road? We might think so—and perhaps it is. Prince and Bentler's 1972 study reported that more than a third of their subjects who divorced cited their crossdressing as one cause. Yet Docter's analysis in 1988 of his research subjects suggests they do not appear to be extraordinarily at risk for divorce. Overall, the rejection of such behavior by a spouse certainly can't be seen as lending itself to marital health and stability, but it also does *not* seem to predict an inevitability of distress and divorce. This is an issue we shall discuss again, when our talk turns to relationships.

Religious Affiliation

Surveys and interviews consistently reveal a broad pattern of religious affiliations. As might be expected, since the research has largely been done in the United States or in societies sharing a similar religious heritage, most crossdressers identify themselves as Christians. Studies report differing levels of affiliation, but consistently show more identification as Protestants than as Catholics. For example, Prince and Bentler's 1972 study found 57% identifying as Protestant, and 23% as Catholic; the 1997 follow-up by Docter and Prince reported 38% Protestant and 24% Catholic. Judaism, the next most reported religion in studies, showed reports from .3% (Meyer and colleagues' 1971 study) to 7% (Croughan and associates' 1981 study). Religious affiliation does not appear to be associated with either an increased or decreased likelihood of crossdressing.

Intriguingly, Sell's research found a related feature that may be significant. In her study, the vast majority of people identifying as 'third gender' experience two facets associated in other parts of the world with shamans: mediation and transcendent spiritual events. More than three-quarters (77%) recounted being asked to mediate between men and women because they are viewed as having a perspective wide enough to see both sides. Many also mediate with other groups (e.g., racial, cultural, sub-cultural, age-differentiated). More strikingly yet, 93% reported one or more transcendent spiritual events and/or what others would term 'paranormal' abilities. Sell notes that these numbers far exceed what other research finds for members of the general population. "Perhaps," she concludes, "as non-Western cultures recognize, there is indeed an element of spirit or 'calling' involved in our being men, women, or mediators between."

Crossdressing

A common refrain among crossdressers categorized as 'transvestites' is that crossdressing facilitates a full expression of personality that otherwise does not occur. While crossdressed there may be an experience of greater access to feelings coupled with an enhanced pleasure in living. Docter and Prince's 1997 survey of over 1000 male crossdressers found four-fifths (80%) feel crossdressing allows them to express a different part of themselves. Similarly, a 1999 online survey hosted by 'Yvonne' found that 74% responded affirmatively to the query, "In your opinion, do you exhibit a different personality *en femme* than when you present as a man?" Such experiences reinforce the behavior.

Neil Buhrich, in 1978, published an article in *Acta Psychiatrica Scandinavica* based on interviews with 33 crossdressing males in a transvestites' club. He found these males commonly reported feeling more at ease when crossdressed. There was also less experience of the burden of traditional masculine demands. Similar reports were made by a comparison group of 24 transsexual males. However, Buhrich found that the transvestite males showed more compulsive and narcissistic behaviors than their transsexual counterparts. Such 'narcissism' is often seen in conjunction to crossdressers' attention to their appearance. It may be transvestites are more conscious of the gender boundary they step over and back, thus eliciting more attention to their (temporary) gender presentation.

Transsexuals and transgenderists (those living full time in a gender different than the one assigned them at birth) might be expected to crossdress most or all of the time. But that is not necessarily so, at least for transsexuals. Although we must reckon with how times have changed, in the 1971 research by Meyer and colleagues, of the 599 self-identified transsexual participants, fully 23% denied ever crossdressing at all—though whether that reflects regarding their behavior as noncrossdressing where others would judge it as crossdressing is unknown. More than half (52%) reported some crossdressing, and the authors noted a distinct difference between male and female transsexuals. Though the latter were less likely overall to try crossdressing, those that did seemed more committed to the practice.

With a different population in view (heterosexual transvestites), Prince and Bentler found that their subjects generally embraced crossdressing. Most (72%) expressed the hope of expanding their crossdressing activities and the vast majority (85%) preferred full costume (including wig and makeup) to partial crossdressing. Among individual items, there was a preference for lingerie (32% indicate most interest in these kinds of items), but more than one-fifth (21%) simply stated they liked all feminine items. Most had never tried to "pass" in public as a woman. A mere 1% of their sample expressed a hope of restricting their behavior in an effort to stop it. Still, more than two-thirds (69%) had experienced a "purge" (doing away with their feminine items) at one time or another. A generation later, almost all (93%) the crossdressers surveyed by Docter and Prince also expressed a preference for complete crossdressing, but remained reticent about appearing in public while crossdressed. Struggles over crossdressing were still evident; three-quarters (75%) had at one time or another purged.

If for no other reason than cultural norms, crossdressing creates at least some degree of internal conflict for most crossdressers. While negative feelings may lead to purging, it neither stops the behavior nor accurately predicts how crossdressers will continue to feel. In fact, Prince and Bentler discovered a wide range of feelings about crossdressing among the men who practice it. Less than a quarter (22%) reported feelings of shame or guilt, and those feelings were dissipating. More than three-quarters (78%) expressed positive perceptions of their crossdressing. About a third (32%) felt free of guilt, and more than one-fifth (21%) believed crossdressing had made a valuable contribution to their life.

Seeking Counseling

Given such a generally positive appraisal of crossdressing, we should not be surprised most transgender males do not seek counseling concerning it. There may be some irony that much of what mental health professionals think they know about crossdressers comes from a very narrow segment of the transgender population. Most never seek counseling, either for their crossdressing or anything else. In this respect, apparently, they are like the population at large.

The 1972 survey by Prince and Bentler found that more than three-quarters of the 504 respondents never sought a professional's opinion about their behavior. The 1981 research by Croughan and associates of 70 subjects used broad parameters in order to designate about half (49%) as a 'treated group'; they were placed in this group if they had ever been seen by a professional in connection to their crossdressing. Within this group, half of the men self-referred for treatment—a number less than one-quarter (24%) of the total pool, and also similar to earlier findings. If anything, numbers seem to have declined since.

When counseling is sought, it often is for relational issues. This proves true for 1-in-7 (16%) of Croughan and associates' group of subjects. The online survey of 1999 found that almost 15% of respondents who had been married, are married, or are in a relationship had tried marriage counseling, and almost three-quarters (72%) felt their counselor was accepting of crossdressing, yet most (62%) did not feel the counseling ultimately proved helpful.

Expression of Gender Identity

Gender identity is clearly of strong interest to crossdressers. In the 1972 Prince and Bentler survey, subjects were asked which statement from a list applies to them. The choices were:
   o   "I feel myself to be a woman trapped in a male body";
   o   "I feel myself to be a man who just has a feminine side seeking expression"; or,
   o   "I feel myself to be a man with just a sexual fetish for feminine attire."

The first and last alternatives were not strongly endorsed (12% for each); the middle choice was the one strongly endorsed (69%).

In a study of 222 male crossdressers in America (N=126) and Australia (N=86), published in 1981 in *Archives of Sexual Behavior*, Neil Buhrich and Trina Beaumont reported that when crossdressed more than three-quarters of the men claimed they feel like a woman. Interestingly, almost a fifth (18%) also reported feeling this way when dressed in masculine clothing. A generation after the Prince and Bentler study, the Docter and Prince survey of 1032 male crossdressers found nearly three-quarters (74%) of these men identified themselves as a man with a feminine side, and more than half (60%) preferred the masculine and feminine gender identities equally.

Gender identity may differentiate crossdressers from noncrossdressers, but it likewise can differentiate some crossdressers from other crossdressers. Buhrich and Beaumont's 1981 study separated results for 'nuclear' (satisfied with crossdressing, less intense feminine identification, and stronger heterosexual interest) and 'marginal' (desire for at least partial feminization by hormones or surgery) transvestites. Marginal transvestites seem more likely to report feeling like a woman when crossdressed than do nuclear transvestites (90% to 69%). A similarly large margin was found in percentages for this feeling even when dressed as a man (26% to 9%).

The 1983 comparative study cited earlier, involving male transvestites, transsexuals, homosexuals and others, also demonstrated this differentiation among crossdressers, though using broader groups. While transvestites were most likely to identify themselves as males with a feminine side (46%), more than a third (37%) preferred characterizing themselves as persons "who enjoy opposite sex clothing," and 11% favored the description "woman trapped in a male body," though they were not categorized as transsexuals. Still, this last choice was dwarfed among transvestites when compared to its selection by transsexuals (64%). More than a quarter (27%) of transsexuals preferred the even stronger descriptor, "woman."

Concluding Note

What have we seen through various psychological tests as well as surveys and other research instruments that allow those of us who are transgender to speak for ourselves? We find that being gender variant means just that—different in gender. It does *not* mean different across the board in a host of other ways. We who are gender variant seem very much like the rest of us in being healthy, productive, and generally happy people. That does not mean all is a bed of roses. Being gender variant when most folk are gender conforming does have its effects. In our society it is like being a round peg in a square peg world. What that means is what we must now turn our attention toward.

10.

Round Pegs in a Square Pegs World

We who are gender variant feel like round pegs in a square pegs world because our culture is based on a gender division that leaves no place for us. Not being square pegs we aren't even allowed on the table. Yet we have to be accounted for, so we are treated as if we were square and jammed into one or the other gender hole. No wonder that hurts!

For some time, our society sought to use both social policy and legal regulations to bludgeon gender variance into gender conformity. It didn't work. It still doesn't. For the most part, laws have changed to reflect this reality. Unfortunately, policies have proven more resistant to change.

The Law

Transgendered people have had a checkered history with the law, especially when practicing behaviors like crossdressing. This fact is not due to greater engagement in different forms of law-breaking than other people, but because transgender behavior itself was against some laws. Crossdressing was often illegal in the past, though sanctions against it in the United States were typically mild. Moreover, past and present, restrictions commonly have been overlooked, only partially enforced, or allowed to have exceptions. Today there are few outright prohibitions of crossdressing although a variety of other laws are used to curb *public* crossdressing. However prosecuted, cases based merely on an individual appearing in public crossdressed are today routinely thrown out of court.

Other issues have emerged as prominent. Discrimination in the workplace against those of us who are transgendered remains a problem despite antidiscrimination measures becoming more common. Housing discrimination also persists. Identity recognition is an issue for some, and various places handle the matter differently. The most serious issue remains violence. Efforts to extend hate crime legislation protection to those of us who are attacked simply for being gender variant has met with varying success. The legal picture continues to develop in our society, but to this point it can be reasonably said that most progress has occurred at local levels. The federal government, rather than leading the way, has lagged behind in many matters.

In the past, some of the areas of law bearing on crossdressers have been the following:

o   *Anticrossdressing laws*—specific regulations prohibiting crossdressing.
o   *Antimasquerading laws*—local ordinances against disguises; these have often been applied against crossdressing.
o   *Antidiscrimination law*—this probably has been the most significant area of law, especially with regard to employment and housing.
o   *Disorderly conduct laws*—these have often been used as a pretext for arresting homosexuals and crossdressers.
o   *Identity recognition issues*—the legal transition from one gender identity to another has been a significant issue for transsexuals.
o   *Moral turpitude legal concept*—this concept provides a catch-all provision that makes possible legal charges based on social value standards.
o   *Use of public restrooms*—a matter most of us take for granted and give no thought to is an issue of substantial practical concern for many who others see as crossdressing.
o   *Vagrancy laws*—historically such ordinances have been used to harass or arrest crossdressers in public.

To the above list might be added other laws, such as prohibitions against 'annoying persons,' or ones that prohibit 'lewd dress,' that reportedly have been used against any of us perceived to be crossdressing.

By and large, laws banning crossdressing are gone, though harassment by law enforcement officers remains common. Yet, while some laws have largely disappeared, that does not mean legal *issues* have all been resolved. Significant legal obstacles remain. The most significant probably are those concerning discrimination (in employment, housing, and health care), and identity recognition.

Discrimination

Discrimination against transgendered people is common. In some cases this discrimination is legal and justified by appeal to a mental health standard regarding transgender realities as mental disorders. Thus, for example, the U. S. military prohibits enlistment of those of us who are gender variant—explicitly including transvestites and transsexuals. The policy reads, in part: "The causes for rejection for appointment, enlistment, or induction are transsexualism, transvestism, voyeurism, and other paraphilias (302)."

Discrimination in employment settings has been common. Crossdressing, even when done in private and away from the place of employment has resulted in dismissal—an action upheld in a U.S. District Court. From the mid-1970s through the mid-1980s, a series of lawsuits in federal court consistently determined that Title VII legislation—which protects against discrimination based on sex—was not applicable to transgender people. This was particularly deleterious to transsexuals, even post-operative transsexuals, who were ruled not protected by the federal act because Title VII did not explicitly consider discrimination based on a change-of-sex.

Identity Recognition

Although those of us who are transsexual are able to obtain medical services (e.g., hormonal therapy and sex reassignment surgery) in the United States, we remain faced with problems associated with our gender identity. Recognition of the legitimacy of change from permanent assignment in one gender to permanent assignment in another has been slow in coming. This creates the practical awkwardness, inconvenience, and occasionally danger accompanying disagreement between gender presentation and declarations on legal documents. It also restricts life opportunities in important areas like employment and relationships. Congruence of presentation and identity documents is a crucial matter.

Later we shall discuss to what extent changes have transpired that may make a more level playing field in our society. But given this historical backdrop it should be easy to see why so many of us who are gender variant choose to stay in the shadows. Indeed, we have yet to learn all the reasons why secrecy seems so wise to so many of us.

'In the Closet'

Plenty of evidence over the last several decades suggests that there are perfectly rational reasons for why so many of us who are gender variant keep our behavior a closely guarded secret. We remain 'in the closet.' Most of us are unwilling to risk the social response we might face if we made something like crossdressing public. Some of us learned in childhood that our behavior should be kept secret. As adults we are aware of the stereotypes and myths held about crossdressing, even by our loved ones. Few of us are willing to face the potential harm that can result from a hostile response to our gender identity.

In fact, report after report of research affirms the keen concern we who are gender variant have to keep that gender difference secret. More than 40 years ago, the article on transvestism in the *Encyclopedia of Sexual Behavior* estimated that more than 90% of crossdressing is done in secret. Medical doctor Vernon Coleman's 1996 report in the *European Medical Journal* on British crossdressing males found that more than two-thirds (69%) of his respondents confessed a fear of being found out. This is a consistent result found in research.

Why are those of us who crossdress so reticent if we both enjoy the experience and see nothing wrong with it? There are several possible reasons. First, most of us have little interest in being social crusaders, no matter how much we privately might yearn for the same degree of freedom and acceptance others enjoy. Instead, we choose secrecy as the most practical route to minimizing risk while maximizing gain. Many of us distinguish between total secrecy, where no one is let in on what is going on, and relative secrecy where one or more others are trusted by us with our secret. While a small minority of us publicly out ourselves, for most of us it is a significant enough venture to share our secret with at least one other person. As would be expected, this is most often a significant other—a spouse or other intimate companion.

The large-scale study of male crossdressers released in 1972 by Prince and Bentler found that more than half (58%) had told someone about their cross-dressing. Among those who are or have been married, four-fifths (80%) had spouses (or ex-spouses) who knew. Only 7% had confined their secret to just one other person; if they told at all, it was a secret likely shared with more than one individual. Perhaps surprisingly, the vast majority of recipients of this secret (91%) proved either neutral (35%) or accepting (56%); less than one-in-ten (9%) were antagonistic. Not surprisingly, women were far more accepting than men (77% to 23%).

Data like that just cited might make us wonder even more at the reluctance to let the 'true self' be seen. Yet this situation needs closer scrutiny. First, recall that we all experience growing up an emphasis on the need to gender conform. Adult messages in mainstream society reinforce these early messages. Rational or not, the fear generated by our society's gender messages retards disclosure. Further, we must consider the considerable courage it takes to risk our sense of self, a central part of which is our sense of gender. Also, we should consider the acceptance of others in the light that most of us—gender variant or not—are cautious and highly selective in disclosing any secret. In other words, we all do our best to ensure that any reaction we receive will not be punitive or rejecting. Seen in that light, the numbers look less happy—only slightly more than half of those selected to be told actually prove to be accepting. If this is true for those carefully chosen for the news, what might be expected from the general public?

Public Attitudes

Social work professionals Mary Boes and Katherine van Wormer, writing in the *Social Worker's Desk Reference*, remind us that, "the most extreme forms of discrimination, including ridicule and violence, are reserved for transgendered persons . . . ." Though they make specific reference to transsexuals, to some degree the observation is pertinent for all of us who are gender variant, especially when that shows in public. Yet this reality is not the whole reality. Both attitudes and laws have been changing in recent years. The complexity of the social situation in the United States—and elsewhere—makes the following question pertinent: Are we on our way to a society where we who are trans-gender are accorded respect for the unique realities we embody? The evidence needed to answer such a question is mixed.

To understand how those of us transgender—especially those of us most visible by virtue of crossdressing—are received in society we all must look underneath polite public behavior to the attitudes most of us hold. As we shall see, the evidence is mixed as to how far some of us have gained a measure of respect or acceptance from the rest of us. Quite clearly there are those of us who,

118

though not gender variant, welcome those of us who are as valued within the wider social fabric. Just as obviously, there persist others of us whose behavior marginalizes or ostracizes those of us who are gender-different.

In our culture, differences have been found in the perceptions of men and women toward transgender behaviors and people. In general, women are more tolerant. Why? Social psychologist Gregory Herek, writing in *American Behavioral Scientist* in 1986, advanced the provocative notion that heterosexual males in American society are culturally constructed homophobic as an important aspect of their heterosexual masculinity. In short, to be an American heterosexual male largely means identifying oneself as *not* homosexual and as *not* feminine. Intolerance or hostility toward other males who display homosexual or feminine identity or behavior has become part of self-affirmation for heterosexual males. This construction lessens the likelihood of most men interacting knowingly with gay men—interactions which might challenge their preconceived attitudes.

Similarly, the construction of masculine identity in our culture may also predispose men toward transphobia. If, as research suggests, men rely more on clothes for self-expression, including as gendered beings, then the stakes are raised by males who dress like women. As researchers Stephen Gould and Barbara Stern, writing in *Psychology and Marketing* in 1989, put it, "That fashion conscious men are more gender conscious suggests that these men connect fashion with their self-identity and internalized maleness, their concept of what it means to be a man." Gender variant males crossdressing may be unconsciously seen as a threat to self-identity by other males.

Crossdressing, especially by males, often engages strong feelings in others. In a society where various sexual and gender lines are both rigidly and narrowly drawn, crossdressing constitutes for some a challenge they decide must be met not only forcefully, but perhaps also with physical force. As Viviane Namaster remarked in her 2000 book *Invisible Lives. The Erasure of Transsexual and Transgendered People*, "Given the cultural coding of gender into a binary framework, a high incidence of violence directed against TS/TG people is not surprising." Perhaps not surprising, but certainly irrational and definitely not what we as a society want to uphold.

Transphobia

Before looking at the limited information that exists on crimes against those of us who are transgender *because* we are transgendered, let us consider a couple preliminary matters. *Transphobia* is an irrational anxiety over the existence, and especially the exposure to gender variant behaviors or people. The very unfamiliarity of the term in contrast with the well-known term 'homophobia' suggests how little attention has been given to negative social reactions to transgender people. Yet Herek's claim that "prejudice against men who display feminine behavior is nearly as common as prejudice against homosexuality in our society" is hard to dispute. In this climate it is easy to see that those crimes against we who are different in gender that are motivated by repulsion of our transgender status are significantly underreported.

Hate Crimes

All of us should be able to see that crimes committed against those of us who are transgender *because* we are gender variant are no different in their nature than like crimes committed against homosexuals because of being different in the pattern of sexual attraction, or against racial groups because of race, or against Muslims because of religious identity. These crimes are all hate crimes. To date, though, federal legislation on hate crimes only recognizes crimes motivated by race, religion, national origin or color. At present, from a federal legal standpoint, crimes against transgendered people motivated by the fact the victim is transgendered may be hateful, but they are not legally hate crimes meriting involvement by federal law enforcement. The lack of recognition of such crimes as hate crimes has carried with it at least two very unfortunate consequences: there has been little incentive to collect data on a national level substantiating the extent of the problem; and, there remain no specific national provisions to protect potential victims or to punish perpetrators motivated by their hate of transgender.

It is against this backdrop we must look at the relative lack of information we can review. Nevertheless, what data we do have is dismaying. For example, in a study published in 1997 by the Gender Public Advocacy Coalition (GenderPAC), a serious incidence of violence against those of us who are transgender becomes apparent. The study utilized a questionnaire designed to assess transgendered people's lifetime experiences with violence. The questionnaire was not randomly distributed—infeasible given the nature of the target population—but distributed through events, volunteers, and the internet. In a 12-month period, 402 cases collected from respondents yielded disturbing information. The data from these cases found that well over half (59.5%) reported having been a victim of harassment or violence. Other highlights of the study are:

- o   Verbal abuse is the most common adverse act; over half (56%) of the cases involve such an incident just within the previous year.
- o   Assault, either with a weapon (10%) or without one (19%) has occurred at least once in nearly a third (29.6%) of cases.
- o   Being followed or stalked has occurred at least once in nearly a quarter (23%) of the cases.
- o   Robbery is involved in about 1-in-7 (14%) of the cases.
- o   Rape, or attempted rape, has happened in some 1-in-8 (13%) of the cases.

While most of us will deplore such acts (and all of us *should*), we are likely to interpret these events as the actions of a fringe or criminal element—certainly not folk like ourselves. Yet one of the more sobering indicators that such acts are tacitly accepted by our society comes from another finding in this study: law enforcement officers and facilities are not uncommonly implicated in adverse incidents (e.g., nearly 8% of the cases involved an unjustified arrest). Moreover, the researchers remind us that acts of violence against transgendered people elicit little outcry from the public, occasion little study, and to date have produced inconsistent and often partial legislative movement to provide protection.

A 1999 online survey hosted by 'Yvonne', of more than a thousand male crossdressers, revealed that a substantial minority either had personally experienced public harassment or knew someone who had. Specifically, more than 1-in-10 (13%) had been confronted either by law enforcement or security while crossdressed, about 1-in-6 (16%) had been either verbally abused or physically assaulted while crossdressed in public, and 1-in-4 (25%) personally knew someone who had been either verbally abused or physically assaulted while crossdressed in public. Similarly, a 1992 study by psychologist Bryan Tully of transsexuals in London found that more than half (52%) of the male-to-female (MtF) transsexuals involved in the research had been physically assaulted.

Without minimizing the risk transgender females face, the data seem to indicate transgender males may be especially vulnerable. Males who crossdress may be viewed, especially by other males, as voluntarily lowering social status and becoming weak, thus inviting disdain and censure at best, and violence at worst. In fact, those of us who perpetrate the hostility typically believe it is warranted and place responsibility for what happens on the victim. But who is really responsible for the treatment we who crossdress in public generally receive? Do any of us *invite* the scorn, ridicule, and sometimes worse behavior we receive? Therapist Gianna Israel, in an online article, remarks, "the problems transgender men and women face are not one necessarily of self-creation, but primarily originate from others' opinions and judgments."

Experience of Children & Adolescents

If adults are vulnerable, children and adolescents are even more so. A study of 'School Climate' conducted in the fall of 1999 by the Gay, Lesbian, and Straight Education Network (GLSEN) returned responses from 496 lesbian, gay, bisexual and transgender students in 32 states. Survey results revealed more than 90% of these students had been subject to homophobic remarks, most often from other students (94.4% of those reporting such remarks), but frequently enough from faculty and staff, too (36.6%). Nearly two-thirds (61%) had experienced verbal harassment, almost half (46.5%) sexual harassment, and more than a quarter (27.6%) physical harassment, including physical assault. No wonder, then, 41.7% reported not feeling safe at school. The *SIECUS Report* covering this study noted that, "transgender kids probably suffer even more harassment and discrimination than lesbian, gay, or bisexual students."

GLSEN's survey for 2001 had an even wider reach: 904 LGBT youth from 48 states and the District of Columbia. Of these, 4.3% self-identified as transgender or other gender identity; 95.7% regarded themselves as identifying at one of the two gender poles (though their sexual orientation placed them under 'transgender' in the widest sense of the term). Their school experience had been marked by exposure to homophobic or transphobic behavior. Nearly all of them (94%) heard homophobic comments (e.g., 'You're so gay'), or labels (e.g., 'Faggot,' 'Dyke'), often or frequently, and nearly a quarter (23.6%) heard such remarks from faculty or school staff.

Such behavior by others fosters a hostile environment. In such an environment anxiety and fear over personal safety arise. In probing issues of safety at school pertinent to this population the survey found that these youth "most commonly reported that they felt unsafe in their school because of their sexual orientation or their gender expression; with over two-thirds of youth (68.6%) reporting that they felt unsafe in their school because of sexual orientation and almost half reporting they felt unsafe because of their gender expression (45.7%)." Their fear is rational, as shown by the numbers: more than two-thirds experiencing verbal harassment over gender expression, nearly a third experiencing physical harassment over the same, and about 1-in-7 experiencing physical assault for their gender expression.

Apart from experiences such as those listed above, transgender students suffer in other ways. School attendance is impacted by their fear. GLSEN's 2001 survey found such fear motivated nearly a third of the students to skip class at least once in the past month (31.9%) and to miss at least one entire day of school in the past month (20.8%). Even when they are present they may be more likely than other students to refrain from participation in school events, such as dances (where they might be afraid to bring a same-sex or same-gender partner), or classroom discussions (e.g., on LGBT issues). No wonder, then, that many transgender students choose not to be 'out' about their gender identity or sexual orientation because such things being publicly known increases their level of risk.

Educator Linda McCarthy, writing in the journal *Multicultural Education* in 2003, asks some hard questions: how will educators address issues affecting transgender youth in school settings? Will they respond at all? Are professional educators willing to educate themselves on the issues accompanying nonnormative gender expression? Are school administrators willing to shoulder responsibilities to support transgender youth? Finally, can educators take seriously and speak out against gender oppression, as they do for racism and sexism? The answers remain unknown in too many schools.

Are attitudes changing?

But what about the rest of us? The safety and well-being of transgender children, youth, and adults, like that of any minority group, depends on the sufferance of the majority—we who are gender conformists. What are our attitudes? Certainly they are not uniform. Different climates exist in different places. Let us consider two scenarios.

In the first, where ordinances or policies prohibit public crossdressing, the message is clear: those who display gender variance are wrong and merit punishment. In this situation most of the public is likely to hold an attitude mirroring the law or policy. Coercive and punitive acts become justified to discourage transgender behavior—and negative attitudes flourish. This is why even where an organization may believe it has compelling reasons to forbid crossdressing it must be explicit in justifying the prohibition and accompany it with education. Otherwise, the policy itself fosters a sense that transgender behavior is wrong and the people who do it are bad.

But what of a scenario where people know the law does *not* forbid public crossdressing and that, in fact, crossdressers are explicitly recognized as a class meriting protection from acts against them based on their gender identity or sexual orientation? Most behavior then, even if colored by rejection or hostility, will seek to remain generally within the law. A sizable number of folk, though, skirt the law or violate it in small ways, or harbor attitudes at variance from the correct behavior they feel impelled to show publicly. Only a small minority ever act out more extreme responses. But this number would be even smaller if not for some aggressors sensing a tacit approval of their acts by many others.

We must be unequivocal and united in our rejection of violence and discrimination if we are to see them end. A corrective response to negative public reactions, whether in behavior or attitude starts in two spheres: legal and educational. We briefly considered the first earlier, so let us now focus on education. We shall elaborate a little later on research about its effects with reference to attitudes concerning transgender realities. But a preliminary remark or two are in place here. First, no teaching is value-free; the best teaching believes that accurate and honest conveyance of facts will reinforce the desirability of basic human values such as respect and tolerance. Educators need not feel compelled to push any agenda other than adhering to reason and evidence.

Second, historically educational efforts concerning transgender realities have progressively encouraged a socially more tolerant stance. For example, the long struggle of women to win the right to change what is deemed acceptable gender dress is evidence of how gender crossing behavior can come to be re-evaluated to the benefit of society. More accepting attitudes toward female crossdressing first meant less enforcement of laws against the behavior and finally abandonment of such statutes. Anticrossdressing ordinances, once drafted largely with women in mind, became relics of the past. Fewer and fewer places retain laws against crossdressing and even those that do, widely ignore them—though crossdressing men may still be the exception. As attitudes change, laws against a behavior like crossdressing are first ignored, then repealed, and at last changed to afford protection for those who engage in a behavior now seen as harmless at worst. This transition is where our society seems to presently be.

But exactly how far along are we? Public attitudes have been probed by survey and interview research. A national poll commissioned by the Human

Rights Commission, conducted with 800 randomly selected registered voters and 6 focus groups, and reported at the end of the Summer of 2002, reveals the following:

o more than three-quarters (77%) think transgendered children should be permitted to attend public schools;

o more than two-thirds (70%) are familiar with the term 'transgender';

o more than two-thirds (68%) support hate-crime laws inclusive of protection for transgendered people;

o more than two-thirds (67%) agree that it is possible for a person to be born of one biological sex but psychologically identify as a member of another sex;

o almost two-thirds (61%) agree to the need for legal protection from discrimination for members of the transgendered community; but,

o more than half (57%) incorrectly assume that present laws already protect transgendered people from being fired because of their transgender status; and,

o half (50%) agree that a transgendered adult should be allowed to hold a job teaching in a high school.

Of course, these findings tell only part of the story. The same study finds that more than half (60%) do not agree that a transgendered adult should be allowed to hold a job teaching in an elementary school, serve as a scout master, or work in day care. And in the nation's schools the experience of transgender youth shows improvement in some respects (e.g., intervention by faculty and staff increased), but not in others (e.g., harassment and violence also increased).

What is most worrisome for the transgender community is that some of the positive impression people reflect in the survey might be the result of a misapprehension of what it means to be transgender. For instance, when provided an actual description of a 'transgender person,' the percent of those who regard transgender people unfavorably rises by nearly a third, and rises by more than a quarter among those who regard transgenderism as "morally wrong."

What Does This Mean for Us?

We may well ask what all this means today. Most observers of the situation concur that transgender is a more visible phenomenon now than in the past. Increasing numbers of us who are gender variant have gone public, often through the relative safety of the internet. Public awareness—and discussion—seems more pronounced than ever. In this climate there are both accepting and rejecting responses. The 'problems' of crossdressing in particular and gender variance in general are now being debated in a more vigorous way than at perhaps any other time in history. What it shall mean for us all remains to be seen. As to the question of what difference we may make in the ongoing social debate, that is a matter to which we shall return at a later time.

11.

Partners & Allies

One truth we all know through experience: we cannot thrive in life alone. All of us, gender variant or not, need allies. We crave intimacy. Regardless of our gender identity, it is a human need to have relationships and for at least one of those to be warmly supportive. It bears repeating: this is a human *need*.

Although not all of us who are transgender are presently involved in intimate relationships, many of us are. We have talked about various aspects of life for those of us who are gender variant, and we shall continue to do so. But we need as well to take some time considering those of us who are gender conforming but also in close relationship with a transgender person. To understand transgender realities requires us to examine the partners and allies of transgender people.

Partners, Family Members, and Friends

Relationships pose challenges for as long as they endure. In our society, having a transgender partner, family member, or friend poses special challenges. Our responses to such a person are inevitably individualistic, but they reflect the weight of cultural values as well as personal factors such as previous experiences and personality. No one sentence can summarize how we who are partners, family members or friends *will* respond, nor can anyone fairly say how we *ought* to respond, save the caveat that all of us should be accorded respect and civil behavior. Unfortunately, that often does not happen in families. Why?

Response Patterns

Let's begin with a foundation. We can start with a basic outline of response patterns. At any given moment, we who are close to a transgender person are likely to find ourselves in one or another of four basic response statuses—basic postures of response that may become stable patterns. These are: *rejection*, in which we refuse to tolerate the transgender behavior and/or identity; *tolerance*, in which we put up with at least some transgender behavior and/or identity; *acceptance*, in which we favorably receive our partner's transgender identity and be-

125

havior; or, *celebration*, in which we support and encourage the transgender identity and behavior. Many of us, perhaps most of us, start with rejection.

Rejection

Rejection may be passing (transient) or permanent. If it begins as transient—typically because we react in a *culturally conditioned shock* response to an unexpected disclosure or discovery—it may move either to permanent rejection or to some form of tolerance. It is hard to imagine this initial shock persisting very long. Likewise, it is difficult to imagine a person moving from surprise immediately to acceptance or celebration. Transient rejection serves as a status that simultaneously accomplishes at least three distinct ends: it expresses a ready-made cultural vehicle of response to transgender (one requiring no particular thought or preparation to use), thus discharging our initial feeling and anxiety, and it fills time while we sort things out. But it does these things at the price of a loss of civility and respect—hardly a promising start to redefining a relationship.

Our initial reaction may lead to permanent rejection. We may concur with a negative social judgment, be unable to overcome our strong negative feelings, or simply find it too overwhelming a reality to want to cope with. In such instances, separation and an ending of the relationship are almost inevitable. The qualifier 'almost' is applicable because we may issue an ultimatum, such as the transgender person seeking therapy or voluntarily ending what we see as objectionable behavior, which may save the relationship, at least for a time. Of course, transient rejection may also give way to tolerance.

Tolerance

Tolerance may be partial or complete. Tolerance, whether partial or complete, is characterized by *endurance without approval*. We agree to the continuance of transgender behavior but we offer neither sanction nor favor. In *partial tolerance* we draws limits with respect to the behavior that will be endured. That might mean the kind of crossdressing suffered (e.g., unseen), and/or when it is permitted (e.g., only when the crossdresser is alone). Perhaps most tolerance is partial. Probably less often *complete tolerance* is offered, where we make no attempt to set limits but endure whatever the transgender person does. In this case, depending upon how much internal adjustment we can make, our movement may be back to rejection or on to acceptance.

Acceptance

Acceptance may be conditional or unconditional. What differentiates acceptance from tolerance is that acceptance does not endure what is not favored, but rather *receives transgender identity and behavior favorably*. Where tolerance grants the transgender person the formal right to be who they are, at least to some extent, acceptance views being transgender as all right—different, perhaps, but not less

126

human, nor mentally disordered, nor sinful or shameful. The qualitative difference between tolerance and acceptance is significant. Our internal feeling state is different.

In light of these remarks, it may seem illogical to speak of 'conditional' acceptance. But favor need not be unconditional and often in life is not. For example, a parent may show favor to a child's school behavior as long as it is compliant to school rules and successful in academic performance. In such a case, the parent's favor is conditioned; some degree of getting into trouble or bringing home poor grades may be tolerated, but it isn't accepted. Similarly, *conditional acceptance of transgender behavior means favorably receiving some kinds of behavior and/or all behavior—but only at certain times or in certain contexts.* For instance, we might think it a good thing for the person to be crossdressed, but still not agree that it needs to be public. Thus a condition is set on our favorable reception.

Unconditional acceptance offers a favorable reception no matter the kind, degree, timing, or context of the transgender behavior. This kind of acceptance is harder for many of us to offer. Often what limits our acceptance is one or another fear, which we shall examine shortly. Of course, it is possible for us to move from partial to complete acceptance. But it is also possible to withdraw acceptance if some unforeseen, undesired outcome is the result. As with any other status, this one need not prove permanent. Some of us may change our feelings or perceptions and move from acceptance to tolerance. Others of us may move to celebration.

Celebration

Anecdotal evidence and survey evidence alike suggests that the rarest status is celebration. This status may take either a private or a public form. *In private celebration we offer full support and encouragement of transgender identity and behavior, but desire for these to remain a private matter.* This wish is not motivated by duplicity or shame, but by an appraisal that to be public would be unacceptably risky or dangerous. *Public celebration means we not only support and approve transgender identity and behavior, but also wish that to be publicly known.* Some of us even become active in efforts to educate the wider public or to change public policy and law to ensure equal treatment for all people.

Hopefully, reviewing these statuses raises the question as to what factors make most likely we will occupy a particular status at a given time. To answer such a query requires examining several other matters. We will begin with certain themes that emerge from research on intimate partners.

Response Themes

A review of various sources suggests certain themes are important. First, knowledge is power. Second, secrecy is dangerous. Third, personal values and self-knowledge are critical. Each of these themes merits some elaboration.

First, as in most matters, *knowledge is power.* The more we know, the better the predicted outcome for our relationship. Yet most of us—like most other members of the general public—know little, if anything, about transgender realities before finding ourselves in relationship with a gender variant person. With respect to spouses, for example, psychologist Richard Docter, in interviews with 21 wives of crossdressers discussed in his 1988 book *Transvestites and Transsexuals: Toward a Theory of Cross-Gender Behavior,* found the vast majority (85%) either had little or misleading information prior to learning about their husband's behavior. In the absence of knowledge, ignorance breeds isolation, misunderstanding, hostility, and many other undesirable, unpleasant reactions.

Second, *secrecy is dangerous.* Secrets prevent equality and mutuality in a relationship. To equalize power in a relationship and promote trust there must be both an absence of secrets between the parties and reliable, factual information about gender variance. Beyond understanding the transgender person, it is crucial for us to also understand ourselves. One aspect of this is being armed with knowledge about a group we now find we belong to—partners, family members, and friends of a transgender person—so that we can combat a sense of isolation and resist the myths we may encounter from an ignorant public.

Third, *personal values and self-knowledge are critical;* we who are exposed to transgender behavior are especially confronted by the need to re-examine matters most people take for granted. This offers an opportunity to us for change and growth. Those of us who are in close touch with our own values, who know ourselves, are more likely to make choices we can be confident about. Depending on how much we already value things like openness, tolerance, or acceptance, we may be more or less likely to reject transgender identity and behavior. For example, if we already champion acceptance of racial and religious diversity, we may be more likely to accept transgender realities than someone who believes in rigid separation of groups with different characteristics. Personality qualities such as openness to experience also play a role. Self-knowledge matters, but it is most likely to assist us in keeping a relationship alive when our knowledge is accompanied by our desire to learn more and to grow.

These themes merge at a starkly basic level: we all are faced with a choice—stay in the relationship, or leave. Making the best decision is largely predicated on how the themes described above come together. A relationship without secrets, where both parties seek understanding, and where each understands the self and is open to the other has a good prospect for continuing and growing. On an individual level, no less than for the transgendered person, our personal success hinges on healthy values, resolving value conflicts within ourselves, facing our beliefs that may be erroneous, confronting our fears, and exercising personal power. Just as much is at stake for the transgender person, so also much is at stake for us.

Achieving Acceptance

For many of us the critical decision after the period of initial shock is whether to move to permanent rejection or to tolerance with the hope of someday being able to achieve acceptance. Of course, some of us choose tolerance with a different hope—that we will succeed in persuading the person to become gender conforming. We will return to that idea shortly, but here we will take a moment to consider how we might move from tolerance to acceptance.

Obviously, the initial obstacle is the strong feelings we may have. Let us consider two aspects to this. First, our feelings complicate matters for the other person. Understandably, the transgender person will be affected by our rejection. Though there may be any number of ways the person might respond to us, we might do well to remember, for example, that since crossdressing often is done to reduce stress, increased stress may prompt *more*, not less crossdressing.

Second, our feelings complicate matters for us, too. Many of us permit our feelings great power over our decision-making. Certainly feelings matter. They are a source of information. At the same time, they are only *one* source of information. Prizing feelings above other facts can lead to poor outcomes. Strong feelings may seem compelling merely because they are strong. Yet even strong feelings have trouble sustaining themselves for long and have to be actively renewed by certain thoughts to keep their intensity. This process means that interrupting one's thoughts, or changing them, can rob a feeling of much of its power. In fact, changing one's *mind* about something can change one's *heart* as well. If we desire to achieve acceptance, then our strong feelings must be challenged. But how does this happen?

First, and foremost, the themes we considered must be engaged. A conviction that knowledge is power, and that such power can be achieved, is essential. Without a sense of control that comes from understanding, rather than manipulating, a genuine balance and health in the relationship will not happen. To attain such understanding means not merely knowing about transgender realities pertinent to the situation, but specifically knowing about the person's experience and expression of these. In other words, to overcome secrecy and keep open channels both parties must engage in disclosure and in questioning. We need to feel free to ask whatever we like and to express our fears. When these things take place, a reexamination of personal values may find shifts based on new knowledge and the trust encouraged by disclosures freely given and received. One sign of health and growth in any of us is a willingness to reexamine personal beliefs, challenge exposed stereotypes, and develop more humane values. This should go on in *both* parties.

We may never grasp emotionally what something like crossdressing means to a loved one. But if we can defeat the power of anxiety elicited by certain behaviors, then we have a chance to construct something more positive than mere tolerance. Since acceptance means coming to value in some degree the behavior, and not feeling negatively about it, time, patience, and empathy (imaginatively putting one's self in the other person's place and trying to feel what they feel) are all needed. Winning acceptance in one's self, if chosen as a goal, is worth taking time and effort to achieve.

The key to putting all of this together remains one thing above all: *talking*. In their booklet *He, She, We, They* a group of partners of male crossdressers emphasize that one theme—talk—repeatedly emerged from a questionnaire administered to partners of crossdressers. They mean by it more than confront; answers from respondents included terms like 'discuss,' 'negotiate,' 'compromise,' and 'keep on working on it.' Negative reactions need to be balanced by positive input. Talking is not a once-for-all event, but an ongoing process.

Counseling and/or Support Groups

But sometimes the talking between two people needs some skilled assistance. Some of us turn to counselors for help. While finding the right counselor is a challenging task at any time, finding one well-educated on transgender issues can be particularly difficult. Some therapists are not only hostile to transgender people, but also unsympathetic to those of us in close relationship with them. So, it is a good idea to be straightforward at the start in asking about the counselor's educational background, especially with regard to any training on transgender issues. It also is only fair to find out immediately what, if any, biases the counselor may hold toward transgender people. For example, a readiness to refer a client to another counselor is often an indication of such bias.

In terms of counseling issues, psychotherapist Kathleen Cairns, writing in 1997 in *The Canadian Journal of Human Sexuality*, noted that the range of adjustment we make to a behavior like crossdressing is very wide, with those of us going to a therapist because of our unhappiness over the crossdressing being only one subgroup. Thus an initial task for a therapist is grasping *how* we have coped with the situation, without presuming any particular response. In some instances, our coping mechanisms may be unproductive. Self-defeating responses include hostility, depression, or alcohol abuse. So another important therapeutic task is helping us to increase understanding of our behavior and finding better ways to cope. These should occur in a nonjudgmental context.

Some of us seek counseling together with the transgender person. Of course, we have every right to ask for such to happen if we feel we need it. Likewise, the person in our life who is transgender might ask for this too. In either case, we shall both benefit if we can agree on a counselor and work together in the counseling process. Adding a third party to the conversation can be very beneficial, but it poses challenges of its own. For counseling to be most effective we must be willing to open ourselves to others, accept their openness and questions, and work as diligently as we hope they will.

What also may prove useful in our struggle to adjust and manage our situation is finding connection with others facing like issues. Support for us can be a potent assist in dealing with our relationship with a transgender person. Just as the transgender individual may desire contact with other gender variant people for support, so we may wish the company of those who understand firsthand what it is like to be in our shoes. Support groups can help us overcome the profound alienation and isolation that may follow discovery of gender variance. Generally, we do not actively seek a transgender person; we suddenly discover that is whom we have. We are not the first to make such a discovery.

How we handle this discovery and what we learn reflects a variety of personal factors. It is time we turn to some of these. It is time to reflect on who we are. Once more, there is some research that comes to our aid.

Female Partners

Our first attention should go to the group of us who live most intimately with a transgendered person as a spouse or partner. We who live in such a relationship might benefit from what studies have shown about us. Although our group includes both men and women, it is the latter who have received the most attention. Psychiatrist George Brown, writing in 1994 in the *Archives of Sexual Behavior*, reported perhaps the largest study of its kind, with data from 106 women gathered over a six-year span. Instruments used in his research included a questionnaire, and interviews with three-quarters of the women. All were involved at present with crossdressing males, and 75% of them were married to the person. The women ranged in age from 19-69 years old. Their relationships ranged in duration from 2 weeks to 46 years (average length of 13.1 years). Most (60%) did not find out about their loved one's crossdressing until they had been in the relationship for some time.

Character

Like we might, many of these women probably wondered if there was something about themselves that made them more likely to end up in a relationship with a gender variant person. Are such partners flawed? Brown found that women who are in relationships with crossdressers do *not* suffer from character flaws. His study addressed some earlier speculation that female partners of crossdressers suffer from low self-esteem and high dependency. Instead, Brown found such traits were not general characteristics. Nor is he alone in this conclusion. Psychologist Richard Docter also did not find this true of the group of 21 spouses he interviewed and tracked over four years, as reported in his 1988 book, *Transvestites and Transsexuals*. Brown, in fact, proposes the following: "An alternative hypothesis to deficient self-esteem would be that these women have high levels of openness, a personality trait that fosters novel ideas and rejection of rigid stereotypes." In short, maybe we who are such partners have the kind of character that would allow us to be positively related to many different kinds of people. If there is something different about our character, maybe it is *good*.

Of course, just as among gender variant people, among those of us in close relationship with them there is much individuality. For example, feminist Annie Woodhouse, in her 1989 book *Fantastic Women. Sex, Gender and Transvestism*, reported rather less openness in five women she interviewed. These women endorsed conventional gender expectations. Since these women were relatively negative toward crossdressing, it seems likely that their attachment to conventional views of gender complicated how accepting they could be. Woodhouse urges us not to 'blame the victim' by being critical of such women.

Finally, we should note the work of researchers Vern Bullough and Thomas Weinberg, who also explored the female partner's self-esteem. They interviewed 70 women married to a crossdressing husband. In a 1988 article in the *Journal of Sex Research* they reported a correlation between adjustment to the crossdressing and self-esteem. Women with high self-esteem rated their marriages as happier than did those with low self-esteem. Among these women a feeling of control over their own life proved critical; those who felt such control possessed higher self-esteem. Women with lower self-esteem did not feel such power, worried over public exposure, and tended to view themselves as failures in their role as wives. It may be that ability to adjust is more critical than a particular situation.

False Beliefs

Consistent with the notion that our perceptions and thinking matter is another finding: various beliefs we might hold can complicate our relationship with a transgender partner. Among such beliefs might be the following:

o   My partner can be cured. I can help him (or her) change.
o   I'll never be able to be more accepting or tolerant than I am now.

Both beliefs are unrealistic and clinging to either is self-defeating.

It is a relatively common belief we may be able to help our loved one to cease being transgender. Betty Ann Lind, writing in *He, She, We, They. Partners of Cross Dressers*, reports that the majority of crossdressers' wives she surveyed who knew about the crossdressing before marriage thought that marriage would cure it. Brown's study found that a quarter of the women initially believed a 'cure' might be found for the crossdressing. This belief dissipates over time for almost all of them. Knowledge and experience counter the belief. Understanding both the nature and prognosis for transgender identity and behavior can help alleviate our negative feelings, including any self-reproach we may have for being unable to get a loved one to change.

The second belief, like the first, is often a product of the initial shock of discovery. In the midst of the surprise it can scarcely be wondered that we may say, 'I'll never be able to be more accepting or tolerant than I am now.' And right now we may not be very accepting! Yet time dulls the effects of surprise and heals many wounds. We human beings have a marvelous ability to habituate to all kinds of situations without a permanent decrease in our levels of happiness or satisfaction. Indeed, Brown reports in his research that partners of crossdressers frequently do become more accepting over time.

Fears

Still, regardless of our level of self-esteem, or our growth in acceptance, given our society's anxiety over gender variance, we should not be either surprised or dismayed that alongside false beliefs we might also have fears. Four common ones are: Is my partner homosexual? Will my partner want to go all the way and change his/her sex? What if others find out? What does it say about me that I am in such a relationship? We need facts to help us confront our fears.

Is My Partner Homosexual?

Most transgender males identify themselves as heterosexual, and this is especially true among those who are married. Indeed, the classic 1972 report by Virginia Prince and Peter Bentler of more than 500 male crossdressers noted that 89% characterized their sexual orientation as heterosexual. The 1997 study by Richard Docter and Prince, patterned on this earlier research but utilizing more than twice the pool of subjects, found an almost identical rate: 87%. A 1983 study by Vern and Bonnie Bullough and Richard Smith found that 82% of transvestite men say they are more sexually attracted to women. In sum, research consistently finds a heterosexual orientation for most crossdressers.

Will My Partner Want to Change Sex?

Another fear is that our partner will seek to change sex. Perhaps surprisingly, for most of us this fear is not very pronounced. That is fortunate, because the research shows that most transgender people are not transsexual. The 1983 study by Bullough, Bullough and Smith, for example, found that less than half of transvestites (47%) held any interest in a sex change, and of those who did only a miniscule number (2%) were actually favorably inclined toward surgery. In fact, of those who had some interest, nearly half (46%) had looked into the possibility and rejected it. In his study of over 400 adult British males, physician Vernon Coleman found that more than three-quarters (77%) said they would not have a sex change operation even if the opportunity presented itself.

Still, this is not a completely irrational fear. The 1983 study noted that one-quarter (25%) of the subjects had at one time or another taken sex hormones. Some gender variant people are transsexuals and do desire to change their body sex. In such cases, regardless of whether the relationship ends or not, it changes dramatically. Yet some of us in such circumstances choose to stay. For example, a study published in 1981 in the *Canadian Journal of Psychiatry* of 41 female-to-male (FtM) transsexuals (ages 18-63), and 21 female partners, found them in stable and long-term relationships. And this was in a less socially tolerant time than our own. In the range of human experience and relationships, some people are capable of finding satisfaction in situations that others find unimaginable.

What If Others Find Out?

The fear of discovery may be simply our fear of being embarrassed (if we see transgender as shameful), or a fear of being harmed by others. Such harm can range from social isolation to violence. Interestingly, Peggy Rudd, herself partner to a crossdresser, wrote in her 2000 book *Crossdressers: And Those Who*

Share Their Lives, that her research with 850 crossdressers disclosed their own greatest fear is over the potential harm that might come to we who love them. If nothing else, then, this is one fear both parties are likely to have in common.

Richard Docter, writing in his aforementioned book *Transvestites and Transsexuals*, discovered the most commonly mentioned fear was having the husband's crossdressing discovered by a visitor. Yet, while nearly three-quarters (71%) of the wives mentioned this fear, its average weighting on a 7-point scale (0 being "no problem"; 6 being a "very great problem") was only a 3.7— midway between "a moderate problem—not especially difficult," and "a difficult problem." It may be that the underlying concern is less what others will think of the husband and more what they'll think of the woman living with him.

What Does This Relationship Say About Me?

So what does it say about us if we find ourselves intimately involved with a transgender person? Does it mean we are also gender variant, or homosexual? Obviously, the ultimate answer to such queries can only come from within. But the research does not indicate that as a group we spouses and partners of transgender people are either gender variant or homosexual. With respect to the latter fear, George Brown's study found that women married to crossdressers are *not* more likely than other women to have engaged in a homosexual experience. Of course, our fears may not be so specific. We may have general doubts about our sexuality or sexual identity. Or, our concerns may not have anything to do with sexuality but rather be of a more ambiguous nature or attached to vague worries about what others might think and say should the word get out. Whatever they are, our fears belong to us and only we have a final say on the power they will exercise in our life. We can draw comfort from knowing the evidence does not support negative judgments on us for being in such relationships and, in fact, may speak well of our capacity for love and acceptance.

Family

Perhaps the greatest fear our transgender loved one faces is rejection by us who are family. What lies at the root of one family member rejecting another? Transgender therapist Gianna Israel, in a 2003 online article entitled 'Contentious Family Issues,' says that most rejection occurs when we who find out about our loved one's gender variance cannot bridge the gap between their gender experiences and our own. She notes how, ironically, the transgender person often becomes caretaker to us, helping us manage our shock and distress at the very time when the transgender loved one may need our support the most.

In our own shock at discovery, we tend to forget or minimize what is at stake for the other person. When self-disclosure is made by a loved one the content of that disclosure may outweigh for us any recognition of the courage required to make such a disclosure. We may find it hard to think about what it means to risk one's very soul in the manner a transgender family member does when coming out about gender identity. To our shame, we may react in a careless, hurtful manner, saying or doing things we will have plenty of time to regret later.

Clearly, disclosure of gender variance in a society like ours is both risky and controversial. Perhaps nowhere is this more the case than when it comes to the question of whether children should be told a family member, especially a parent, is a transgender person. Let us consider the matter.

Children

Research suggests that most children don't know a parent is transgender. Some, of course, do. The study by Brown, and another by sociologist John Talamini reported in his 1982 book *Boys Will Be Girls: The Hidden World of the Heterosexual Male Transvestite*, both found that about one-third of the children knew. More recent research, such as that reported in various online surveys, suggests this percentage has not increased. Moreover, whether the children are told or not, it appears rare that they are actually exposed to visible markers of the gender variance such as seeing a parent crossdressed. Should those who don't know be told?

Is telling a good idea? One might argue the answer depends on the outcome, but since that is only known after the fact it is not a terribly helpful reply. So what have been outcomes? In Talamini's study, apparently no negative outcomes followed from the children being informed. None of them adopted the behavior, or demonstrated cross-gender identity or role problems. Similarly, Israel thinks it is a myth telling young children will do them harm, such as by prompting development of confused ideas about sex or gender. If anything, she observes, younger children generally handle the news better than adolescents.

On the other hand, Brown's study reported that three mothers told how their young sons (school-age) had "spontaneously cross-dressed on more than one occasion without assistance or overt encouragement from either parent." In seeking to understand this, Brown drew upon previous research and indicated several possible explanations, but opted as the most likely explanation that it reflected a short-lived identification phase. In light of the possibility that children might respond like this, should they be told? Harry Benjamin, in his 1966 *The Transsexual Phenomenon*, expressed his belief that children should be "protected" from learning of a father's crossdressing because of potential damage to their development. He felt sons were at particular risk since the boy's identification with his father might suffer irreparable damage. Two decades later, Richard Docter likewise argued that being open and honest runs a risk for younger children that may exceed the benefits. This general view still appears to be the majority opinion. But is this merely expression of an irrational fear?

There exists little if any empirical evidence that harm actually occurs from disclosure, save to the one disclosing. In fact, the fear of harm itself may be the most damaging result. Some parents might therefore choose to let the gender variance be known by their children. If the decision is made to tell the children, Israel believes it should be a fairly straightforward process. In a 2005 article for the *Journal of GLBT Family Studies*, she recommends keeping the following in mind: first, in the face of anything new and different in the family, children need to be reminded they are loved and accepted unconditionally. Second, they also need reassurances things will be okay. Third, they need help to learn that a parent being different is about the parent, not themselves. Finally, they may need help in facing harassment from others, especially bullying peers.

Unfortunately, revelation of a parent's transgender reality may come about because the parents have decided to separate or divorce. This decision raises the stakes for the whole family, and most particularly for the children. We should see it as unconscionable that we might use society's transphobia as a way to manipulate our children. Regardless of how we might feel in separating, our children remain *our* children. The gender variant parent should be permitted a relationship on *hir* own terms.

Parents

Setting aside preconceived notions is difficult for anyone, but perhaps particularly for us who are family members, and especially if we are parents. In fact, the research suggests that the one group who may have the most trouble accepting the news that someone is gender variant is we parents. Social work professor Ski Hunter, in his 2007 book *Coming Out and Disclosures*, observes that the grief reaction is much like that by parents of gay or lesbian children. We often experience *shock* and *denial*. We may respond with disbelief and the disclaimer, "We didn't raise our child to be like this!" We may experience a sense of loss as we slowly comprehend that our hopes and desires for our child no longer fit.

Hunter points out how our response may vary according to different factors. For example, we may be able to sustain our denial if our child is living away from home or if *sie* refrains from displaying a cross gender role. However, as in the stages of grief associated with death, denial may give way to *anger*. Common in anger is blaming or scapegoating the child. In time, anger may be displaced by *bargaining*. This process can take several forms. We might, for example, try to strike a bargain based on a threat such as disinheritance; if the child gives up the transgender behavior, then we won't punish. Or we may attempt to bargain based on a bribe; we might offer money for school, or starting a business if the transgender is kept secret.

Hunter tells us that as our child's reality sinks in, a number of other reactions are possible, including depression, illness, and even suicidal behavior. We might turn to drugs, withdraw from other family members, and even blame the other parent, perhaps leading to separation or divorce. If nothing else, such extreme responses should remind us how central our culture has made gender, and how critical gender conformity has become to our judgments about ourselves and others.

However, our decisions are not predestined. We always have within our power the right and ability to choose different response patterns, no matter our initial reaction. Hunter says that when we parents have more moderate emotions different outcomes happen. For example, he observes we might *create a family ceremony* to mark the 'rebirth' and new acceptance of our child. Continuing with the parallel to the stages of grief associated with death and dying, Hunter remarks that *acceptance* is reached when we confront our sense of loss for the child we knew and no longer exert efforts to try to change *hir*.

We might expect, as Hunter remarks, that our relationship with our child *before* we learn of the transgender identity may be a pretty good predictor of how well we handle the discovery. If we accept society's negative stereotypes about transgender, we may find it very hard to move to acceptance. In some cases, though, our child's revelation can lead to greater closeness; we rise to the challenge and may even surprise ourselves by the grace under pressure we display. In fact, psychologist Ritch Savin-Williams, in his 2001 book *"Mom, Dad, I'm Gay." How Families Negotiate Coming Out*, points out that even those of us with strong, conservative religious convictions can have positive outcomes with our child if we love unconditionally. It is up to us.

Siblings and Other Family Members

Growing up with someone tends to lead us to believe we know that person very well. Our long familiarity through our family of origin makes it especially likely we will have trouble adjusting to the discovery that a family member is a transgender person. If we only find out after the person has become an adult and started a new family the news may be especially difficult. But our response may be partly cued by how we see our loved one's partner responding to it. An online survey in 1999, hosted by 'Yvonne,' sought to assess how supportive family might be. Respondents were more than 1,000 male crossdressers (ages 16-76). Of these men, 539 were married to spouses who knew of their crossdressing. The survey found that in marriages where the spouse is supportive, other family members who knew of the crossdressing were more likely to be supportive. Interestingly, a substantial difference was found among siblings: a spouse's support was correlated with twice the likelihood that siblings would be supportive, too. Even more pronounced was the correlation with supportiveness among extended family. When the crossdresser's spouse is supportive, extended family members are more than four times more likely to be supportive.

Families, like individuals, have habits and boundaries. The safety and comfort of the familiar is stripped away by discovery of transgender realities. To make a successful transition to a new family identity, one where the transgender person has a place, requires adjustments of perception and behavior alike. Some of our families are unwilling to expend the effort to make such changes. For some of us it proves easier to discard 'the stranger' the transgender person appears to have become. For those of us most bound to cultural conventions of gender, the mismatch we perceive in a family member is hard enough, but if that person then attempts to eliminate the mismatch by changing body sex rather than gender presentation, we may regard this act as crossing a line that puts the transgender person out of our family. In fact, we may be tempted to cope with the situation by justifying our behavior as a legitimate response to the 'outrageous decisions' of the 'transgressor.' In short, we choose to interpret the transgender person as the one leaving the family rather than see ourselves casting the person out.

Who is family?

When transgender individuals find themselves cast off from family, most move from mourning the loss to efforts to construct a new family. In this regard, we may legitimately ask who constitutes a family anyway. The idea that family is a matter of biological relations persists despite decreasing relevance. The fact is that many of us find our sense of family—bonds of respect, affection, and loyalty—among a group of people who may include only a few, and perhaps none of those to whom we are genetically related. Among transgendered people, no less than among any of us, family are the people who love, support, and welcome us any time and always. And no less than anyone else, transgendered people need family, seek family, and build family as best they can. Even a single such other person can make a family happen—and prove to be the difference in how the challenges of life will be met.

Some adopt a broad understanding of family and thus identify the people of their church, or support group, or closest friends as 'family.' Others seek out and form new intimate bonds, finding housemates, roommates, or spouses. Being different appears to encourage and elicit creativity simply to survive and adapt, and transgender people as a group seem to have an abundant supply of creativity. This resource serves them well in identifying different people to be in a family with, or crafting a different way to be in a family. One way or another, many of our loved ones find paths to end isolation or estrangement after we divorce them from our families.

How unfortunate, though, that our response hurts our family rather than heals it. When we reject a transgender family member we are responding to our own hurt from what we construe as deceit and betrayal. We may believe we *have* to act in this manner, cutting away a cancer to save the family, or trying to shock the loved one into coming to his or her senses. When it doesn't work, when the family stays broken, and the transgender person makes a new family, what have we left? We are burdened with our loss. And we stay so burdened as long as we insist on our righteousness over our relationship. For exactly as long as we cling to our justification for rejection we shall remain bereft of relationship. That seems a high price to pay for endorsing a dubious cultural value.

138

12.

Turn Ons

One of the more curious facets of being human is our intense interest, even concern, about the sexual habits of others. What makes it curious is not that we should be interested, for sexuality matters, but that we should regard our interest as perfectly okay even though we would be horrified at the suggestion that anyone else has a right to know about our own sexual lives! Often we explain this discrepancy—if we bother to address it all—by saying that we are less interested in the particular habits of an individual than in the general patterns of groups. And no groups excite more interest than minority groups, because we tend to believe that anything as important as sexuality must be affected by whatever is the quality—gender, sexual orientation, race, ethnicity, or religion—that sets the minority apart. For groups we disapprove of we tend to assume that disturbed sexuality is one characteristic we will find. If the minority is transgender people, we are especially likely to presume a sexual dysfunction is both present and central if we view sex and gender as Essentialists do.

In our earlier discussion on what psychological testing shows about the sexuality of we who are transgender, it emerged we are not significantly different from everyone else. We might recall the studies assessing sexual functioning using the Derogatis Sexual Functioning Inventory (DSFI), which employs 255 items to measure 10 dimensions. DSFI results reveal that transgender males do not deviate dramatically from so-called 'normal' male heterosexual subjects. Despite such findings, many of us still suspect that something unusual, and perhaps unhealthy, is involved in transgender sexuality. Given that crossdressing serves to visibly mark transgender, and given that historically crossdressing was commonly viewed as showing an interest in same-sex sexual relationships, two of the principal areas of interest have been the sexual orientation of those of us who are transgender, and the role crossdressing plays in our sexual behavior.

Transgender and Sexual Orientation

Some of us believe that all transgender people are homosexual. Those of us who believe this are incorrect. There has been an unfortunate tendency to automatically link gender variance with homosexuality. This is a byproduct of the medicalization of sex. It generates a stereotype that for the convenience of creating one large box lumps together all of us who are too much different from the culture's ideal of heterosexual masculinity and femininity as expressed in gender-conforming ways.

Linking Gender Variance and Homosexuality

In this manner, for instance, all crossdressers are presumed to be at least latently homosexual because of not conforming to gender expectations in dress. The reasoning is that if someone is different in one way (gender), it is easy to imagine that person different in another way (sexual orientation) as well. This supposed link is strengthened by assuming that crossdressing is meant to elicit sexual interest by others of the same sex. Certainly crossdressing can be used for such a purpose. Just as certainly that is most often not the motivation.

Unfortunately, those of us who are transsexual are especially likely to be labeled as homosexual because many people insist that anatomical sex, rather than gender identity, is what matters in determining sexual orientation. The logic comes from Essentialism: since a person always remains genetically the same sex, and sex can be used to determine sexual orientation, then a genetic male, even if altered by hormones and surgery to appear female, remains 'really' male. Thus a genetic male, professing a desire for a male sexual partner, must be homosexual.

This way of reasoning prioritizes sex over gender. But it has been challenged in recent years. In an alternative to the view just described, gender can be seen as what determines sexual orientation. A genetic male who experiences the self as female, and alters the body accordingly, should be regarded as a woman in gender. The desire for a male sexual partner by a woman is seen correctly as heterosexual.

Let us put this all together. *Sexual orientation* refers to relatively fixed patterns of erotic attraction. To be *heterosexual* means our sexual desire is aimed at others whose gender identity varies from our own. Because most people are gender conforming this means we can also say that our sexual attraction is toward others whose body is of a different sex. But gender, not sex, is the decisive determinant of sexual orientation. Heterosexual men are attracted to women regardless of the precise anatomy involved. Similarly, *homosexual* means our sexual desire is directed toward others whose gender identity matches our own. Men are attracted to men; women desire women. Again, because most people are gender conforming, most people who identify as men have male bodies and those who identify as women have female bodies. Therefore, generally speaking, homosexual desire means both a desire for others who have a similar gender and a similar sex. The only time most of us get confused is when considering the sexual orientation of transsexuals because of the mismatch between sex and gender. In this case we would do well to be guided by what real people in real relationships say, and in that respect gender matters more than sex.

Most of us who are transgender are not transsexual. We do not see our body sex as wrong. Nor do most of us desire to have sexual relations with others whose bodies are like our own. Consider, for instance, those of us who are transgender males. We can regard ourselves as males and also see ourselves both as men and as persons with a feminine side. Or we might regard ourselves as men who also have a separate feminine identity. If we see ourselves as heterosexual because we desire sexual relations with those who have female bodies, then such a self-identification can be established on either basis just described, because we have a male body (sex) and identify as men (gender).

Obviously, this matter can be confusing and *has* created confusion. This seems especially unfortunate because sexual orientation has been made inordinately important in a way that places stress on *all* of us, gender conforming and gender variant alike. Some things, however, are clear from the data gathered by researchers. First, *most* of us who are transgender identify as heterosexual. If we go by the numbers found in the various studies we have discussed, some four-fifths or more of transgender males who crossdress identify as heterosexual. Second, *some* of us who are transgender identify as homosexual. While most of us who are homosexual do not crossdress, some of us do. However, for many of us as gay men or lesbian women who crossdress the purpose is different than that motivating crossdressing for transgender heterosexuals. *Drag*, for example, intends to make a public criticism of our culture's restrictive ideas about sex, sexuality, and gender. Thus, third, we all would do well to refrain from making casual assumptions about the sexual orientation or crossdressing behavior of transgender people.

Changing Clothes, Changing Gender, Changing Sexual Orientation?

Interestingly, some research suggests that crossdressing may be associated with changed patterns of arousal. In a pair of studies, researcher Neil Buhrich and colleagues explored whether sexual partner preference changes when a male crossdresses. First, in a study with a small subject pool published in 1977 in the *Archives of Sexual Behavior*, Buhrich and Neil McConaghy looked at a dozen transsexual males. When dressed in masculine clothing two-thirds declared their sexual interest was predominantly women. When dressed in feminine clothing less than half expressed a principal interest in women, while half reported a predominant interest in men. Later, in a study published in 1981 in the *Archives of Sexual Behavior*, Buhrich and Trina Beaumont investigated the matter with 236 male members of transvestite clubs in both Australia (N=97) and the United States (N=136). After excluding 24 subjects who reported no fetishistic arousal related to crossdressing, the remaining subjects were classified based on their reports of sexual preference in partners and sexual behavior. A change was found between partner-preferences in some of the men when they moved from masculine attire to feminine clothing. Interest in having a male partner was more likely when crossdressed, though a majority of men remained exclusively

141

heterosexual no matter how they were dressed. These studies do not suggest that crossdressing makes men homosexual, but they do encourage us to conceive of sexual attraction patterns related to gender as more fluid and less fixed (i.e., polarized between heterosexual and homosexual) than typically conceived.

Transgender Sexuality and Crossdressing

Apart from presumptions about sexual orientation, there remain the speculations and curiosity many of us have about the role of crossdressing in sexual arousal and activity. In order to best understand this matter we must again try for a broader perspective, one that connects with experiences we all may have. We need to reflect a moment on the more general role of clothing in sexuality.

Human sexual interactions are sense-intensive. Touch, vision, smell and taste all play important roles. So, too, do clothes. They fascinate the eyes and titillate the touch. Some clothes are purposely designed to do exactly such things, to be a part of human sexual discourse. There need be no surprise, then, that clothes come to play for some of us a different or more extensive role than merely enticing an encounter with someone else. For many of us wearing sexy clothes helps us feel sexual. They facilitate sexual interactions. For some among us various clothes become sexual objects in their own right, enjoyed as adjuncts to masturbation. For others among us the pleasure in the opposite gender's clothes extends beyond looking at and touching them to putting them on. The wearing of them can produce sexual pleasure with no other action required, though wearing them may be accompanied by other behaviors, such as masturbation or intercourse.

Because garments can excite sexual arousal an interesting question might be asked: Why is it okay for clothes to possess an erotic quality only for so long as they remain either unworn or on someone else? No one is bothered by the idea of a man being aroused by the sight of lingerie, especially when worn by a woman he hopes to have sex with. No one is disturbed that he finds the feel of such clothes pleasurable when he comes into contact with them. Why, then, are so many distressed if he puts such items on?

Think about it. In our culture, sexual arousal is viewed positively. Indeed, individuals who have trouble with either desire or arousal are regarded as suffering from sexual dysfunction—and may receive a diagnosis of a mental disorder in the reigning psychiatric model. It seems curious, then, that the ability to attain arousal and satisfaction from crossdressing is seen as a bad thing by this same model—as are a number of other 'paraphilias' (like sadism and masochism). Apparently, to escape being considered mentally disordered one's sexual interests and behaviors must be such that he or she wants sex, attains arousal, and pursues the same avenues for sexual satisfaction as the mental health professionals who set the parameters for sexual disorders. We might well be inclined to ask, 'Who died and made psychiatrists lord and king over my sexual life?' Yet they only reflect the mainstream culture's values and attitudes. That, of course, is the key insight: our beliefs about how clothes should figure in our sexual behavior are socially constructed. They are not a given of Nature or an intrinsic property of the clothing.

In the case of crossdressing, the real issue is probably not just the component of sexual arousal. As we have seen already, arousal associated with clothes is common. The reason crossdressing is objectionable to most folk likely has more to do with gender presentation than it does with mere sexual excitement. As long as the feminine garments are unworn or worn by a woman they are legitimately sexual adjuncts and do not compromise any sense of the man's masculinity. Men are free to enjoy feminine clothing as long as the apparel remains at some distance from their own gender expression. Of course, all the same considerations are true for women who find articles of masculine clothing erotic.

Crossdressing and Sexual Arousal

But when a man puts on a woman's clothes and is aroused, then there seems to many of us a profound confusion both of sex *and* gender issues. Psychologist Ray Blanchard has introduced a controversial notion that gets at the sense of unease many people feel. He suggests that 'autogynephilia' is at work—the individual is sexually aroused at the self-presentation as a female. In such a mixing of sex and gender the real presence of another person may become superfluous. And *that* can certainly produce problems in significant relationships.

Curiously, though, crossdressing in the context of a sexual interaction isn't always seen by the couple as changing gender presentation; he remains 'he' and she remains 'she' no matter who wears what. The whole matter is as much *perception* as it is *presentation*. Some men who never otherwise don women's garb may do so spontaneously in the play of lovemaking by trying on their partner's sexy clothes. Some women find men's clothes sexually stimulating in the context of lovemaking. In other words, it is possible and actually happens that a man or a woman puts on one or more articles of a lover and is not seen as deviant. Despite crossdressing during sex being associated primarily with heterosexual men designated as transvestites, the phenomenon is wider than that.

Examining the Link Between Crossdressing and Sexual Behavior

But let's stay focused on self-identified crossdressers. The link between crossdressing and sexual arousal needs to be explored. First, we should note that crossdressing typically is lifelong, rooted early in developmental experience. In fact, studies from 1951 to the present consistently show a majority of those who crossdress as adults began doing so as children, with many starting before age 5. For example, sociologist H. Taylor Buckner reported in 1962 that of his 262 subjects, 54% had begun crossdressing before age 10. A decade later, the study in *Psychological Reports* by Virginia Prince and Peter Bentler, with 504 subjects, found an identical result. In 1981 in the *Archives of Sexual Behavior*, Neil

Buhrich and Trina Beaumont reported that 94% of their 222 subjects had started before adulthood and almost half of them before age 11. A. M. Verschoor's 1990 report on 292 subjects found that 61% of those later identified as transvestites had started crossdressing before age 12 and 87.5% of those later identified as transsexual had begun crossdressing by that age. Richard Schott's 1995 study in *Archives of Sexual Behavior* on 85 subjects reported 97% cross-dressed before puberty. In the same journal, in 1997, Richard Docter and Virginia Prince, in a study of 1,032 subjects, found 66% began crossdressing before age 10. That same year, writing in the book *Gender Blending*, Bonnie and Vern Bullough reported on 372 subjects, finding 91% had begun crossdressing by age 14 with more than a third by age 6. The early origin of crossdressing is perhaps the most certain result of all research on crossdressers.

Why does this matter? It matters because many of us believe crossdressing is exclusively, or at least primarily, a sexual fetish—a way to become aroused and gain sexual relief. Certainly, we are sexual beings all our life, but childhood sexuality is not the same as adult sexuality, nor is it accurate to presume that childhood crossdressing starts with an aim to gain sexual arousal. There may be a sensual element in the early experience of crossdressing, but that should not be confused with crossdressing as a prelude or accompaniment to masturbation. Some of us who crossdress *never* do so for sexual satisfaction; some of us *rarely* do so for sexual pleasure; some of us *occasionally* do so for sexual arousal and relief; and some of us *often* do so for sexual reasons. The point should be clear: we err if we generalize from the experience of a few to all.

The presumed link between crossdressing and sexual fetishism has complex roots. But we can identify as especially important the following: those adult males who in psychotherapy were identified as transvestites often were there because their crossdressing was associated with sexual behavior that had gained them unwanted attention. So, in his 1966 classic *The Transsexual Phenomenon*, Harry Benjamin confidently expressed the view that any experienced clinician would find sexual roots in the majority of transvestites. Moreover, thought Benjamin, though many older transvestites claim to crossdress for emotional rather than sexual reasons, this claim had to be modified in light of their tendency to minimize the sexual nature of crossdressing in an effort to conform to our culture's views. Benjamin's view persists among some mental health professionals, but a recognition that a clinical population may not be representative of all crossdressers, coupled with greater research, has largely tempered his judgment.

By the 1980 publication of the American Psychiatric Association's *Diagnostic and Statistical Manual of Mental Disorders, 3rd edition,* it was generally accepted that some men's crossdressing can, at some point, become largely or entirely non-sexual in character. Research since then has further confirmed this conclusion. So any connection between crossdressing and sexual arousal must be qualified to some degree. We can say with confidence that some crossdressing by some crossdressers is for sexual arousal and relief. We cannot accurately say that all crossdressing is for such a purpose.

So, an emphasis on a connection between crossdressing and sexual arousal may be misplaced. For most crossdressers, sexual behavior is neither the only reason for crossdressing, nor always an accompaniment to it. There is no denying that sexual arousal and an association between crossdressing and sexuality are important matters to consider. But they are not the only ones, and may not even be the defining ones. In fact, Neil Buhrich, in interviews with 33 crossdressing men reported in 1978 in *Acta Psychiatrica Scandinavica*, found that sexual arousal (i.e., "fetishistic pleasure") was not a frequent reason offered for their crossdressing. In other research, Jack Croughan and associates, in a study published in 1981 in the *Archives of Sexual Behavior*, found that crossdressing done because of a desire for sexual arousal and relief was an insignificant precipitating behavior, occurring just over 5% of the time.

Research since then seems to confirm that though a link sometimes exists between crossdressing and sexual behavior, it is not as prominent as many of us believe. For example, a 1999 online survey hosted by 'Yvonne,' of over 1,000 male crossdressers (ages 16-76), discovered that less than one-fifth (19%) said that crossdressing was pursued solely for sexual pleasure. For more than 4-in-5 of these men, crossdressing was about more than sexual arousal. Clearly, while crossdressing cannot be entirely separated from sexuality, the connections are both more complex and less pronounced than popular mythology often presents.

Such statements may remain unsatisfying to many of us. We may persist in wanting to know how common crossdressing for sexual arousal and relief actually is. There has been research in this regard, but like most other matters it has not yielded uniform results. For example, Richard Schott's 1995 report in the *Archives of Sexual Behavior* concerning a sample of 85 males (including both transvestites and transsexuals) revealed that more than three-quarters (78%) reported certain items of feminine clothing had produced sexual arousal in them during childhood. Similarly, the 1999 online survey we mentioned a moment ago found that sexual arousal accompanied crossdressing, at least sometimes, for 90% of the respondents. Further, 85% of them admitted masturbating while crossdressed. But what exactly do such numbers mean?

We may find it hard to see how such results square with the research we discussed earlier. If most crossdressing males report crossdressing for sexual purposes, then how can anyone argue the link between crossdressing and sexual activity is weaker than often presumed? To make sense of this we need to highlight some critical qualifiers. Let's list them: first, even though most of us who are crossdressing males report having crossdressed in connection with some sexual behavior, that's not the same thing as saying that most of us report crossdressing for that purpose most of the time. Crossdressing is dress behavior, and dress behavior occurs in a variety of contexts for a number of reasons. We will return to this basic idea in a moment.

Second, even though some of the sexual behavior accompanying cross-dressing occurs during adulthood, most of it seems to occur in adolescence and early adulthood rather than later on. The association of crossdressing and sexual arousal generally persists through adolescence into adulthood, though it tends to gradually weaken with aging. Mental health professionals have recognized that finding for decades now. It is time for everyone else to catch on.

Third, regardless of *when* the crossdressing for a sexual reason occurs, or *how often* it occurs, most of us who are adult crossdressers insist that our cross-dressing is not primarily about sexuality; there is no compelling reason to doubt us. It may be that our enjoyment of crossdressing associated with sexual behavior is analogous to gender conforming individuals who enjoy sexual behavior while wearing lingerie. We wouldn't say all or even most of their dress behavior is for sexual reasons simply because some of it is, so why would that be said of us? A consistency in logical reasoning is more likely if we apply to ourselves what we use in evaluating others.

Transvestic Fetishism

In those for whom sexual satisfaction is difficult or impossible without crossdressing, and causes personal distress or impairs functioning (e.g., in relating to others), the behavior is called 'transvestic fetishism.' The perspective of crossdressing as a psychological disorder results from a modern preoccupation with one, rather limited aspect of a complex behavior: obtaining sexual arousal and relief. That this focus is limited is pointed out by research scientist Ron Langevin, who wonders why anyone seeking sexual relief would bother to put on the clothes inasmuch as fetishism hardly requires such an act. Rather, such behavior indicates *gender* needs play a role. Yet it is sexuality many focus on.

The term 'fetish' (spelled in more than one way) comes from outside medicine and psychiatry, deriving from the language of anthropology and religion. Already by the end of the 18th century it was being applied among French physicians to a certain kind of sexual 'perversion.' They settled on explaining it as a phenomenon attached to the more 'primitive' of the human senses: touch, taste and smell. The idea of fetishism gained prominence especially through the influence of psychoanalysis. Sigmund Freud adopted the term in his small 1905 book, *Three Essays on the Theory of Sexuality*. The basic idea of a sexual fetish is that it is an object that takes the place of another person; it symbolically stands in for a person. Virtually any object can be a fetish, though the term is most commonly applied to articles of clothing.

Psychiatrist Robert Stoller, influential in the modern psychoanalytic development of how crossdressing has been understood, stands in a long line of psychoanalysts who extended Freud's ideas by applying them to crossdressing. Stoller conceived of transvestism as a fetish for the clothing of the opposite sex.

He documented its occurrence in women as well as in men. For the behavior to qualify as fetishistic, according to Stoller, the person must experience something more than mere sexual arousal to the clothes of the opposite sex, for most males find the sight of female lingerie to be stimulating. What distinguishes transvestic fetishism is the use of the clothing to replace a sexual partner.

At present, in the current psychiatric model of the *Diagnostic and Statistical Manual of Mental Disorders, 4th edition* (DSM-IV), the criteria for 'transvestic fetishism' are two. First, for a period of "at least" 6 months, there are "recurrent, intense sexually arousing fantasies, sexual urges, or behaviors involving crossdressing," and, second, these must either cause "clinically significant distress" or cause "impairment in social, occupational, or other important areas of functioning." The latter of these two criteria—distress or impairment—is a basic aspect of the DSM logic, which we shall discuss much later.

Interestingly and importantly, 'transvestic fetishism' in DSM-IV is curiously qualified by two distinguishing marks. First, it is applied only to *males*. This is despite the fact we have solid evidence that crossdressing for sexual arousal also occurs in females. Second, it is applied only to *heterosexual* males. This is despite our also having evidence that some homosexual males crossdress for sexual arousal. Clearly, cultural values are in play; in our society we care much more about the sexual behavior of heterosexual males than of either homosexual males or females, whether heterosexual or not.

How common transvestic fetishism is remains a matter of controversy. The general thinking in recent years is that it is less common than once believed. In DSM-IV neither the prevalence (i.e., how many people in the entire population), nor the incidence (i.e., how many new cases are identified in a specific period of time) of transvestic fetishism is speculated upon.

Masturbation

As we might suspect, some of the sexual behavior that occurs associated with crossdressing is masturbation, or 'self-pleasuring.' Masturbation is common in both sexes, though nearly universal among males. It tends to occur regardless of the availability of a sexual partner. Still, in the absence of a partner it provides an important sexual outlet for both gender conforming and gender variant individuals. Given all these factors, we might expect masturbation to be common in adolescence—and so it is.

The relation between crossdressing and masturbation has been investigated in various studies. Perhaps the most detailed of these is the 1981 study by Jack Croughan and associates, mentioned earlier, using interviews with 70 adult male crossdressers. It found that more than three-quarters (79%) had masturbated while crossdressed during adolescence. A majority (54% of all subjects) masturbated most of the time (20% of all subjects), or all of the time (39% of all subjects), when they crossdressed. But while such numbers indicate a general association between crossdressing and masturbation, it is hardly universal or overwhelmingly strong. After all, even in adolescence, a fifth (21%) of all subjects did *not* masturbate while crossdressed, while nearly half (46%) did so only a minority of the times they crossdressed. Interestingly, the overall proportion of subjects who masturbated while crossdressed remained the same in adulthood, but the numbers masturbating most (24% of all subjects), or all of the time (50% of all subjects), while crossdressed increased.

The same researchers also probed the kind of fantasies engaged in by their subjects while masturbating crossdressed. They asked for retrospective reports of masturbatory fantasies during adolescence as well as for their adult fantasies. They then categorized these fantasies. Among the results are the following:
- most report having fantasies while masturbating crossdressed, both as an adolescent (59%) and as an adult (63%);
- ranked, in order, the predominant fantasies during masturbation included: *heterosexual thoughts*; the *self as a woman*; and the *crossdressing self*;
- fantasies where homosexual thoughts predominate were found in only 1% of subjects in adolescence or adulthood.

The researchers noted that masturbatory fantasies differ proportionately between crossdressers who have never sought or received treatment for crossdressing and those who have; the latter are *less* likely to report fantasizing, but much *more* likely to report fantasies of the self as female (4-5 times more often) among their fantasies.

As we noted at the beginning of this conversation, there seems to be a keen interest in whether or not the sexuality of those of us who are transgender is 'deviant.' We saw that testing did not support the notion that it is, but does the research we just examined suggest otherwise? Certainly, we might think that a fantasy of the self as a different gender from our assigned one is deviant, but consider it in another light. Those of us who are gender conforming, when we masturbate, probably picture ourselves in our gender identity in whatever fantasy we indulge. How is that different from what a gender variant person does? By definition, a gender variant person embraces a gender identity different from the assigned one, at least a good portion of the time. When crossdressed, many males experience a feminine gender identity, so their internal representation is analogous to what a gender conforming person has. In that light, perhaps the fantasy is not so odd after all.

Socially Disapproved Sexual Behaviors

But perhaps transgender sexuality is correlated with some other kind of deviancy. Speculation in that regard has centered on two things: fetishism and bondage related to sadomasochism.

Fetishism

Leaving aside the matter of transvestic fetishism, are crossdressers likely to be drawn to fetishes? Because transvestism and fetishism are both paraphilias, when they are diagnosed as both occurring in the same individual this coincidence is termed 'comorbidity.' The belief that there exists high comorbidity among the paraphilias is a perception not uncommon among mental health professionals, despite being based on a relatively small number of studies.

Perhaps the most often cited name in such research is that of psychiatrist Gene Abel, who with various colleagues has published a number of papers on the paraphilias. For example, in 1992, Abel and C. A. Osborn, in a report published in *Clinical Forensic Psychiatry* and widely cited, found that among 859 men diagnosed with a paraphilia, fully one-third of those diagnosed with fetishism also received a diagnosis of transvestism. Impressive as the percentage is, in actuality only *12* men received a diagnosis of fetishism. So, in fact there were just *4* men out of the 859 subjects who received a dual diagnosis of fetishism and transvestism. Both the small size of this group and its other characteristics (e.g., criminal offender status) should make us hesitant about any generalizations. Indeed, with respect to the work of Abel and colleagues supporting the notion of high comorbidity among the paraphilias, Devon Polaschek in the edited volume *Sexual Deviance: Issues and Problems*, writes that despite the popularity of their findings it is clear the data is skewed and replication of results has been a problem. In Polaschek's estimation, even among criminal offenders there is "sparse evidence" for comorbidity of paraphilias.

Perhaps the best study in respect to a possible connection between fetishism and crossdressing is that reported by Chris Gosselin and Glen Wilson in their 1980 book *Sexual Variations: Fetishism, Sadomasochism and Transvestism.* They intentionally compared heterosexual male crossdressers with sadomasochists and others involved in rubber and leather fetishism. This was a large-scale study (N=593)—the transvestite group alone numbered 269 crossdressers. Using self-report data obtained from a variety of instruments (e.g., the Sex Fantasy Questionnaire), they looked at the sexual fantasies reported from these three groups and a control group. Crossdressers most resembled the control group in their fantasies, except for crossdressing occupying a preeminent place on their fantasy lists. As a group, the crossdressers' fantasies were unlike those of the sadomasochistic and fetish groups. On the other hand, in terms of actual experiences, there was considerable overlap among the three groups of interest, with about a third of the crossdressers drawn to a leather fetishism and/or sadomasochism. What to make of the findings from these studies remains unclear.

Bondage

Speculation about a relationship between crossdressing and bondage has been around for decades. Harry Benjamin, in his 1966 book *The Transsexual Phenomenon*, identified this as the most dangerous 'concomitant deviation' a male crossdresser might pursue—but offered no research results to support his contention. Similarly, sociologist Taylor Buckner, apparently following Benjamin, wrote in 1970 in the journal *Psychiatry* that transvestism was often found associated with fetishism, dominance, bondage, and sadomasochism—but distinguished "pure transvestism" from these other patterns—and also offered no evidence about the reported connections. Apparently, most of this impression is formed from case studies drawn from a clinical population rather than from systematic research of a larger, nonclinical group.

By contrast, in their classic 1972 study published in *Psychological Reports*, Peter Bentler and Virginia Prince asked 504 men if they enjoyed crossdressing the most when the activity was bondage-related. They specifically asked about a variety of scenarios, such as being forced to wear feminine articles as punishment or being dominated by another person. The results indicated that sadomasochism constituted, in the authors' words, a "trivial" component of crossdressing. Likewise, Jack Croughan and associates, in their previously discussed report of 70 crossdressers found just 4% had engaged in sadomasochistic behavior.

On the other hand, Neil Buhrich and Trina Beaumont's 1981 report in the same journal that year found that bondage *fantasies* among male crossdressers were common. In their research with 222 subjects from Australia and America, they discovered that over one-third reported fantasies of bondage, most usually of themselves bound while crossdressed. They speculated that fantasies of bondage in this population may be more frequent than for the general population, although they had no data to support that suggestion.

More recently, some data seems to support the notion that crossdressers are more likely than the general population to try certain behaviors commonly viewed as deviant. The 1999 online survey hosted by 'Yvonne' of over 1,000 crossdressing males found almost one-third (32%) had experimented with bondage while crossdressed, and of those, more than 1-in-5 (22%) said it was a regular aspect of their crossdressing. Of those who had not tried it, nearly half (48%) expressed a desire to experiment if given the chance. Although this is a survey based on a self-reported convenience sample, it may echo findings in more carefully controlled research.

Of course, logically the mere presence of a fantasy does not ensure any given behavior; many 'ordinary' people fantasize about a wide range of sexual behaviors they never engage in—including bondage. A similar situation exists with fantasies found in pornographic literature. The appearance in pornographic material of bondage scenarios with forced crossdressing occurs in mainstream pornography as well as that aimed especially at transvestites. Culture scholar Steven Connor, writing in *Women: A Cultural Review* in 2002, points out that it was during the 19th century—a time when gendered distinctions in dress were much debated and when new dress practices eroticised certain garments—that clothes emerged as an important element in sadomasochistic fantasy. He argues that a man's fantasy of being humiliated by forced crossdressing was "a humiliation devoutly to be wished by any red-blooded, yellow-bellied man," and reflected a response to the era's increased appropriation by women of masculine fashion.

But what we should make of such fantasies or activities today remains a matter open to debate.

Intimate Relations with a Partner

Any sexual arousal associated with crossdressing may be accompanied by masturbation, but may also be a part of sexual relations with a partner. Of course, where a partner is involved, more than just what the crossdresser desires is involved. Yet, research indicates that crossdressing behavior does occur with a partner present, and may involve sexual interaction. In fact, findings have been reasonably consistent regardless of whether it was the crossdresser or the crossdresser's partner reporting. An educated estimate is that *between half and two-thirds of crossdressers have had sex at least once while crossdressed.*

Crossdressing During Sexual Relations: The Crossdresser's Perspective

In his 1994 study of the partners of male crossdressers, published in the *Archives of Sexual Behavior*, psychiatrist George Brown found the following:

o   crossdressing in her presence had occurred for 94% of partners;

o   for half (50%) of the women, crossdressing in her presence occurred once a week or more;

o   almost half (48%) of the women reported at least one sexual encounter where their partner was crossdressed;

o   more than one-third (39%) of the women experiencing a crossdressed partner during a sexual encounter reported they were at least occasionally aroused by the crossdressing; and,

o   regardless of whether they ever had engaged in a sexual encounter with their partner while he was crossdressed, a quarter of the women (25%) admitted to some sexual arousal while seeing their partner crossdressed.

It bears mentioning that these women were *not* drawn from a clinical setting; suggesting any idea of pathology in the partners' sexuality is unwarranted.

Other research has examined this occurrence. Vernon Coleman reported in his 1996 book *Men in Dresses: A Study in Transvestism/Crossdressing* that his survey, involving 414 adult British men, found more than half (55%) had participated in sex while crossdressed. The 1999 online survey of male crossdressers hosted by 'Yvonne' found that the respondents reported even more frequent crossdressing during sexual activities. Some 60% of the respondents had been at least partially crossdressed on at least one occasion of lovemaking. Almost a quarter reported they either "always" or "frequently" were crossdressed when having sex with their partner—and 70% claimed that the partner enjoyed it.

Most crossdressing males want to incorporate crossdressing into lovemaking. Jack Croughan and associates, in the 1981 article we discussed earlier, found that heterosexual intercourse was the most desired form of sexual behavior while crossdressed. Prince and Bentler, in their aforementioned 1972 survey of 504 male transvestites, found that "there was a general factor of preference for

151

feminine clothing during intercourse." While one-fifth (20%) liked being fully crossdressed during sex, the most popular single items were nightgowns (27%), panties (18%), padded bras (18%), and stockings (17%).

This preference for being crossdressed appears to correlate with changes in sexual behavior. The 35 spouses in Richard Docter's 1988 study, *Transvestites and Transsexuals: Toward a Theory of Cross-Gender Behavior*, reported varying effects on the sexual behavior of their husbands when crossdressed: a third either displayed no change or a reduction in sexual behavior, while the remaining two-thirds displayed heightened sexual arousal. Apparently, for some males crossdressing enhances the pleasure of the activity.

But is this because of fetishistic arousal? One problem in our sex-obsessed culture is interpreting *any* pleasurable association with crossdressing as sexual in nature. For many crossdressers there is a general sense of well-being and specific pleasure in being crossdressed. That can carry over in a sexual setting to erotic pleasure. The one feeling merges into the other. Put simply, the pleasure of self-experience and expression in crossdressing enhances the pleasure of sexual experience and expression in making love to another person.

What separates sexual fetishism from nonfetishistic sexual behavior is whether the stimulus (crossdressing) is both *necessary* and *sufficient*. If the partner is inconsequential because it is being crossdressed that matters, then transvestic fetishism is present. What may muddy the waters, though, is a situation where the crossdresser insists on crossdressing during sexual relations, but still desires such relations with the partner. In this case it may seem the crossdressing is necessary but not sufficient. Investigation into *why* this is important to the crossdresser can be beneficial. If it is because the crossdresser desires to be crossdressed in order to be fully self-realized, then it stands to reason that apart from this condition the crossdresser may still be able to sexually perform, still love and desire the partner, but will remain to some degree sexually unfulfilled.

It perhaps says more about our personal biases than about the real experience of transgender individuals to find a fetishistic element. In light of what we have learned it seems reasonable to think there is a congruence of gender identity in crossdressing that facilitates the person's greater openness and responsiveness sexually. If those of us who are gender conforming try to connect that experience to our own, is it so hard to understand that a transgender person is like ourselves in finding more pleasure sexually when accepted fully and permitted self-expression in lovemaking? Of course, partners may be oblivious to this fact, lost as many of the rest of us are within the harmful stereotypes about transgender.

Crossdressing During Sexual Relations: The Partner's Perspective

Those of us who are gender conforming may also find it difficult to comprehend women who would have sexual relations with a crossdressed man. Perhaps this difficulty, though, is less among younger women than older ones. As one counselor reported in a 2008 email to me on this matter, she knows "many intelligent, beautiful, and feminine ladies" who find a crossdressed man "very, very sexy." Younger women's greater openness to crossdressing men is showing in research, too. A survey conducted by Mark Clements Research in 2000 in Los Angeles, New York, and Chicago of women ages 21-39 revealed that slightly more than 1-in-5 (20.8%) said they would be willing to date a man dressed in a skirt. Similar levels were found for the percentage of those surveyed who stated they viewed men wearing skirts as "very" or "somewhat" acceptable (24%). Perhaps surprisingly, the survey found a similar degree of support for accepting even a brother or father who engaged in such dress (20.3%). A like percentage even expressed a willingness to share their own skirts with a man (22.3%).

Still, some of us willing to accept a man in a skirt might find it unappealing to have sexual relations with one dressed in feminine apparel. Why would a woman *want* to engage in sexual relations with a man dressed as a woman? In his provocative study of crossdressing men plying the sex trade in Costa Rica, *From Toads to Queens: Transvestism in a Latin American Setting*, Jacobo Schifter offers his conclusions as to why some women pay to have sex with crossdressed males. He says heterosexual women find appealing the 'sensitivity' of such males: "As several clients put it, transvestites are 'sweeter, more sensible and caring, and have a better sense of humor' than other, more 'masculine' men. Thus, the women can become more intimate with transvestites than is possible with their usual sex partners." Schifter found some lesbians also enjoyed sexual interactions with crossdressed males because they could relate to the feminine gender identity while experimenting more openly with alternative forms of sexuality.

In the intimate relationship of marriage, sexual behavior generally reflects not just the sexuality of the individual partners but the quality of their relationship. Both parties working to promote the well-being of each of them separately and together characterizes healthy relationships. Dialog and compromise are tools used to resolve difficulties. To the degree that sexual enjoyment reflects pleasure in the partner and not merely physiological arousal, those able to see and love the whole person do better than those able only to see and accept part of the partner. In marriages where the spouse enjoys sexual relations with a crossdressed partner the source of the pleasure may stem from the joy of loving the partner as a person, no matter how clothed, or perhaps precisely because the partner is crossdressed and that act brings the loved one most fully into being.

We must be careful, in other words, with our judgments. A wife who finds sexual pleasure with a crossdressed husband is hardly to be pitied in a world where too many women find little if any sexual joy with anyone. At the same time, we should be careful in judging women who do not find a crossdressed partner sexy. In fact, some find crossdressing an obstacle to sexual fulfillment. What may surprise us, though, is that their number may be less than we suspect. Docter found in his sample that less than half (43%) of the wives believed that crossdressing had a harmful effect on their sexual relationship, and even then the average weighting was in the range of 'moderate difficulty.' On the other hand, a few held that it had a strongly positive impact. As in all things sexual, tremendous variety exists in individuals *and* in couples.

Docter's group of wives offered him a number of strategies they found constituted useful compromises in marital sex. Docter lists four:

o *passive acceptance*—the wife sets aside her desires and submits to her partner while trying to ignore the crossdressing;

o *crossdressing as a prelude to sex*—the agreement is to permit crossdressing before sex to facilitate arousal, but not to continue it into lovemaking;

o *partial crossdressing allowed*—the couple agree on what the husband can wear to add sexual excitement without distressing the wife; and,

o *play acting*—the couple verbalize, or act out, a mutually agreeable sexual fantasy.

Again, success is predicated on negotiated agreement.

Clearly crossdressing during sexual interactions poses an issue both parties must grapple with. In some instances the crossdresser may be open to compromise, crossdressing on some occasions of lovemaking and refraining at other times, or limiting what is worn, or submitting to a partner's approval of clothing. But compromise and negotiation require both parties. Some partners may be willing; others may be reluctant or refuse to do so. Therapist Arlene Istar Lev, in her 2004 book *Transgender Emergence: Therapeutic Guidelines for Working with Gender Variant People and Their Families*, points out what some of us may see as an uncomfortable truth, but others of us will celebrate: partners vary in their flexibility in adjusting to their sexual relationship after learning their lover is a transgender person. Lev acknowledges some people have little flexibility when it comes to sexual desire; others find ease in dealing with their lover's reality.

One thing is reasonably sure: while a few relationships can move from having been sexual to being nonsexual, most that go that route do not endure. If the parties desire to pursue a successful sexual relationship, honest conversation and negotiation seem indispensable. If the needs of either party are entirely set aside, a festering dissatisfaction is likely to erode the relationship. For some partners this may be, or become, the chief obstacle in keeping the relationship, and it is beyond the scope of this brief coverage to do more than encourage the basic human instinct to strive together in truth and in love.

13.

Sinner, Sick, or Sane?

We are a point where we need again to focus on our judgments. One important reality every one of us who is transgender lives with is knowing we will be judged because of our gender variance. Much like racial or ethnic minorities may be evaluated negatively simply *because* of race or ethnicity, we discover we are often looked down upon *because* of our gender difference—and for no other reason. To some degree this is an experience many who are gender conforming can relate to personally. Many women, for example, know firsthand what it is to be prejudged by a man simply because of being a woman. Such judgments do not arise from a natural hierarchy that predisposes those at the top to sneer down upon the lower ranks. Instead, these judgments are derived from cultural values we can and should question.

The Social Construction of Judgments on Transgender

Social Constructionists continually remind us that what is built can be modified or removed. Indeed, the history of any society reveals that socially constructed judgments do change, to greater or less degree. In broad strokes we can follow the French philosopher and historian Michel Foucault by picturing a historical process that selectively changes what it says about some sexual matters. For example, homosexuality was for a time 'officially' regarded as *sin*. Under the medicalization of sex, it came to be regarded as a *sickness*. With more passage of time and social changes motivated by better understanding, it came to be seen as *sane*. In short, a social construction of one sexual orientation as sin later was reconstructed as sickness and still later as sane.

Viewing things in this manner bothers many of us. We want things to be unambiguously clear, especially where morality is concerned. A thing must be 'right' or 'wrong.' Yet in practice we know that most things judged either way reflect individual values and the application of different models of moral reasoning. We know from hard experience that our own moral judgments are not universally endorsed. In truth, pressed on the matter, we grasp that a number of our moral judgments simply reflect our cultural inheritance. They are not judgments we have personally carefully considered before embracing. In light of this, most of us acknowledge the wisdom of examining the cultural baggage we have had attached to us in order to see if, in fact, we want to keep it.

As well, with a little reflection we recognize moral judgments are often qualified by developmental experience. Things we were taught as children are wrong may be wrong for us when immature, but not when we become adults. Our own growth and maturity changes our perspective—and our judgment. If this is true for us as individuals, why should it not be the case for societies? The fact that we have been able to change our view of some things from sin to sickness to sane does not mean the thing has changed, but that our understanding of it has. In that regard, to cling to a judgment against the weight of better knowledge seems awfully immature.

There are many signs that our society is shifting its view on transgender. If so, it is a reflection of the many individuals within our society—folk like ourselves—who have grown beyond a need to endorse an earlier generation's judgments. Our development, we hope, is based on better understanding. Access to facts, openness to human experience, and generosity of spirit allow us to see matters in a manner more favorable than others. A great help in this has been the emergence of perspectives like Social Constructionism, or Queer Theory, both of which have marshaled reason and evidence to deconstruct Essentialism.

Nevertheless, for those of us still doubtful as to how best to regard gender variance, there remains a need to tackle head on matters like whether being transgender really is sane, or constitutes a sickness. The remainder of our time together shall be spent looking at this matter from different angles. To begin, let us consider if transgender people are more prone to psychological illness.

Transgender and Psychopathology

Not surprisingly, given that our minority status comes from our culturally unusual pairing of sex and gender, we who are transgender have been studied with reference to whether we are more likely to experience psychological disorders than are others. We discussed earlier research into the personality characteristics of transgender people (especially those of us who are male and viewed as crossdressers) and saw it reveals few, if any, distinguishing traits. Overall, we transgender individuals appear to be as mentally healthy and 'normal' in our general personality makeup as anyone else. What about in other respects? Again, we saw how being transgender does not seem to mean having had a broken family, an unhappy childhood, less education, unsuccessful careers, or lack of intimate relationships. Nor are transgender people in our society necessarily unlike those in other societies in these respects.

In research in a society that shares our cultural background, a population study done in Sweden, reported in 2005 in the *Journal of Sex and Marital Therapy*, found that satisfaction with life in general, psychological health, and current psychiatric morbidity were *not* significantly linked with the behavior of crossdressing. Typically, research across societies supports the notion that we who are transgender are more like than unlike the general population. Yet the notion persists that our way of being—or 'lifestyle' as so many pejoratively put it—is associated with various forms of psychological or behavioral problems. Given this reality, further examination is merited.

Crossdressing and Mental Health

There are any number of ways we could tackle this issue but let's do it by examining research with respect to specific subgroups under the transgender umbrella. This might enable us to see if *any* group of transgender people is more likely to have a psychological disorder. It will also help us get at the deeper worry we may have that being transgender is itself a disorder, or prompts the occurrence of mental and emotional problems.

Transvestites

A study published by psychologist Peter Bentler and Virginia Prince in 1970 in the *Journal of Clinical Psychology* involved nearly 200 male transvestites. They received a standard psychopathology inventory test along the lines of the Minnesota Multiphasic Personality Inventory (MMPI). It consists of more than 500 statements to which the respondent must answer 'true,' 'false,' or 'cannot say.' A total of 10 clinical scales are reported, which provide a measure of any psychopathology. The research discovered no gross psychiatric symptomatology in its subjects. It did note, though, that on average these men were slightly more constrained in their impulses. If anything, this is a behavioral trait that tends to keep people out of trouble rather than violate social rules through impulsive acts.

On the other hand, in their 1981 study in *Archives of Sexual Behavior*, Jack Croughan and associates, in interviews with 70 adult male crossdressers divided into two groups by whether they had ever received treatment in regard to their crossdressing, found elevated lifetime frequencies of alcoholism and unipolar (i.e., 'major' or 'clinical') depression. Does this 'prove' being transgender is itself an illness? If so, we could argue by the same logic that being an American Indian is an illness, since there are also high levels of alcoholism and depression among them. The parallel example should caution us that perhaps this finding is better viewed as a predictable outcome from the negative cultural factors, such as social rejection, that we who are transgender often experience. As Croughan and associates observe, over 95% of the crossdressers they interviewed had, in fact, experienced some negative consequence because of crossdressing. Yet it is important to note that these researchers also concluded that no obvious relationship could be found between crossdressing and nonsexual psychiatric disorders. What they saw was that transgender people who acknowledge crossdressing pay a price—but that doesn't mean they are crazy.

Peter Fagan and associates reached a similar conclusion in their 1988 report published in *The Journal of Nervous and Mental Disease* on "distressed transvestites." These were 21 heterosexual male crossdressers who had sought psychiatric consultation at the John Hopkins Sexual Behaviors Consultation Unit between 1979-1987. They were compared with 45 married heterosexual males. With reference to disorders coded on Axis I of the DSM system (then DSM-III), the researchers found "the difference in frequencies of axis I disorders between the two groups tended to be different but not at a significant level . . . ." Although more than a third (38%) of these distressed transvestites met diagnostic criteria for an axis I disorder, the researchers noted that whether the presence of such a condition was "an independent phenomenon or a reaction to an adverse consequence of transvestism such as discovery by a spouse, threat of marital separation, or legal difficulties is not known." Indeed, what may be most remarkable is that only a little more than a third of the transgender people distraught enough to seek psychiatric help actually met the criteria for a diagnosis. Given the greater degree of social tolerance today, that percentage could well prove less.

Transsexuals (or, broadly, people diagnosed with Gender Identity Disorder)

Transsexuals are commonly regarded as more likely to show psychopathology than transvestites. As a group transsexuals are often believed to suffer severe psychopathology. Despite the widespread acceptance of this notion actual evidence supporting it is weak. Let us review some relevant studies.

We saw that the MMPI was used to assess transvestites; it also has been used with transsexual subjects. In 1979, 27 MtF transsexual candidates for SRS were administered the test. The data obtained was then compared to that gained from 50 male medical patients (24 kidney transplant candidates and 26 possibly having a psychophysiological disorder). The results found an absence of psychopathology in the transsexual subjects.

Also reported in 1979 was research involving 17 FtM transsexual candidates for SRS, in a comparative study with 40 lesbians and 59 female heterosexuals, focused on self-esteem and psychological well-being. The researchers used the Tennessee Self-Concept Scale (TSCS), an instrument comprised of 100 self-descriptive items. The TSCS measures more than just self-esteem. It examines a variety of aspects of a person's self-concept, including both external (e.g., social) and internal (e.g., identity) factors. While the FtM transsexuals individually varied in measures both of self-concept and adjustment, as a group they were not appreciably different from the other groups.

Transsexuals awaiting SRS were subjects in a 1981 study. The 22 persons were administered both a standard mental ability test and a comprehensive personality test. For the former, the Wechsler Adult Intelligence Scale (WAIS)—the most widely used measure of adult intelligence—was employed. It has both vocabulary and performance tests. For the latter, the MMPI was used. Results on the WAIS proved mixed: subjects score congruent to their genetic sex except on a measure of conceptual styles, where scores were congruent instead with their gender identity. The MMPI disclosed no major psychopathology processes involved in the subjects.

More contemporary research continues to provide similar findings. For example, consider a 2000 comparative study published in *Acta Psychiatrica Scandinavica* by I. R. Haraldsen and A. A. Dahl, using three distinct groups. Two of the groups were clients diagnosed using a structured clinical interview employing DSM criteria. All three groups—86 transsexual clients, 98 individuals diagnosed with a personality disorder, and 1068 adult controls—were administered the Symptom Checklist-90 (SCL-90). This popular instrument, created by Leonard Derogatis, employs 90 items designed to detect through self-report psychological symptom patterns along nine scales. The transsexual group did not show levels of psychiatric symptoms outside the range considered normal. This finding agrees with other studies and offers empirical support to the conclusion that regarding transsexualism as a severe mental disorder is erroneous.

Nor is the situation different with children diagnosed with Gender Identity Disorder (GID). Kenneth Zucker and Susan Bradley's 1995 book, *Gender Identity Disorder and Psychosexual Problems in Children and Adolescents*, reports research using the Child Behavior Checklist (CBCL) to assess and compare children referred clinically for gender issues with other children, including siblings of gender-referred children. The results show no significant differences across groups on the CBCL's Activities or Social scales. Mean scores for the gender-referred children did not reach a level of clinical significance on *any* scale—not even with regard to total social competence and school competence, two areas where there were noticeable differences from other children. *Difference does not equal disorder.*

Another question of interest to researchers has been whether 'gender dysphoria'—the hallmark symptom in the DSM model for GID—coexists with other disorders. This phenomenon, known as 'comorbidity,' is common in psychological conditions; depression and anxiety, for example, often occur together. As reported in the *Archives of Sexual Behavior* in 1997, Collier Cole and associates investigated this question. Studying 435 people (318 male; 117 female) diagnosed with gender dysphoria associated with transsexualism, they found that less than 10% displayed indications of mental illness. They concluded that transsexualism does *not* appear to belong to any general psychological disorder.

So consistent have been such findings—and so slender any support that transsexualism is itself a disorder—that some societies have abandoned the notion that it should be used as a credible diagnosis of mental illness. This is a matter of great importance, and one for us to return to at the end of our time together. Right now, there remain some loose ends to tie up. We must, if we can, lay to rest the worries many of us entered the conversation with, worries that transgender is either a disease or makes having a mental illness more likely. So let us look at yet another speculation.

Crossdressing & Obsessive Compulsive Disorder (OCD)

One persistently hypothesized link is between transvestism, specifically transvestic fetishism, and obsessive-compulsive disorder (OCD). Research into this matter has depended largely upon case study reports. For example, Carmita Abdo and colleagues reported in 2001 in *Acta Psychiatrica Scandinavica* two cases of men who were diagnosed both with transvestic fetishism and OCD. They note four possible explanations for this co-existence: the two conditions may be independent and associated in these men by chance; crossdressing may be a symptom of the OCD; OCD may be a symptom of the transvestism; or, they may represent different points along a spectrum of like disorders—a position they favor with reference to these individuals.

Their position reflects a search among some researchers for a common pathway that might link together the various paraphilias, or certain of them with other psychological conditions. To date, however, all such efforts have proven unsuccessful. No solid body of evidence exists that transgender people suffer from OCD or are more obsessive or compulsive in general. That some personality research suggests a modestly greater tendency toward maintaining a neat and orderly environment, or preferring deliberate to spontaneous acts, is hardly worrisome. In fact, the real concern seems again to be about the sexual behavior of the transgender crossdresser. Some mental health professionals regard crossdressing accompanied by sexual activity as showing a compulsive element. But that remains a subjective impression perhaps colored by cultural values. For example, many of us envy people we see as lucky enough to have sexual intercourse more often than we do. We are unlikely to see such people as burdened with obsessions that lead them to compulsive acts. At the very least, much more work remains before we should grant much credibility to the hypothesized link between crossdressing and OCD.

Transgender and Harm

Some of us do not couch our worries over gender variance in terms of the individual and whether or not the person is psychologically disordered. Instead, we express concern about *the harm to society* posed by transgender people, especially when publicly visible in crossdressing. Given the very real harm those of us who are transgender experience at the hands of gender conformists, such a concern seems not merely ridiculous, but offensive. Yet, rational or not, such a fear warrants attention.

Some people fear that crossdressing, like an infectious disease, is catching. Specifically, they worry that crossdressing behavior by an adult—especially a parent—presents an influential learning model for children, who then are at special risk to grow up transgendered. Some parents do not want even minimal exposure of their children to crossdressing and will cover their child's eyes if, for example, they think they see a crossdressed male in public. As we learned earlier, there is little if any support for this notion. The idea is similar to the concern voiced by many people against allowing homosexuals to adopt children. Despite the compelling body of evidence that children of homosexuals are no more likely to grow up homosexual than anyone else, many people persist in this irrational fear. The phenomenon is an aspect of what is called 'homophobia,' and the parallel with other transgendered people is 'transphobia.'

The Harm of Transphobia

Transphobia is indeed harmful, both to the person who experiences anxiety from having it and to the person against whom aggressive behavior is directed because of it. It would be erroneous, though, to locate the source of the problem in the transgendered person; *the problem is the phobia.* And it takes many forms. Some people who are in relationships with transgendered people experience this transphobia as a persistent discomfort that they attribute to the willful behavior of the transgendered person. The irrational belief runs something like this: 'If only he/she would choose to be normal (i.e., dress conventionally, or be heterosexual, etc.), then I wouldn't feel uncomfortable.' By locating the source of their anxiety in the transgendered person, they follow an old, familiar path: blame the minority because they are different.

How is it that we so seldom consider that it is the person with the phobia who needs help to change? The essence of any phobia is an *exaggerated* anxiety or fear, one all out of proportion to the danger actually posed by the stimulus. What, exactly, is the danger posed by a man wearing panties under his pants? How does a man in a dress endanger civilization? Posing such questions reveals the irrationality of the response by the person who claims that a transgendered loved one is hurting them by behavior like crossdressing.

This line of illogical reasoning is often more than the response of a few individuals. It also has been a response basic in racism, religious persecution, ethnic cleansing, and a number of other social responses in which being different has been a pretext for judgments that the minority person is inferior or evil. Simply being different—whether by virtue of skin color, religious belief or practice, ethnic custom, or crossdressing—is not enough to morally justify harmful acts against the minority, which may include social marginalization or ostracism, discrimination, or physical aggression. For those who feel the gender variant harm society, the burden is on them to demonstrate it factually; the burden is not on the transgendered to prove their innocence.

The 'Logic' of Objections

The judgment some of us make that crossdressing is deviant, and thus intrinsically harmful to society, often stems from the perception that crossdressing threatens the gender divide and that this divide must be maintained or the natural order of things will deteriorate into chaos. This is simply the Essentialist view reinforcing the gender status quo. Others of us see the threat as more ex-

161

plicitly sexual—crossdressers are viewed as seeking illicit sexual satisfactions through their behavior. In either instance, some of us go a step further by explicitly linking crossdressing to moral turpitude. Some of us simply find the sight of someone crossdressed emotionally upsetting and believe that no one has the right to offend us by such public display. Those of us thinking along these lines are apt to say, 'Whatever someone does in the privacy of their own home is all right by me, but they shouldn't be out in public.' Further—as the testimony of many transgender persons confirms—even in one's own home a similar restriction may exist, as though by keeping the behavior completely removed from the sight of others stops a contagion from spreading. In this case, though, the 'disease' is simply *dis*-ease—a feeling of discomfort whose source is projected away from the self and onto the crossdresser.

The irrationality of the logic often used becomes more apparent when we look at some of the things we tolerate with hardly a thought, despite mountains of evidence as to the threat they pose to all of us. For example, we socially approve the consumption of alcohol though we know that use of the drug impairs judgment, alters social functioning, and leads to many kinds of harm, from lowered inhibitions that get people in trouble, to rape while intoxicated, to drunk driving, to cirrhosis of the liver. We still at least tolerate smoking in many public venues despite the evidence concerning the health threat of secondhand smoke. Compared to such widespread harms to health and the attendant threats to social order, the very occasional sight of a man in a skirt seems rather insignificant in the scheme of things.

The *Benefits* of Transgender Identity and Behavior

Maybe we would do better to take a less common approach and ask whether being transgender carries any benefits. Instead of spending all our time wondering if being transgender is an illness or crossdressing causes harm, perhaps we should consider if there are benefits from being gender variant. For this 'road less taken' journey let us consider research investigating 'third gender' people in our society and the benefits of crossdressing.

'Third Gender' People

We can return to the work of clinician Ingrid Sell. She published an important article in *The Psychotherapy Patient* about Americans who identify as 'third gender' people. Her study of 30 such folk, including both biological males and females, with ages ranging from 29-77, found that compared to the general population a disproportionate number (43%) work in health and helping professions. Most of us would consider this a highly positive career choice. The desire to help others is typically seen as prosocial and desirable. Perhaps 'third gender' individuals are more disposed to such work by virtue of their unique gender and the experiences it creates for them living in our gender dichotomous culture. We have no way of knowing if such a small sample is representative of a larger population, but it certainly does not speak ill of such people.

Sell found they also are more likely than the general population to be engaged in highly creative and artistic endeavors; nearly half (47%) are writers, musicians, or other performers—and 17% earn a substantial portion of their income from their art. These activities may flow from their gender nature, or be creative responses to the pressures of living in our society. Either way, they reflect positive avenues of self-expression and social contribution.

Likewise, as Sell points out, more than three-quarters (77%) recounted being asked to mediate between men and women because they are viewed as having a perspective wide enough to see both sides. Many also mediate with other groups (e.g., racial, cultural, sub-cultural, age-differentiated). Being in-between has advantages for others, as many societies have noted in using 'third gender' people in mediating roles.

An especially important mediating role is as a spiritual person standing between the Divine and people. As Sell remarks, a striking 93% of 'third gender' people report one or more transcendent spiritual events and/or what others would term 'paranormal' abilities. She notes that these numbers far exceed what other research finds for members of the general population. How can such things not advantage all of us, if we let them?

The Benefits of Crossdressing

What then of crossdressing? Let us begin with listing five of the healthy benefits allegedly conferred by crossdressing:
- o   It meets a basic need not otherwise met.
- o   It provides relaxation (a positive stress-reducing response).
- o   It boosts mood and self-confidence.
- o   It enhances interpersonal relating.
- o   It facilitates maximal performance on various tasks.

Let us briefly examine evidence for such claims.

Crossdressing Meets a Basic Need

Peggy Rudd, spouse to a crossdresser, writes in her 1990 book *Crossdressing with Dignity: The Case for Transcending Gender Lines*, that she believes crossdressing for the crossdresser "is a basic human need." Others express a similar sentiment. That, unlike Rudd, many making this claim are crossdressers should not automatically disqualify its validity. Instead, we would be better served considering what basic need is thus met. Simply put, crossdressing uses clothes to experience and express something basic to the person in a way that does not otherwise happen. Exactly what that is does not have to be the same for every person. What the different ways may have in common is both the sense that the need is basic to them and that it is crossdressing that meets it. If this contention is true, perhaps we can find traces of support in the other four benefits.

Crossdressing Reduces Stress

The successful use of crossdressing to reduce stress and provide pleasant relaxation is well-attested in the testimony of crossdressers. In their 1981 research published in *Archives of Sexual Behavior*, researchers Neil Buhrich and Trina Beaumont reported that fully a third of the 222 adult male crossdressers involved in their study said their frequency of crossdressing increased when they felt tense. But this statistic alone probably underestimates the use of crossdressing to relieve tension. When their data is closely examined it emerges that nearly three-quarters (71%) of the subjects increased the frequency of their crossdressing in response to tension at least some of the time, while only 8% said the frequency decreased because of stress.

In his 1996 study, *Men in Dresses: A Study in Transvestism/Crossdressing*, Vernon Coleman reported that nearly half (48%) of his study's respondents indicated this purpose as the reason (or one of the reasons) for crossdressing. Coleman remarked, "As a physician I would much rather see a man under stress deal with pressure by cross dressing than by taking tranquillisers." We might do well to at least see this as less harmful than reducing stress by getting drunk and then taking to the roads with the rest of us. Reducing stress without harming others is a prosocial behavior.

Crossdressing Boosts Mood and Self-confidence

Undoubtedly associated with stress reduction are other benefits often associated with crossdressing: elevation of mood and self-confidence. This idea makes sense in what we have learned about the way men relate to clothes. Some research finds men rely more than women on clothes to raise mood and boost self-confidence. Other research suggests that traditional masculine values lead to signs of psychological distress. Perhaps crossdressing, if it does nothing more than to allow temporary respite from the rigors and pressures of masculinity, affords male crossdressers the kind of relief that elicits more positive mood.

Crossdressing Enhances Interpersonal Relating

Some mental health experts believe that crossdressing is associated with impaired interpersonal functioning. But at least some research suggests this idea is incorrect. Logically, a relaxed person who experiences a sense of congruence with the self is far more likely to succeed in the challenges of interpersonal relating. Many crossdressers and their partners attest that better relating accompanies the crossdressing and that when the behavior is frustrated interpersonal interactions suffer. What impairs relating, then, is *not* crossdressing.

If the crossdresser's interpersonal behavioral traits improve, but relationships suffer when crossdressing is going on, then what is happening? The crossdressing itself might be implicated as the problem, but only if clothing somehow communicates negative results all-by-itself. Of course, that would be an absurd conclusion; clothes are part of a system that relies on the wearer and the perceiver to determine the outcome of any interaction between them. So if the crossdresser's interpersonal traits improve with crossdressing, then perhaps what is happening is the *other* person's interpersonal traits are *declining* with exposure to the crossdressing, or even just knowledge of it. Who has the problem?

This perspective helps make sense of what the research reveals: interpersonal functioning in couples where crossdressing occurs depends on how the crossdressing is regarded. We can assume the crossdresser always or almost always views the behavior positively. If the partner concurs, then the outcome will be positive, or at least neutral (i.e., no significant effect). If the partner disapproves, the relational outcome will be negative. The best conclusion we can make is that crossdressing can enhance interpersonal functioning by the crossdresser and thus contribute to a better relationship, but such an outcome is not inevitable. The well-being of any relationship likely depends on the values, feelings, and behaviors of both partners. Thus relational success or impairment is better regarded as a function of the relating between the two and not merely the characteristics of just one or the other.

Crossdressing Facilitates Maximal Performance

Crossdressing, as evidenced by various test situations, may actually facilitate the attainment of maximal performance. Once more this makes sense if we accept the reasoning that people who feel more relaxed and more themselves are thereby likely to also feel greater confidence, more competent, and perform closer to their actual potential. However, we must again qualify this conclusion by noting that any environment where the crossdressing is negatively evaluated is likely to have an effect on the crossdresser that offsets, perhaps even eliminates, the benefits of crossdressing itself.

The Benefits of Crossdressing for Nontransgender People

The risks of harm those of us who are transgender face daily might be alleviated somewhat if noncrossdressers could see ways they might be advantaged by crossdressing's existence. The very idea probably surprises—crossdressing as a social *benefit*?! So accustomed are many of us to regard gender variance as bad that the mere thought of crossdressing elicits distaste. Many of us barely tolerate crossdressers—so long as they stay at a distance—but accepting, even celebrating the notion that transgender folk offer *good* to all of us may seem completely absurd. Yet there may be some matters worth considering. Let's look at three.

Vicarious Cross-gender Experience Through Crossdressers

Crossdressers through public crossdressing express in actual practice a secret longing the rest of us experience from time to time. That secret desire is to somehow experience what it might be like to cross a gender line and walk for awhile in the shoes of another gender. Men and woman are endlessly fascinated with the presumed differences that separate them. There is a commonly perceived 'gap' between the dominant genders that seems nearly impossible to bridge. Yet crossdressers bridge it.

In so doing, perhaps only for an instant they provide opportunity for vicarious experience. Certainly that seems to be in play when we seek out entertainments where we know crossdressing takes place. A significant difference between that and what happens on the street is that we go expecting to see the crossdressing, rather than being caught be surprise, and we diffuse anxiety by reminding ourselves that what we are seeing is merely play—purely for entertainment. Yet that entertainment offers the vicarious thrill of gender crossing.

Transgender Experimentation Through Situational Crossdressing

More of us than would like to admit it actually do crossdress! We may reject the identity of crossdresser, typically hold the behavior in low regard, yet in very narrowly circumscribed situations still engage in it. Some of us do it on occasion as an erotic act of play with a sexual partner. Others of us do it in order to draw comfort from a lover's clothing in their absence. Some of us even do it for laughs at costume parties, while others of us try it once just to see what it's like.

There is no reason why such behavior cannot be regarded as transgender experimentation. In fact, if it were, imagine how different might the social response become to transgender. If we could see that even the briefest engagement in crossdressing offers us the possibility of empathy—an imaginative placing of our own self in the experience of some other self—how much more tolerant we might become! Every act of crossdressing, no matter the motivation or brevity, is an act ripe with potential. We could choose to find in it a microcosm of a larger universe of experience some of us dwell within all of the time.

Communal Experience in Sanctioned Social Crossdressing

Throughout history every society that heavily invests itself in keeping the genders separated and in strongly enforcing gender conformity has faced the need to manage the pressures that thereby arise. One important way to do so is through festivals, such as Carnival or Halloween. These times temporarily suspend normal gender conventions in dress and behavior. In permitting gender crossings they act as safety valves, reducing pressure. Holidays where crossdressing is sanctioned offer a perfect avenue for those who otherwise might never consider such behavior to alleviate gender pressure in a sanctioned way.

Conclusion: Sanity and Society

If we put all the various strands together, perhaps what we arrive at is something rather simple: the health and well-being of gender variant and gender conforming people alike is largely in our own hands. Our judgments have a critical effect on how well we do—or how much we suffer. We can, if we have the will, make a society where we can be sane regardless of our gender identity. In light of the benefits accruing to us all, why would we want to do otherwise?

14.

Shoulder to Shoulder

Should we resolve to make our world a better place for all of us, the question becomes—How? Some of us might still wish for a world comfortably fitted to just our gender experience, even at the expense of the experience of others. But most of us recognize the inherent injustice in such selfishness. We grasp that being a good citizen means reasonable accommodations to the needs and freedoms of others. Being a decent human being means desiring for others the same things we wish for ourselves. In light of all we have learned, we know it is both unnecessary and futile to try to eliminate gender variance. Every effort to force gender conformity on transgender people has failed as predictably as any effort to make a gender conformist become gender variant would fail.

Given time and effort we may move from a begrudging tolerance to full acceptance and someday even a celebration of the diversity seen among us. As we consider how we might walk shoulder to shoulder with those whose gender identity and expression may be very different from our own, let us examine a number of possibilities for offering support to transgender people, beginning with a review of some matters we already have touched upon.

Public Policy and Legal Reforms

Earlier, we saw that being round pegs in a square pegs world is not easy. But there are indications that the good will of many of us is helping shift our society in ways of benefit to us all. Let us consider five different indications of such prosocial change.

Public Attitudes

Some recent evidence suggests that the American public may be becoming more tolerant of those of us who are transgender—or at least more willing to protect our basic human and civil rights. For example, about three-quarters of Americans surveyed support broadening federal hate crime legislation to include protection for transgender people. Some legislative changes aimed at ensuring us the same rights and protections (not more) that other citizens possess now is in place. In various states around the country (e.g., California, Florida, New

York, and Texas), inclusive safe schools legislation has been introduced. These acts offer one indication of trends in attitudinal shifts.

Judicial Rulings

Shifts in the law are helping too. Some of these are legislative and others are judicial. Within the courts, the case of *Price Waterhouse v. Hopkins* (1989) has been especially important. In its judgment the U.S. Supreme Court offered in the majority opinion that in a suit brought under Title VII, when an individual demonstrates that gender served a motivating part in an employment decision, the employer is liable unless it can provide by a preponderance of evidence that the same decision would have been made on legitimate grounds apart from consideration of gender. In January, 2001, an Ohio case brought in U.S. district court against United Consumers Financial Services (UCFS) by a person referred to as 'Mrs. Doubtfire' successfully utilized Title VII protection. The individual had worked only 10 days as a temporary employee when, after a complaint by a fellow employee that a man dressed as a woman was using the ladies restroom, 'Mrs. Doubtfire' was questioned by management about her gender. UCFS sought dismissal of the suit on the grounds that Title VII offered no protection in such a case. But Judge Kathleen McDonald O'Malley rejected that motion, pointing to the U.S. Supreme decision in *Price Waterhouse v. Hopkins*. UCFS then reached a satisfactory settlement with the plaintiff. Although court decisions in our country have provided an inconsistent support for transgender people, the tide has clearly turned. More and more often transgender people are finding protection under the law in their lawsuits against discriminatory practices.

Legislative Protections

While the situation in the courts remains muddled, a clear trend toward providing legal protection, especially against discrimination and hate crimes, has emerged. Mirroring what is taking place elsewhere in the world, in the United States we are seeing more proactive legislation, especially at the state and municipal levels. Many legislative bodies have amended their laws to recognize violence based on the victim's gender identity as hate crimes. By 2008, at least half of the states had explicit laws with respect to human rights protection and/or antidiscrimination. According to the International Foundation for Gender Education (IFGE), by the Spring of 2004 some 71 municipalities in the U.S. had added gender identity as a protected class in their human rights ordinances, and that number continues to grow. These are signs of social change.

Identity Recognition

As pointed out before, those of us who are transsexual are able to legally obtain medical services related to changing body sex (e.g., hormonal therapy and sex reassignment surgery). A significant challenge remains in accompanying such changes by legal recognition of a different sex identity. In a society so anxious to have sex and gender coincide, we might think there would be a ready willingness to grant this recognition. But the Essentialist insistence that gender follow sex has meant resistance to legally recognizing sex based on anything other than birth designation. Thus getting a change in a birth certificate is an issue in many societies. Still, there have been important changes in some places.

In this regard, the State of California has been more progressive than many in providing helpful legal provisions. The Department of Motor Vehicles (DMV) instituted changes so that pre-operative transsexuals, living in the gender identity and role they would possess post-operatively, can hold a license with that name and gender on it. This provides important protection against potential misconstruing of intent concerning appearance and manner of dress.

Identity recognition issues are important for many matters ranging from the mundane (e.g., use of public restrooms) to the profound (e.g., marriage). Though changes in such everyday documents as the driver's license are critical, there are many documents in our society that record either sex or gender, which our society's documents tend to treat as the same. At the present time, changes are occurring piecemeal and mostly locally, complicating life for those of us who are trying to live in a gender different from our birth assignment. As a partial response to this situation it has been suggested we need a widely recognized document to guide the drafting of local policies and ordinances. Fortunately, such a document exists.

The International Bill of Gender Rights

At the beginning of the 1990s, working independently and without knowledge of each other's efforts, two women initiated action to craft a gender 'Bill of Rights.' In Pennsylvania, JoAnn Roberts, an author on crossdressing and a co-founder of the Renaissance Transgender Association (1987), wrote such a document and began circulating it. In New York, Sharon Stuart, a former Judge Advocate General (JAG) officer, published a proposal for such a document in the newsletter for the International Foundation for Gender Education (IFGE). In 1992, the International Conference on Transgender Law and Employment Policy (ICTLEP) had its first annual meeting. Subsequently, Stuart began drafting a formal Gender Bill of Rights that utilized both her own earlier proposal and the work of Roberts.

In 1993, the *International Bill of Gender Rights* (IBGR) was drafted in committee and adopted at the 2nd annual ICTLEP. This was reviewed, amended, and adopted with revisions at the annual meetings in the next few years. The IGBR affirms the primacy of individual self-determination, independent of biological or social factors. It also affirms the resolution that neither Human nor Civil Rights shall be denied in consequence of such choices. Ten 'gender rights' are enumerated in the version of July 4, 1996:

1. The Right to Define Gender Identity.
2. The Right to Free Expression of Gender Identity.

3. The Right to Secure and Retain Employment and to Receive Just Compensation.
4. The Right of Access to Gendered Space and Participation in Gendered Activities.
5. The Right to Control and Change One's Own Body.
6. The Right to Competent Medical and Professional Care.
7. The Right to Freedom from Involuntary Psychiatric Diagnosis or Treatment.
8. The Right to Sexual Expression.
9. The Right to Form Committed, Loving Relationships and Enter into Marital Contracts.
10. The Right to Conceive, Bear, or Adopt Children; The Right to Nurture and Have Custody of Children and to Exercise Parental Capacity.

Though the IBGR has no force of law on its own, it serves as a model for legislative bodies and as a guide to individual organizations and persons. Today efforts continue to shape laws and policies aimed at securing a better world for us all. This document remains a guiding force.

The Role of Education

The success of social change depends largely on education. There is a place for discussion of transgender in America's classrooms. As gender historian Elizabeth Reis, writing in 2004 in *Radical History Review*, puts it: "Transgender is out of the closet, and it should be in the classroom as well." Talking about gender variance should be seen by all of us as relevant, for as Reis points out, issues of gender identity and self-presentation affect us all—including those of us who see ourselves fitting neatly into a dominant gender. Education—the presentation of reason and evidence in an open and balanced manner—can and does have a positive effect. That does not make it easy. We have seen already how educators themselves can be part of the problem. Increasingly, they are trying to be part of the solution.

Educator Linda McCarty points out that in years past multicultural education was principally concerned with racial and ethnic groups and issues. Today gender and transgender groups and issues are increasingly being recognized as important and legitimate aspects of multicultural education. As McCarty says, "Non-normative gender expression is not new. . . . What is new, however, is that the concept and identity of transgender is culturally available as never before. Increasingly, young people, especially high school aged youth, are exploring what it means to be transgender or 'genderqueer.'" Schools, then, have been faced with finding ways to cope with this expanded awareness and exploration. Many of them have responded by addressing what transgender realities mean for school climate, curriculum, policy, and activities, though the 'T' ('transgender') in GLBT ('gay, lesbian, bisexual, transgender') still remains underserved.

A 2002 study reported in the *College Student Journal* found that when college undergraduates are directly exposed to crossdressers and able to interact with them in a classroom setting, their discomfort with crossdressing diminishes. The study reports results gathered in 37 classes over a period from 1989-2002. During that time, students enrolled in human sexuality courses were exposed to crossdressing members of The Society for the Second Self (Tri-Ess), an organization offering support for crossdressers. Prior to meeting their guests, the students read information about crossdressing and formulated questions to ask. Participating Tri-Ess members provided autobiographical sketches and then students were encouraged to ask their questions. Afterward, the students were provided an opportunity through interviews and discussions to appraise what they had learned. Results obtained show widespread reduction of discomfort.

However, not everyone may be affected equally by interactions with crossdressers. In a study reported in 2004 in the journal *Sex Roles*, scholars Cindi Ceglian and Nancy Lyons examined whether an individual's gender type might affect the level of comfort with crossdressed men. A total of 157 undergraduate students (117 female; 40 male) were administered the Bem Sex Role Inventory (BSRI), which uses 60 characteristics to gender type a person as 'feminine,' 'masculine,' or 'gender-neutral' (i.e., androgynous). They also were tested with regard to their degree of comfort with crossdressing. After this testing, the students were exposed to two male crossdressers, who interacted with the students in a classroom setting. Then the students' levels of comfort were again measured. All three gender type groups showed increased levels of comfort (or decreased levels of discomfort) after interacting with the crossdressers. The greatest degree of change proved to be among the male students, who initially were more negative than the female students, but whose scores became similar to those of the women after interacting with the crossdressing men.

Especially in the case of transgender children and adolescents, more than education is needed in our schools. Formal policies against discrimination and harassment based on sexual orientation and/or gender identity are needed, with a firm commitment to enforcement of them. A 1999 *SIECUS Report* on sexual harassment points out that school districts permitted to develop their own policies are free to add such matters, and emphasizes that because provisions about sexual orientation do not cover gender identity that the latter should be expressly incorporated. The report also mentions that such action is important in light of the possibility of schools losing federal funding for failure to do enough to protect sexual minorities. Such policies need to extend to everyone within the school—students, faculty, staff, and administration.

Support Groups and Organizations

Fortunately, we who are transgender—and those who love us—have support. There is no exaggeration involved in saying that the venues for transgender people to meet other transgender folk have explosively multiplied over the last few decades. The same is true for spouses, family, and friends of transgender people. We can take time only to name a few of the better known organizations, and as we do so it must be remembered many more exist to help.

Support for Transgender People

Today, the number of independent support groups, affiliated support groups, educational, activist, and support organizations for gender variant people is astounding. Many of these maintain a presence on the internet.

Tri-Ess

One organization ranks first in historical importance and ongoing influence for many transgendered people, especially those for whom crossdressing is important: the 'Society for the Second Self,' or more simply and popularly, Tri-Ess. Its origin in the 1960s is rooted in the experience of perhaps the single most significant figure in the transgender community in North America in the last century—Virginia Prince. In 1987, Tri-Ess gained national attention after several members of one chapter appeared as guests on the *Donahue Show*. By the decade's end a board of directors had been established, some reorganizing transpired, and a vision statement was articulated. A significant change during this period was recognition and inclusion of spouses and partners of crossdressers as equal members. The organization's Board of Governance designated the three 'S' words as a motto: 'Support, Serenity, Service.' Support comes from the acceptance and encouragement of other crossdressers. That support generates internal serenity—a peace with one's self, accompanied by a sense of pride. This eventually leads to a desire to give back by offering service to others. The organization's philosophy is also expressed in twin Bill of Rights affirmed for both the crossdresser and the noncrossdressing partner.

Other Important Organizations

An important educational resource is The International Foundation for Gender Education (IFGE), founded in 1987 by Merissa Sherrill Lynn, also founder of the Tiffany Club (1977). IFGE is headquartered in Waltham, Massachusetts and maintains an active and extensive website on the internet (IFGE Transgender Tapestry). At that website, IFGE's purpose is stated as "overcoming the intolerance of transvestism and transsexualism brought about by widespread ignorance." However, the website also notes an expansion of consciousness within the organization has led to a rededication to educating toward the "emancipation of all people from restrictive gender norms." The organization is *not* a support group. Rather, IFGE provides information and serves as a clearinghouse for materials related to anything considered transgressive of our society's established gender norms. Five values of the organization listed on the website are: individual uniqueness and dignity; personal wholeness; respect for human diversity; freedom from society's arbitrarily assigned gender definitions;

and respect, acceptance, enforcement, and protection of gender-related human and civil rights for all.

Another prominent educational organization is the American Educational Gender Information Service (AEGIS), founded by noted educator Dallas Denny in 1990. Among its leadership are some of the foremost names in transgender study and support, including Gianna Israel, a counselor who specializes in transgender issues, and JoAnn Roberts, who was instrumental in the creation of the widely adopted *International Gender Bill of Rights*. Many other organizations offer help of one kind or another. For example, the Gender Public Advocacy Coalition (GenderPAC), founded in 1995, is a nonprofit human rights organization headquartered in Washington, D.C. that seeks to promote political and legal changes. Similarly, the National Center for Transgender Equality (NCTE), founded in 2003, is a nonprofit social justice organization headquartered in Washington, D.C. and devoted to ending discrimination and violence against transgender people through education and advocacy. These and many other organizations maintain websites where more information can be obtained.

Support for Partners, Family, and Friends of Transgender People

We are in a similar situation with respect to support for those who are in close relationships with transgender persons: there are too many to even list here. Once more we shall have to be highly selective. We may begin by remembering that some organizations, like Tri-Ess, offer support to nontransgender people as well as transgender loved ones. To be as useful to as many of us as possible, let us consider a few organizations with a wide reach.

PFLAG

Perhaps the best known nonprofit organization with a national span is 'Parents, Families, and Friends of Lesbians and Gays (PFLAG). Although the name suggests an interest only in people defined by homosexual orientation, the organization's Vision Statement immediately makes clear that transgender persons and their family and friends are included. PFLAG can claim some 200,000 members and supporter, with local affiliates in 500 communities, making it the largest grassroots-based family organization of its kind.

FPC

Family Pride Coalition (FPC) is another nonprofit organization with a national scope. It began in 1979 when a group of gay fathers banded together to form the 'Gay Fathers Coalition.' Lesbian moms were included in 1986, leading to a change in name to 'Gay and Lesbian Parents Coalition International' (GLPCI). The organization under this name spawned, in 1990, 'Children of Lesbians and Gays Everywhere' (COLAGE), which became an independent organization in 1999. The current name for FPC was adopted in 1998. Headquartered in Washington, D.C., FPC has about 200 membership-based LGBT parenting groups and some 35,000 supporters. Its website lists as its 'Strategic Objectives' three primary areas of labor: advocacy, education, and support.

SSN

Straight Spouse Network (SSN) operates an international support system with 74 support groups in the United States and 7 abroad. A nonprofit organization, its 'Welcome' page at its website declares that SSN "provides personal, confidential support and information to heterosexual spouses/partners, current or former, of gay, lesbian, bisexual or transgender mates and mixed-orientation couples for constructively resolving coming-out problems." Its 'Our Mission' statement offers three goals: reaching out, healing, and building bridges. The last of these includes not only building bridges between partners, but also collaborating with professional and community organizations to foster understanding at the levels of couples, families, and communities.

The bottom line is this: there are organizations reaching out to us. All we have to do is reach back. Yet for some of us, the thought of any association with an organization widely known is intimidating or sparks concerns about our privacy. For some of us there is more appeal in seeking a private counselor. This is true not only for those of us who are gender conforming, but for many of us who are gender variant. Thankfully, there are many mental health professionals working diligently to develop and provide supportive counseling.

Mental Health Reform: Supportive Counseling

Shifts in cultural consciousness are accompanied by changes in mental health conceptions. There exists a reciprocal interaction; we who are counselors cannot help but be influenced by our culture, especially its implicit values, yet we also exercise influence on our culture, bringing about the possibility of important shifts in cultural consciousness. Who leads in this fragile dance is less important than that it happens and that consciousness of our role can assist us who are mental health professionals in better fulfilling our ethical obligation to challenge society to move toward better health.

Ethics and a Shift in Sensibility

For decades now this delicate dance has swirled around transgender. In 1977, for example, in responding to a report detailing behavioral therapy to eliminate transgender behavior in a 5-year-old boy, psychologist Robin Winkler suggested that the case raises "a fundamental question, to whom does the therapist owe first allegiance: to the client (or in this case the client's parents), to the therapist's own values, or to prevailing relevant social norms?" Even then the early shifting social views about transgender made clinical work fraught with the possibility of conflict between these value sources. Today Winkler's question is more important than ever in light of an expanded awareness of the role culture plays in counseling individuals.

Dallas Denny, in a historical review published in a 1999 issue of the *SIE-CUS Report*, speaks of an emerging sensibility—a transgender model—that has moved the perception of pathology away from the transgendered and to the society that will not tolerate difference. He remarks, "This shift has forced a reevaluation of traditional clinical categories to which these people have been assigned and cast light upon the often-erroneous and sexist assumptions of clinicians and researchers who have studied these populations." In sum, shifting social realities are demanding an appropriate response from counselors. Mental health professionals can either step to the lead in supporting health-affirming changes or remain mired in a cultural myopia belied by their own research data.

Rupert Raj, who counsels transgendered clients, sees an encouraging change taking place among mental health professionals. Writing in a 2002 issue of *The International Journal of Transgenderism*, Raj finds a shift from a more 'transphobic' stance to one he calls 'transpositive'—characterized by a respectful, collaborative relationship between client and counselor. However, Raj says more work needs to be done, including developing a transpositive therapeutic model and providing ongoing education and training to professionals.

Courtland Lee and Gary Walz, in their edited volume *Social Action: A Mandate for Counselors*, contend that mental health professionals, in order to be effective, must possess three levels of awareness: an awareness of self, interpersonal awareness, and systemic awareness. The last named level entails both the ability "to perceive accurately environmental influences on client development" *and* "skills to intercede at an environmental level to challenge systemic barriers that block optimal mental health." This third level of awareness not only means counselors recognizing that transgender people experience negative effects from a defective society, but it additionally mandates that these *profes*sionals actually *profess* that awareness to the client and to others. There is a moral imperative implicit in professional counseling to make the world the client lives in a better place in which to be a better person.

We are in a state of cultural flux. Not all people, and certainly not all mental health professionals, view transgendered realities as pathological. In fact, among professional helpers changes in attitudes have been progressing for several decades. A study published in 1986 in *Social Science and Medicine* surveyed more than 200 medical professionals (including psychiatrists and psychologists, obstetrician-gynecologists, general practitioners and others) concerning their knowledge about transsexuals and their attitudes towards them. The findings were compared to data published twenty years earlier. The results indicated a more favorable attitude among medical professionals, especially psychologists. Specifically, the trend was toward less pathologizing, more acceptance, and greater readiness to support treatment like SRS. In the decades since these trends appear to be persisting, as marked by a growing number of therapists developing and employing supportive models of treatment for transgendered clients.

Supportive Psychotherapy

For some transgender people, mental health and medical professionals are important adjuncts to the ongoing formation of a positive self-identity. "One way of gaining social recognition is through the sanction of the 'expert'," writes sociologist Sally Hines in a 2006 article in the *Journal of Gender Studies*. "Thus the construction of a transgender identity frequently relies upon medical discourse and practice and access to medical intervention." Therefore, counseling is still valuable for transgendered people (and for their partners). The practical difficulties of living as a person who does not fit squarely within the holes dug at either end of the gender continuum are worthy of exploration, discussion, planning, and empathy.

The Cornerstone of Supportive Treatment

The most basic premise of supportive therapy for the transgendered—its cornerstone—is to *depathologize transgendered realities*. Yet this act is principally one of negation—trying to eliminate an obstacle. It needs pairing with a positive act. Randi Ettner, a psychologist who works with transgendered clients, recommends in a 1999 book entitled *Gender Loving Care: A Guide to Counseling Gender-Variant Clients* employing treatment strategies that both depathologize gender variance and empower individuals. *Empowerment* is a worthy positive partner.

But these twin acts are not as simple as they might seem on paper because clinicians serve as gatekeepers for those transgender clients who are seeking access to transforming services such as sex reassignment surgery (SRS). In the current situation such individuals *must* be diagnosed with a pathology to receive the care they desire, regardless of whether either they or their therapists regard them as 'disordered.' How can clients be empowered as they seek entrance into a medical system that disempowers them? That question remains unanswered.

General Treatment Recommendations

Despite the inherently hostile climate of pathologizing diagnoses, therapists and clients can carve out a healing space. There is not just one right way to do this, although successful treatment tends to incorporate similar elements. To get at some of the key ones, let us see what various professionals recommend.

Norwegian transgender therapist Esben Esther Pirelli Benestad, writing in *The International Encyclopedia of Sexuality*, suggests that in working with transgendered people the term "gender belonging" may be helpful. It refers to the process of developing a sense of belonging (gender identity) that accomplishes twin goals: being self-confirming and generally appropriate. But both goals are framed within boundaries that include cultural roles alongside the client's body status, erotic preferences, and personal synthesis of sexual experiences. In short, counseling work with the transgender person is an ongoing dialog between self and culture.

Sex therapist Richard Carroll, in the 2000 edited volume *Principles and Practice of Sex Therapy (3rd edition)*, offers us four main goals of therapy when working with clients diagnosed with gender dysphoria (a label many transgendered people resent and reject): first, aim at increasing self-understanding and comprehending one's own personal history. Second, explore the relevant and realistic options available. Third, address any concomitant psychological disorders. Finally, develop a life's goals plan. These goals support the client's insight and growth while treating problems such as depression or anxiety that often accompany the reality of living as a transgendered person in a culture of dichotomous gender.

Social work professionals Mary Boes and Katherine van Wormer, in the 2002 *Social Worker's Desk Reference*, recommend for gay, lesbian, bisexual and transgendered (GLBT) clients five steps to what they term a "strengths-based practice" within the context of a caring relationship: "seek the positive; hear the narrative; acknowledge the pain; don't dictate, collaborate; and pave the way for further growth through helping others." These steps avoid pathologizing, recognize individuality and the realities of social context, seek a working partnership goal-directed toward adding growth rather than eliminating what others demean, and encourage positive engagement with others. This is the kind of supportive therapy that can help transgendered clients and those who love them.

Finally, writing in a 1999 *SIECUS Report*, educator Dallas Denny, offers a broad review of the work of mental health professionals with transgendered clients, and identifies the following nine broad functions of the therapist:

1. Assist client exploration of feelings, including any feelings of guilt or shame associated with the response of others to their transgendered reality.
2. Help examine options for self-expression.
3. Function as a sounding board during changes pursued (e.g., transsexual transitioning into a new full-time gender identity and role).
4. Offer support especially during the difficult moments if/when self-expression results in important losses (e.g., loss of friends or job).
5. Suggest alternative and constructive ways to handle problems.
6. Serve as a resource for desired or needed services, including making any appropriate referrals (e.g., for sex reassignment surgery).
7. Treat mental health problems associated with the transgender experience (e.g., a history of abuse by others that might have given rise to post-traumatic stress disorder (PTSD) or a dissociative condition), or other mental health problems regardless of identifiable connection to the transgendered reality.

8. Work with the client's loved ones (e.g., spouse, family) as they process their own feelings about transgendered realities.
9. Provide education to other important figures such as employers.

Of course, we must keep in mind that the actual tasks undertaken by a counselor depend on the real individual sitting across from her or him and not some predetermined 'to do' list.

In addition to the positive recommendations advanced above, some cautions are in order. Transgender clients often experience pressure from therapists to 'come out' to others. The counselor may intend to be supportive in making such a recommendation. However, the client's lived reality may make such a move unwise. Even if there are no obvious obstacles to coming out, if the client is reluctant the issue should not be pressed. After all, the goal remains supporting *client* control and choices—not the promotion of the therapist's own agenda. At the same time, should a client desire and choose to come out, the courage of the decision should be recognized and reinforced even as the practical difficulties are addressed.

The Role of Medical Treatment

Some form of biological/medical treatment commonly accompanies treatment of transgendered people. A transgender person may or may not desire to alter his or her body. If such a desire is present, it may be more or less pressing. The degree of alteration may be minimal or extensive, including everything from some body shaving to complete sex reassignment surgery (SRS). As we have seen, gender variant people are often arrayed along a spectrum ranging from, for example, transvestites to 'marginal' transvestites to transsexuals. Along this spectrum transvestites typically desire, seek, and accomplish less body alteration than do transsexuals.

Individuals can accomplish minor body alterations, such as some body shaving, without expert help. But if a person desires something like complete removal of facial hair through electrolysis, professional assistance is required. Hormonal and surgical procedures also need competent professional help. The entire range of body alterations that involve actual physical changes (and not mere cosmetic changes through application of removable materials like artificial breasts) are collectively called 'biological/medical therapies.'

Biological/medical therapy can be an important treatment strategy incorporated into therapy with transgendered people. Sometimes hormones are used to alter biochemistry to facilitate a greater match between sexual characteristics and the gender presentation through dress and makeup. In some instances, sex reassignment surgery (SRS) is employed.

Hormone therapy

Hormone therapy seems like a logical candidate in cases involving sexual and/or gender conditions linked to hormonal contributions. Certainly, treatment with hormones is an important aspect in the treatment of transsexualism where the patient is transitioning to full life in a body of the sex opposite the one the person was assigned at birth. This treatment, though, is meant to take place in a context where other therapeutic measures are being used, including extensive counseling and living full-time in the gender role the client experiences greatest fit with. These matters precede any sex reassignment surgery. Treatment of transsexuals is typically divided into pre- and post-SRS periods.

Cross-sex hormone treatment used with transsexuals shows changes in several dimensions. In addition to physical changes such as breast tissue enlargement there are psychological changes. A 1995 study published in the journal *Psychoneuroendocrinology*, involving 35 Female-to-Male (FtM) transsexuals and 15 Male-to-Female (MtF) transsexuals, demonstrated that both groups displayed changes relatively soon after treatment began. Both groups were subjected to testing before treatment began and then three months into treatment. The administration of the cross-sex hormones produced alterations in cognitive performance, aggression, and libido—all in the direction expected for gender specific performance. Thus, for example, the FtM transsexuals increased in aggression, whereas the MtF transsexuals decreased in aggression.

Sex Reassignment Surgery (SRS)

Hormone treatment often is used in conjunction with sex reassignment surgery (SRS). The Harry Benjamin International Gender Dysphoria Association's (HBIGDA) 'Standards of Care' are widely used in the treatment of transsexual clients, including the steps preparatory for SRS. First appearing in 1979, periodic revisions have taken place. Though the Standards exist within a system that accepts the medical nomenclature of 'gender identity disorders,' as mental disorders, they do not view this as a license for stigmatization of the client. The 6th version of HBIGDA's Standards, adopted in 2001, express the "overarching treatment goal" of attaining in the client "personal comfort with the gendered self in order to maximize overall psychological well-being and self-fulfillment." Toward this end both talk therapy and biological therapies (endocrine and surgical) may be employed. The Standards offer minimum eligibility requirements in different matters meant to serve as guidelines for clinical care.

Not all transsexuals seek SRS, and it may not be the best course of treatment for a given person at a particular point in time. The American Educational Gender Information Service (AEGIS) and the International Foundation for Gender Education (IFGE) both advocate regarding SRS as a choice rather than a mandated treatment for those identified as transsexual. Yet for many clients SRS is highly desired and highly effective. In 1998, after reviewing 30 years of gender reassignment cases that involved nearly 2,000 patients, researchers Friedemann Pfäfflin and Astrid Junge, in their book *Sex Reassignment*, concluded that the treatment that includes the whole process of gender reassignment is effective, with significant lessening of suffering and positive improvements in areas such as partnership and sexual experience, mental stability and socio-economic functioning.

Counseling for Partners, Family and Friends

Earlier, when discussing partners of transgender persons, we looked briefly at the role of counseling. Let us return for a moment to that issue and ask what supportive therapy might look like for those of us who are partners, family, or friends of a transgender person. Kathleen Cairns, writing in the *Canadian Journal of Psychotherapy* in 1997, recommends attention to several important issues and tasks. First, the counselor needs to *identify and follow the vocabulary the client prefers* in describing the transgender behavior. Second, the counselor should *offer fact-based reassurance*, because clients commonly present with fears based on misinformation (e.g., crossdressing will be inherited by their children). A therapist can and should correct false beliefs with accurate information. Third, a counselor should *be candid* by not reinforcing client hopes that will likely prove unfulfilled (e.g., that the crossdresser can be cured), or by offering certain answers where uncertainty is more realistic (e.g., speculation on the outcome if the crossdresser's behavior is discovered by others). Fourth, a counselor should offer *support of emotional expression*—clients need the safety to feel what they feel (e.g., grief, betrayal) and convey that in the counseling process; resolution of unhappiness or interpersonal problems is unlikely without permitting such release. Fifth, a counselor should *assist in a reckoning of consequences*. The behavior by the loved one may mean for the client a number of consequences such as a sense of a loss of freedom and social isolation; feelings may develop into resentment over what crossdressing is perceived to be doing (e.g., taking away time and money from the family). Finally, the counselor needs to *encourage patience*—adjustment that leads to maintaining relationship, together with relief from present unhappiness may take considerable time. Early exposure through support groups to others whose acceptance of transgender is greater may generate despair in the client so such exposure is best used toward the end of therapy.

Help Is Where One Finds It

All of us long for acceptance—and all of us worry at least occasionally that we won't receive it. Regardless of our gender identity, experience, or expression, we all face times when we feel alone. Likewise, in different moments, for varying reasons, we all find ourselves desperate for the caring support of another. These human needs can be met in almost as many ways as there are people. Help is where we find it. But it rarely comes without effort. We need to look for—and welcome—the support we are offered. There is no shame in asking for help. If we are to work together to reconstruct our society, we must be willing to give and to receive from each other.

15.

GET GID OUT, DSM!

This is a pivotal time for those who study and/or live within the transgender community. There is lively discussion occurring in some quarters that holds promise for eliciting a wider and more profitable discussion in mental health circles than has been generally the case. There is even the possibility of a future wherein mental health professionals no longer regard any of us who are gender variant as psychologically disordered because of our transgender identity. While some of us may attribute the movement toward such a situation one motivated primarily by political and social forces, the fact is that a growing body of research substantiates such a position. It seems increasingly likely that at some point—perhaps in the not too distant future—the mental health community will reach a consensus that transgender realities are interesting and important subjects of research, but that such research need not be conducted under the attendant stigma of a diagnosis of one or another kind of psychological disorder.

Today's key questions include one like this: Should gender variances automatically be subject to psychiatric judgments as 'illness'? Especially in light of mountains of research demonstrating how variable and controversial are notions about where the boundaries of 'normal' gender should be drawn, questions like this one have become very important. Accordingly, teams of researchers, like George Brown and his associates, who tested 188 male crossdressers for both personality and sexual functioning (finding no significant differences in either regard from general male norms) suggested in *The Journal of Nervous and Mental Disease* in 1996 that their data raises the question of appropriateness in categorizing crossdressers as suffering a mental disorder.

Diagnostic and Statistical Manual for Mental Disorders

To put the current discussion in proper relief, we must review the American Psychiatric Association's (APA) *Diagnostic and Statistical Manual of Mental Disorders* (DSM). This volume guides much of the assessment of the mental health of individuals in our society. It is a core text in the training of professional counselors, therapists, psychologists, social workers, and psychiatrists. We would not be exaggerating to say it exerts a significant influence in contemporary mental health circles. This makes it a critical piece in addressing our society's regard of gender variant people. Any substantive social change in how transgender conditions and behaviors are viewed will involve important modifications in the DSM.

This model has never been without its critics and its architects themselves recognize its limitations. In fact, in DSM-IV-TR (2000), the latest incarnation of the model, some important claims are made alongside some equally important cautions. First, the model recognizes that its "utility and credibility" rest on the support of "an extensive empirical foundation" (p. xxiii)—and it claims to be better grounded in empirical evidence than any other comparable classification system. Second, the model claims to represent "the breadth of available evidence and opinion and not just the views of the specific members" of its work groups (p. xxiii). Finally, it claims that changes from earlier versions of the model (e.g., DSM-III), "had to be substantiated by explicit statements of rationale and by the systematic review of relevant empirical data" (p. xxviii).

Alongside such claims DSM-IV-TR offers some important cautions. First, it notes that most—but not all—of the conditions described "now have an empirical literature or available data sets that are relevant to decisions regarding the revision of the diagnostic manual" (p. xxvi). Second, the use of clinical judgment by qualified professionals is essential; the DSM model is not intended to be used like a cookbook (p. xxxii). Finally, the model is a work-in-progress; new information from research or clinical experience may lead to additions or removals of conditions (p. xxxiii). Our present task is to consider whether transgender conditions are among those that should be removed based on the existing empirical evidence and a critique of their handling in the DSM model.

Problems with the DSM Model

Because the DSM represents itself as a scientific instrument that reflects a careful objective process, it is important we test this claim. How scientific is the DSM? Does it adequately meet basic tests we expect for such important tools? In answering such questions we need to be aware of five basic criticisms:

o   First, the DSM model suffers *low reliability*.
o   Second, this low reliability adversely impacts its *validity*.
o   Third, the model is *more a political work than a scientific one*; allegiance to a medical model represents an attempt to fit in within medical science rather than accurately reflect the reality of psychological conditions.
o   Fourth, *culture, not science predominates*; the model owes more to historical precedent and continuity than to empirical evidence.
o   Finally, *the model is ethically questionable*; it too often violates the moral foundation of the mental health profession: 'first, do no harm.'

Given the importance of the DSM, we need to determine if such criticisms are accurate and whether they really matter.

Reliability & Validity Concerns

The issue of *reliability* has been a constant concern since the inception of the model. Reliability refers to the likelihood that professionals will make the same diagnosis of a case presentation. This concern was behind the significant changes between DSM-II (1968) and DSM-III (1980). Yet professionals in the area of assessment continue to find the model low in reliability as compared to other assessment areas, such as intelligence testing. In general, various professionals have claimed that diagnostic reliability has improved across editions of the DSM but they also confess it remains an elusive goal in terms of high reliability across conditions and across clinicians. Even Robert Spitzer, who spearheaded the development of DSM-III and DSM-III-R (1987), has acknowledged the gravity of the issue. In a 2005 interview with Alix Spiegel for *The New Yorker*, Spitzer said, "To say that we've solved the reliability problem is just not true. . . . It's been improved. But if you're in a situation with a general clinician it's certainly not very good. There's still a real problem, and it's not clear how to solve the problem."

Reliability has proven to be a particularly thorny issue in certain areas of the DSM model, including the sexual and gender disorders. A longtime researcher in this area, Nathaniel McConaghy, observed in *Archives of Sexual Behavior* near the turn of the century that many clinicians have neglected DSM criteria because of a lack of operational definitions to guide clinical judgments. McConaghy offers as an example the criteria for diagnosing premature ejaculation disorder. Though the criteria describe certain factors (e.g., the client's age), they do not establish specific parameters (e.g., 'over 55 years old'). This deficit leaves too much leeway for individual clinicians and thus seriously weakens reliability. Such a situation pertains for several of the sexual dysfunctions.

Validity

Reliability has an important impact on *validity*—is what is seen really there? The accuracy of any diagnosis is threatened if reliability is low. A critic like psychiatrist and neurologist Sydney Walker, III, in his 1996 book *A Dose of Sanity*, has charged that lack of a proper diagnosis is an all-too-common problem. Specifically, medical conditions are too often viewed as psychiatric and mistreated. Walker points out that a psychiatric 'diagnosis' is really just a description; it isn't a diagnosis in the way medicine traditionally has understood the term. Walker charges that the DSM model attempts to shortcut the time-honored "cornerstone" of medicine—the deductive differential diagnosis. "In doing so," claims Walker, "psychiatry has replaced the science of diagnosis with the pseudoscience of labeling."

The Political Nature of the DSM Model

The matter of how *political* the DSM model may be is, naturally, open to debate. The concern is that psychiatrists may be more worried about carving out a respectable niche among the sciences and serving their own professional interests than in helping the people they ostensibly serve. Specifically, the American Psychiatric Association has been charged with forming and reforming itself more and more to justify its place within modern medicine. Distinguished psychiatrist Loren Mosher, in a letter of resignation from the APA, asked, "Why must the APA pretend to know more than it does? DSM-IV is the fabrication upon which psychiatry seeks acceptance by medicine in general. Insiders know it is more a political than scientific document."

The construction of the model, and subsequent revisions, has also followed along political lines. Decision-making in changing the DSM model, critics charge, is not as dependent on scientific appraisal as it is on political consensus building among the professionals involved, and especially among those at the higher reaches of the model. These folk principally are a relatively small group of senior members of the APA sitting on the APA Board of Directors and the DSM Task force it appointed. Thus, while work groups (which often were led by a Task Force member and constituted by invitation) focused on their tasks, they were guided by parameters set by the Task Force, a group of 27 who retained the authority of actually proposing to the Board whether to retain, amend, or delete a disorder in the model. Those parameters constituted a conservative approach to change. Indeed, given the strictures within which work groups operated and the hierarchical structure of the decision-making process, any proposed substantive changes face a long and arduous process to approval.

This system of decision-making has been criticized on several grounds. Philosopher and social scientist Jeffrey Poland, writing in *Metapsychology* in 2001, notes that the DSM model supports a "deep cultural entrenchment" which, on the one hand, is strongly attached to the desire to be scientifically credible, yet on the other hand remains substantially wedded to "an overriding concern with achieving consensus in the absence of constraints based on scientific research." Poland examined the *DSM-IV Sourcebook*, a four volume set that explores more deeply the thinking of the DSM model and which presents its rationale and evidence for decisions about disorders. But Poland found that this work did not address fundamental criticisms that have persisted about the model since the new direction undertaken in DSM-III (1980). His review of the first two volumes calls into serious question both the empirical basis of the DSM model and its subsequent claims to credibility on those grounds.

But there is another dimension to this issue we need to consider. Not only may politics be an important part of how the DSM model is shaped, the resulting model is itself used politically. This has at least two dimensions: first, clinicians advantage themselves and their clients through the use of the model in diagnosing disorders for insurance payments; second, they endorse and uphold cultural mores through supporting the model. With reference to the first point, philosopher of science Rachel Cooper, writing in *History of Psychiatry* in 2004, discusses the financial pressures and incentives clinicians face when diagnosing clients. These often lead to providing either a less severe or a more severe diagnosis along economic and social (i.e., 'political') lines rather than genuinely scientific ones. With reference to the second point, the power of the model ought not to be underestimated, as sexologist Charles Moser and psychologist Peggy Kleinplatz have reminded us. In a paper delivered at the APA's 2003 annual meeting, they stated, "The equating of unusual sexual interests with psychiatric diagnoses has been used to justify the oppression of sexual minorities and to serve political agendas. A review of this area is not only a scientific issue, but also a human rights issue."

The Power of History & Culture in the DSM Model

Running parallel to the role of politics, has been the power of *history* and *culture* in shaping the model. The DSM model not only has forebears, but these are rooted in the decision and efforts to shape mental health science along the lines of the medical profession. Thus changes in the DSM editions early on reflected a desire to adopt and conform to medical diagnostic coding. The use of Greek and Latin terms (e.g., 'paraphilias') for descriptors follows a tradition in scientific labeling and reinforces the appearance of scientific credibility. The use of a categorical classification system such as in mainstream medicine lends itself to increasing diagnostic categories rather than reducing them. In all these matters, and others, the DSM model positions itself to enjoy the same prestige and authority as modern medicine does, despite the significant differences between assessing mental health and disease-based physical conditions. The model self-consciously positions itself in the history and culture of modern Western medicine.

Not surprisingly, then, diagnostic categories have tended to persist across time; the labels and descriptive specifics change, but not the general picture. Once a diagnostic category is entered into the DSM model it is difficult to remove. The DSM claim that conditions may be removed on empirical grounds has proven far less true than the reality that they actually have been re-envisioned (e.g., transsexualism has become Gender Identity Disorder; transvestism has become Transvestic Fetishism). Conservative in nature, the model has been resistant to any evidence that challenges long accepted claims while simultaneously welcoming any theory or data that justifies already reached conclusions. Dissent is not encouraged. History and tradition trump empirical reality.

An unintended consequence of positioning the DSM within a broader medical model has been to convey the impression that its diagnostic categories signify disease. With reference to transgender conditions, at least, the case is more *dis-ease* than 'disease.' As Stuart Kirk and Herb Kutchins point out in their book *The Selling of DSM: The Rhetoric of Science in Psychiatry*, the DSM capitalizes on unspoken and largely unconscious cultural notions about normality and abnormality. While appearing humane the medical model as filtered through the DSM actually pathologizes the powerless in society who those in power judge as undesirable; the model perpetuates stereotypes and promotes bigotry despite the science that discredits such acts.

Ethical Concerns

Karen Eriksen and Victoria Kress, in their 2005 volume *Beyond the DSM Story: Ethical Quandaries, Challenges, and Best Practices*, bring us to the weightiest matter. By far the most serious criticism of the DSM model is that *it harms people*. Broadly rooted in the same helping tradition as medical science, mental health professionals likewise subscribe to the central tenet of the Hippocratic tradition: 'first, do no harm.' Yet it seems the DSM model violates this precept.

Diagnostic Issues

Irvin Yalom, an existential psychotherapist, proposes in his book *Love's Executioner and Other Tales of Psychotherapy: For Anyone Whose Ever Been on the Other Side of the Couch*, "Even the most liberal system of psychiatric nomenclature does violence to the being of another. If we relate to people believing that we can categorize them, we will neither identify nor nurture the parts, the vital parts, of the other that transcend category." In his view, every one of us must come to grips with the fact we cannot fully know, define, or explain a person. Instead, "enabling relationships" assume the other cannot be fully known. No transgendered person is *merely* transgendered, nor can classification of a cluster of symptoms adequately capture the individual's lived experience.

Helping professionals intend diagnosis to benefit their clients. Unfortunately, it remains a question whether the benefits outweigh the risks of some unintended consequences. How can diagnosis injure? There are a number of problems that often flow from diagnosis. First, *diagnostic labels can stigmatize clients.* Unfortunately, a long history exists of diagnostic labels being used to further marginalize those outside the cultural mainstream, such as racial, religious, or sexual minorities. Second, *diagnostic labels can change client self-perceptions in unhealthy ways.* They may accept such labels as unalterable and objective statements of truth about themselves, or change their conceptions of self and relations with others in injurious ways. Third, *diagnostic labels can negatively influence mental health professionals.* They can serve to reinforce irrational cultural values that counselors may hold and use to dictate conceptions of the client and strategies for treatment that are narrow, biased, inappropriate, or harmful. Finally, in addition to these, the use of the DSM model when aware of its limitations and flaws may generate a number of other ethical concerns regarding matters such as informed consent and confidentiality, as well as many other important issues.

Treatment Issues

Beyond diagnosis, *treatment* also presents ethical issues. Behavioral treatment of transgendered realities traditionally has involved aversive techniques such as the application of electrical shock or nausea-inducing drugs. Therapist Ron

Langevin, writing in his book *Sexual Strands: Understanding and Treating Sexual Anomalies in Men*, recounts working with a man where his crossdressing facilitated his successful sexual activity with his female partner. Langevin observes, "One would expect then that by making crossdressing aversive, it would hinder his heterosexual relationships rather than helping them." If the 'cure' leaves one worse off than the 'disease,' what is the point of the treatment?

Ethical concerns inhere in every aspect of diagnosis and treatment. An individual's ethics steer his or her moral behavior. Although our discussion here has focused on mental health professionals, we all share a moral obligation to treat one another with at least the same measure of respect and concern to preserve personal integrity and dignity that we desire for ourselves. It is not just a classification system such as the DSM model that requires ongoing ethical scrutiny; all of us profit when we constantly reexamine our decisions about others and behaviors toward them in the light of improving the welfare of everyone.

Transgender in the DSM

We must turn now to a more narrow focus. In addition to the general criticisms of the DSM model advanced above, there are numerous points of critique that have been set forth in reference to specific diagnostic categories. With reference not only to conditions featuring crossdressing, but indeed all of the paraphilias, a number of weighty criticisms have been advanced. Our focus shall remain on transgender conditions where crossdressing is prominent.

Three important criticisms of the DSM model with reference to transgender conditions are:

o   *Cultural bias counts more than scientific evidence.* In understanding and classifying conditions known as 'paraphilias' the model relies more on cultural bias than solid science.

o   *The model's own logic is inconsistently applied.* If the same logic were applied to conditions like GID and transvestic fetishism as was applied to homosexuality, then the same conclusion should be reached: neither warrant inclusion as a 'disorder.'

o   *The diagnostic description and criteria are seriously flawed.* Even if these conditions are retained, their current descriptions are inadequate in light of the ambiguous wording, which leads to problems of application, the inclusion of the concept of 'distress,' which jeopardizes the logical consistency of the category within the model, and the narrowness of the category, which is empirically unwarranted.

Each of these contentions has able advocates, whose arguments we shall now examine.

Cultural Bias

As B. F. Skinner once put it, "no one steps outside the causal stream"—we are all products of our environments and those of us residing in Western culture today are the inheritors of certain ways of looking at things. Among these, in the last century or so, has been a definite medical model of human sexuality and gender. In this model there are two—and *only* two—clearly demarcated sexes and corresponding genders. Despite multiple signs of erosion in this dichotomous model of sex and gender, it still constitutes the conventional wisdom in both culture and among mental health professionals. Various contemporary scholars have charged the DSM model with such cultural bias in its inclusion and treatment of 'paraphilias' within its group of 'sexual disorders.'

In a 1987 essay for the volume *Sexuality and Medicine, Vol. 2: Ethical Viewpoints in Transition,* Frederick Suppe addressed this problem of cultural bias in reference to the paraphilias in the DSM model. He argued that the change in labels from 'sexual deviations' to 'paraphilias' did little to remove the old sense of 'sexual perversions.' The inclusion of these conditions, he charged, was not merited by scientific evidence and raised the specter that modern psychiatry was engaged in "the codification of social mores masquerading as objective science."

As we have seen, transgender realities, by their very existence, challenge a rigidly dichotomous scheme of sex and gender. This is enough to create cultural unease. Labeling what makes us uneasy a psychological disorder seems more humane than calling it a crime. But to do so merely on that ground would violate the DSM's own internal logic, which requires either significant personal distress or impairment in one or more important areas of social functioning, such as at work, school, or in relationships (DSM-IV-TR, p. xxxi).

We might argue, though, that the logic also associates mental disorder with a significantly increased risk of suffering death, pain, disability, or an important loss of freedom (p. xxxi). Certainly, in the past those of us who are transgender were at risk for arrest for things like crossdressing, and we remain at risk from aggressive or hostile behavior by others, including law enforcement officers and even medical professionals. Hate crimes against us remain a serious issue. But the DSM logic expressly notes that the dysfunction must be in the *individual,* as already described, and *not* simply because the behavior is judged 'deviant' by the society, resulting in conflicts between the person and society (p. xxxi).

Despite this official stance, Katherine K. Wilson, of the Gender Identity Center of Colorado, complains that the mental health profession *still* relies too much on subjective notions about sex and gender. At the same time, in her view, the profession considers too little the power of social prejudices. For example, those of us who exhibit variance from cultural norms are subject to societal forces that can generate in any individual significant personal distress and impede social functioning by erecting barriers others do not have to face. This does not mean the problem is *in* us; it is all *around* us, arising from social pressures. When cultural notions dictate ideas about gender, and become enfranchised in diagnostic criteria, the resulting bias is a serious matter. Wilson finds such biases at work, for instance, in the diagnosis of 'Gender Identity Disorder' (GID).

Even more pointed is the criticism offered by psychiatrist Justin Richardson of Columbia-Presbyterian Eastside's Center for Lesbian, Gay and Bisexual Mental Health. Richardson, writing in the *Harvard Review of Psychiatry* in 1996, decries the triumph of personal discomfort over professional commitments to sound science. Clinicians may label someone as pathological not because of psychological dysfunction, personal distress, or problems but because the professional finds the atypical behavior or presentation personally distasteful. The social value those in power apply to atypical behavior determines whether it is a 'problem'—and it often is to those who have the power to declare it so.

The continued presence in the DSM model of GID and other transgender realities makes it easy for individual practitioners to justify to themselves and others what is in reality personal bias. Richardson has taken the DSM model to task on this point. He points out that the GID diagnosis for children makes assumptions about gender-appropriate behavior based on our own culture. The model fails to distinguish a rationale for determining the line between 'atypical' and 'pathological' gender behavior even as culture itself steadily broadens the boundaries of socially tolerated behavior. Who decides, then, what constitutes gender behavior that needs professional intervention?

Indeed, with reference to GID there has been some acknowledgment of at least partial bias in the diagnostic criteria of the DSM model. Consider, for example, the wording of the 1987 DSM-III-R for 'Gender Identity Disorder of Childhood' (p. 71). With reference to crossdressing the bar was set substantially higher for females ("persistent marked aversion to normative feminine clothing and insistence on wearing stereotypical masculine clothing") than it was for males ("preference for either cross-dressing or simulating female attire"). In 1994's DSM-IV (p. 537; cf. DSM-IV-TR, p. 581) the criteria was simplified, but a gender-based difference could still be detected; for boys the wording remained the same (*sans* the word 'either'), while for girls only the latter half ("insistence on wearing stereotypical masculine clothing") was retained. Interestingly, DSM-IV itself acknowledged that, "in children, the referral bias towards males may partly reflect the greater stigma that cross-gender behavior carries for boys than for girls" p. 535; cf. DSM-IV-TR, p. 579).

Another worrisome possibility suggests itself by the origin of GID in the DSM model. As social workers Gerald Mallon and Theresa DeCrescenzo point out in a 2006 article in *Child Welfare*, GID in children was introduced in DSM-III (1980). Two important matters stood in the immediate background: first, homosexuality had recently been removed from the DSM model (in 1973), and second, research on gender-variant boys suggested more than half of them would become adult homosexuals. As Mallon and DeCrescenzo write, "Treatment, which was justified in the name of preventing transsexualism, focuses instead on modifying gender variant behavior and may be easily used covertly to 'treat' future homosexuality."

A similar charge of bias might be made concerning 'Transvestic Fetishism.' Moser and Kleinplatz have contended that viewing crossdressing as psychopathological relies on historical precedent rather than empirical fact. Their claim is that there is "no objective support" for the notion that strong sexual interests like those found in fetishistic transvestism either stem from or constitute psychopathology. In a chapter contributed by Moser to Kleinplatz' text, *New Directions in Sex Therapy. Innovations and Alternatives*, he adds his voice to others in documenting the history of value judgments expressed in ideas of public morality and legal restriction of behaviors that are disfavored because of the unease they arouse in many people, not because of solid empirical evidence of mental pathology. Both Moser and Kleinplatz have tirelessly lobbied their colleagues and the American Psychiatric Association to rethink the matter of paraphilias.

At least one part of their criticism apparently is conceded in DSM-IV-TR. The opening remarks on the paraphilias notes that "the paraphilias described here are conditions that have been specifically identified by previous classifications" (p. 586). Evidently, historical precedent alone was enough to warrant their carry over. In fact, with the exception of homosexuality, the conditions first listed by DSM-I in 1952 remain in the model. Frankly, it is hard to see science prevailing in this situation.

Another serious indication of cultural bias is the restriction of the diagnosis to heterosexual males. This clearly reflects our society's gender hierarchy—the people who matter are heterosexual males; what others do is of little consequence. This issue we will return to in examining the DSM criteria.

Flawed Logic

The principle argument for eliminating GID and Transvestic Fetishism from inclusion within the DSM model is that their inclusion violates the very logic employed in removing homosexuality *per se* as a disorder. This is not a recent critique. Indeed, as far back as the early 1970s debate about retaining or removing homosexuality from DSM-II there was recognition that 'sexual deviations' differed from the logical standard other disorders must meet. In a 1973 Position Statement, psychiatrist Robert Spitzer, the guiding hand for DSM-III, observed not only homosexuality, but perhaps also some of the other sexual disorders in their milder forms, do *not* meet the logic test of the DSM model. In the 1980s, Frederick Suppe was even more emphatic when he charged that the same criteria justifying removal of homosexuality should require the removal of the paraphilias, which include Transvestic Fetishism. Put in other words, if reason and evidence argue for excluding homosexuality as a disorder, and the same reasons and similar evidence exist about Gender Identity Disorder (GID) and Transvestic Fetishism, why are they still retained?

Katherine Wilson, writing in *Psychiatry Online*, correctly observes that homosexuality was seen for a long time by members of the medical profession (and by many in the wider culture) as pathological in itself. It mattered not that homosexual individuals might lead stable, productive, and content lives. After the APA, in 1973, decided homosexuality should no longer be regarded as a disorder, the 1980 DSM-III explained "the crucial issue" in determining a disorder was the *consequences* of the condition rather than its *causes*. This led, in 1994's DSM-IV, to the logic that psychiatric disorders are characterized either by significant distress, or impairment in one or another important area of functioning, or both. Yet, Wilson concludes, this same logic has *not* been applied to GID or transvestic fetishism. Instead, the DSM model leaves open the question whether these transgender realities are, like homosexuality used to be, viewed as *inherently* disordered.

Wilson has made the trenchant observation that *the DSM's logic about GID amounts to saying that too much masculinity in females and too much femininity in males is pathological.* Further, the model presupposes that gender dysphoria is a response to an internal regression, or collapse, rather than a rationally realized response to oppressive forces in the culture. Thus the distress or impairment the transvestite or transsexual faces may not be inherent to a pathological condition but elicited by the necessity of facing all too real social circumstances such as disapproving loved ones or a hostile public.

These, of course, are the kinds of matters the APA had to resolve in the 1970s with regard to homosexuality. Are gay men pathologically feminine and lesbians pathologically masculine? Is the psychological pain of the homosexual, if and when it occurs, an inevitable result of being disordered, or brought about by irrational social pressures? These queries were answered such that homosexuality was removed from the DSM model. When will a similar effort be put into reexamining transgender conditions like transvestic fetishism and GID?

The matter is more than idle dispute over terminology. The inadequacy of the logic is reflected in scientific evidence. For example, as reported in *Sex Roles* in 2000, Nancy Bartlett, Paul Vasey, and William Bukowski conducted research to test the empirical evidence in children diagnosed with GID against DSM-IV's definitional criteria for a mental disorder. They reviewed the literature on GID in children with the goal of seeing whether research findings supported an association between symptoms and one or another of four DSM criteria for a mental disorder: present distress; present disability; a significantly increased risk of suffering death, pain, disability, or an important loss of freedom; or dysfunction in the individual (rather than merely being socially disapproved behavior). They concluded that both because of problems with DSM's definitional criteria and a lack of supportive evidence that the existing form of the diagnostic category for GID in children should not be retained.

Problematic Criteria: Transvestic Fetishism

Logic is only one problem in the DSM model. Another criticism of the DSM treatment of transgender conditions has concerned the criteria. Richard

Docter and James Fleming—both with considerable experience and expertise in the study of transgenderism—refuse in a 2001 article in *Archives of Sexual Behavior* to quarrel with the DSM's broad diagnostic descriptions, but they do urge setting these aside if the component aspects of transgenderism are to be understood. They caution that abundant examples exist of individuals whose experience of gender identity, gender role behavior, or sexual history simply do not fit neatly into diagnostic categories.

Problems with the Criteria for Transvestic Fetishism

Consider the problematic nature of the DSM handling of transvestic fetishism. Three specific areas of concern are: the wording is ambiguous enough to lead diagnosticians to apply the judgment of a disorder to any heterosexual male who recurrently crossdresses; the use of the term 'distress' introduces logical problems, and, the criteria are unwarrantedly restrictive in only including heterosexual men.

Problem 1: The Label

With reference to the first matter, though it is not part of the criteria *per se*, the diagnostic label has been criticized. The first three DSM editions (1952-1980) used the label 'transvestism.' In 1987, with DSM-III-R, the label became 'transvestic fetishism.' This has been retained in DSM-IV. The current label aims at greater and more appropriate specificity, implying that crossdressing in itself is not a disorder. McConaghy expresses the concern that the change to the current label is likely to confuse rather than clarify. He points out that, in fact, the change soon created controversy as researchers debated to whom the DSM criteria, in view of the new label and additional discussion, truly applies.

Problem 2: The Application of "Sexually Arousing"

With respect to the criteria themselves, Wilson notes that the DSM wording (in Criterion A) of "recurrent, intense sexually arousing fantasies, sexual urges, or behaviors involving crossdressing" is subject to interpretation. For example, do the words "sexually arousing" apply only to "fantasies," or to fantasies, sexual urges and behaviors? Wilson argues that the case study offered in the casebook for the DSM-IV supports seeing the idea it applies only to fantasies.

Problem 3: The Idea of "Distress"

Another complaint focuses on the phrase "cause clinically significant distress . . . ." In the volume, *The Philosophy of Psychiatry: A Companion*, philosopher Alan Soble points out several difficulties with the use of this criterion. First, the notion of 'distress' makes the sexual aspect irrelevant. Distressing Transvestic Fetishism is logically no different in kind than, say, distressing psoriasis—distress is distress. Second, DSM-IV claims the distress must be "in the individual," and not "primarily" caused by conflicts between the "deviant" person and society. Yet the source of the distress remains unclear. Third, why couldn't we argue that *not* feeling distress is more pathological than feeling distress?

What makes the issue all the more interesting is the unlikelihood that 'sexually arousing' would often be experienced as 'distress.' For that to occur would seem to require an inculcation of the culture's values that what is eliciting the arousal is morally wrong, *and* for that moral judgment to be imperative enough to cause unease. In fact, in a culture where most people still regard sexual intercourse outside of marriage as immoral, it happens regularly without enough distress to be clinically significant; marital infidelity is not (yet) a DSM disorder. When we take into account that most crossdressing is done in secret to avoid censure from others, it would seem that crossdressers generally go out of their way not to distress others and thus to minimize problems for themselves. Moreover, most of us in this culture reason that sexual arousal in itself is a good thing and that if it stems from behavior that does not harm others it should be left alone—hardly a ringing endorsement of the need for immediate clinical intervention.

Beyond the unlikely instance that crossdressing for sexual arousal will produce enough internal distress to motivate seeking treatment is the fact that crossdressing may be done for reasons other than sexual excitement. DSM-IV recognizes that for some male crossdressers "the cross-dressing becomes an antidote to anxiety or depression or contributes to a sense of peace and calm." Rather than producing distress it *alleviates* stress. Most of us would regard such an outcome as favorable to an individual's well-being, especially since stress is known to precede or exacerbate emotional distress and mental disorders.

We might ask, then, '*whose* distress is the DSM model really concerned about?' The empirical evidence makes it plain that most crossdressers are not distressed by their behavior. More often than not, when crossdressing is the presenting problem it is because a significant other (e.g., spouse or parent) has pushed the person to 'seek help' for a 'problem.' DSM-IV-TR (p. 566f.) itself recognizes this in noting that individuals rarely self-refer for therapy and when others push them to go often claim their real problem is the reaction of others. Is it impairment to distress others? Unfortunately, it matters not that 'the problem' resides outside the crossdresser if the clinician concurs with the person that pushed the crossdresser into therapy. In such instances the therapist acts *as if* the problem arises within the crossdresser and proceeds accordingly. It appears that if others are distressed by crossdressing behavior, then the problem must be with the crossdresser.

Problem 4: The Restrictive Nature of the Criteria

Another criticism of the criteria has indicted the restriction of the diagnosis of transvestic fetishism to heterosexual men. Our culture has come to accept women dressed in clothing styles once associated strongly with males. Crossdressing females excite little attention. But crossdressing men provoke much comment. Could the DSM model's inclusion of transvestism be a matter of a wider, persistent cultural judgment? If not, why are *only* heterosexual men included within the boundaries of the 'disorder'? And why is the *heterosexuality* of these men described in such a manner as to call it into question? After all, we have empirical evidence that some women, both homosexual and heterosexual, crossdress; so do some homosexual men. Moreover, in all these groups there are some who do so for sexual arousal. So why are heterosexual men singled out unless some cultural bias is at work?

The DSM model in the 1980s attempted to preclude this objection by noting a differential diagnostic point about crossdressing: male homosexuals and female impersonators might also crossdress, but the act does not create sexual arousal in themselves, though it might in others. Apparently, crossdressing that elicits sexual arousal in another person is all right as long as it does not also create sexual excitement in the crossdresser! The logical problems in such distinctions should be obvious. They point to the culturally arbitrary way in which heterosexual males who look in most respect like other heterosexual males must be singled out as mentally disordered. It is not, then, crossdressing *per se* that is troublesome. It is not even that crossdressing may elicit sexual excitement that is the issue—'fetishistic' transvestism is a misleading title. The real problem is that otherwise "unremarkably masculine" heterosexual men crossdress—and that behavior profoundly troubles many other heterosexual men.

Problematic Criteria: GID

The most problematic criterion for GID is the notion of 'gender dysphoria.' Literally, it means an ill-feeling (or dis-ease) concerning one's gender. The idea is that the transgender person feels bad (i.e., experiences personal distress) over the internal sense of gender. This is misleading. Typically transgender people—including transsexuals—are comfortable with their *felt* gender; it is their *assigned* gender that is discomfiting. Of course, from an Essentialist perspective, feeling bad about one's assigned gender is problem enough to warrant a label of psychological disorder. Transsexuals recognize the problem as a misassignment of gender at birth, one misled by pairing gender with apparent body sex. Since it easier to correct body sex than misassigned gender, they seek SRS.

Bartlett, Vasey, and Bukowski point out that three of the criteria listed for GID, with reference to children, are problematic. Criterion A, they show, suffers from two problems: first, it treats very different symptoms as equivalent in significance and, second, thus allows the criteria to be met without the presence of a hallmark symptom—the child's expressed wish to be a member of the opposite sex—which violates the DSM's own stated specifications for the disorder. Criterion B inappropriately confuses sex and gender, equating discomfort with one with discomfort with the other, and assigning equal significance to symptoms associated with one or the other (e.g., considering one's genitals disgusting has the same diagnostic weight as avoiding certain types of play). Crite-

194

rion D is weak because it refers to causation ('the disturbance *causes* clinically significant distress or impairment in social, occupational, or other important areas of functioning'), despite the DSM's avowed stance that an association— not causation—is at play. This inconsistent usage raises questions about how to regard the relation of a child's 'distress' to GID—is it caused by the gender identity disturbance, or associated with it more indirectly, such as via social ostracism? As seen earlier, such issues with regard to the criteria and the DSM's logic, coupled with existing empirical evidence, lead the authors to call for the existing form of the criteria, with reference to children, to be discontinued.

Transgender Diagnoses Should Be Dropped from DSM

A longstanding uneasiness has accompanied the transgender conditions found in the DSM. This uneasiness is reflected in the awkwardness with which the model has attempted to handle these conditions. The opposition to their inclusion by people both within and outside the mental health community also reflects this uneasiness. At no point in time has there been unanimous consent to the legitimacy of these conditions inclusion.

There are practical consequences that flow from the decisions mental health professionals make. They impact real people. They affect self-image, relationships, and social functioning. They either contribute to reinforcing irrational cultural notions or they challenge them. At present, the weight of the above arguments suggests that mental health professionals, both in the DSM model and through its application, may all too often be violating the preeminent precept of ethical practice: first, *do no harm*.

Though we have never been far from it, we again are faced directly with the moral dimension of the matter. Nowhere is this more poignant than in regard to protecting those who cannot protect themselves—children. Therapists Susan Langer and James Martin, writing in 2004 in *Child and Adolescent Social Work Journal* with reference to the diagnosis of GID in children, called for reappraisal of retaining it as a diagnostic category. Their critique not only points out the conceptual and psychometric problems that have persistently plagued this category, but also raises ethical concerns. Because our notions of atypical gender are socially constructed, and such constructions vary across time as a result of various factors, locating one conception at a single point in time and within a particular cultural context is more than illogical; it is unethical. Behavior that deviates from the norm by being statistically infrequent is not thereby automatically disordered. To deem such behavior mentally disordered to justify trying to change a child's attitudes, behaviors and even identity is, in the authors' view, ethically repellant. Gender atypicality need not—and should not—be regarded as pathology.

The evidence we have spent so much time considering suggests that transgender realities should eventually be discarded from mental health classification systems. GID already has been in some places. Denmark, for example, removed it in 1994. In December, 2002, the British Lord Chancellor's Office, in a Government Policy paper declared its conclusion that transsexualism is *not* mental illness. The Scottish Executive's Review of the Mental Health (Scotland) Act of 1984 specifically recommended excluding sexual orientation or behavior from the definition of mental disorder. If past trends hold true, Europe will precede the United States in recognizing the illegitimacy of retaining crossdressing conditions as mental disorders, with official bodies such as the World Health Organization and American Psychiatric Association following the cultural shift rather than leading the way, despite having greater access to the very evidence that substantiates greater social tolerance.

Perhaps the noted biologist Joan Roughgarden, in a 2004 article for *GLQ: A Journal of Lesbian and Gay Studies*, best captures the lunacy so many of us find in the DSM logic:

> In any culture, people do what they must to realize that identity. The realization of identity goes far beyond gender; after all, many volunteer to die for their country, their religion, or some other cause that gives them their identity. Do we list patriotic heroes who give their lives for their country in the *Diagnostic and Statistical Manual of Mental Disorders (DSM)* as people afflicted with a life-threatening mental disease? Perhaps we should, and at the same time remove transgendered people from the *DSM*, because soldiers are dangerous, whereas transgendered people are not.

If we find ourselves dismissing the challenge posed by Roughgarden because of her rhetoric, perhaps we may hear the more measured words put by clinician Ingrid Sell. In an important study published in *The Psychotherapy Patient* of Americans who identify as third gender people, Sell found compelling evidence of consistent and significant differences in life experiences that might be mined by mental health professionals to enrich our comprehension of humanity. Citing Sidney Jourard, she raises the specter of a modern psychology that has unnecessarily limited itself, becoming little more than a faithful report of the majority of us who reduce our human experience in order to conform to social pressures. Sell concludes her article with words well-suited to finish our remarks as well:

> [A]s psychologists interested in the full range of human potential, we would do well to look openly, rather than fearfully, at those among us with the gift of bridging gender polarities, as they point the way to a much broader understanding of human possibility, one that includes integrating opposites, holding paradox, the courage of authenticity even in the face of fierce opposition, and ease with transpersonal dimensions.

These are qualities worth celebrating.